PRAISE FOR

*THE PENDULUM: A GRANDDAUGHTER'S SEARCH
FOR HER FAMILY'S FORBIDDEN NAZI PAST*

*"An extraordinary meditation on evil and complicity and on the
role future generations play when trying to uncover a perfidious
past. With a brilliant prose that often reads as poetry, Julie Lindahl
explores and discovers her family's Nazi past. A narrative that is
deeply moving as well as informative in its history."*
—MARJORIE AGOSIN, WELLESLEY COLLEGE;
AUTHOR OF *I LIVED IN BUTTERFLY HILL*

"I opened The Pendulum *and immediately found myself drawn into
it. As a historian, I often wondered how we could profit from the
determined pursuit of haunted family stories by descendants of indi-
vidual perpetrators. Here's the breathtaking answer."*
—JOCHEN BÖHLER,
FRIEDRICH-SCHILLER UNIVERSITY, JENA

*"In the literature of the Holocaust, the story of the perpetrator is rarely
told from 'the inside.' Julie Lindahl has taken on this painstaking
task when she tells us the story of her family. It is written from the
heart but has outstanding literary qualities—a rare but phenomenal
combination. The result is a very important book that is difficult to put
down before you reach the end."*
—STEFAN EINHORN, KAROLINSKA INSTITUTE;
AUTHOR OF *THE ART OF BEING KIND*

"Outstanding insights into the aftermath of World War II and the Holocaust—based on the perspective of both perpetrators and their descendants. The book is indispensable for anyone who wants to see the extent and complexity of the lasting influence of war, not only in its own time but also for future generations."

—ESKIL FRANCK, UPPSALA UNIVERSITY;
FORMER DIRECTOR, THE LIVING HISTORY FORUM

"A powerful book about good and evil that has become even more important in today's climate of mounting far-right extremism and alternative facts."

—HÉDI FRIED, AUTHOR, PSYCHOLOGIST,
AND HOLOCAUST SURVIVOR

"I have never read a book as perceptive, intuitive, and courageous as Julie Lindahl's memoir. She is the first of her generation to describe the reverberations of that terrible Darwinism, that 'Herrenmensch' orientation, and its overwhelming consequences, so profoundly. I thank her with all my heart."

—GERHARD HOCH, THEOLOGIAN AND HISTORIAN
OF NAZISM IN SCHLESWIG-HOLSTEIN

"A powerful, painfully human, and honest work of words and heart. . . . Beautiful in the writing sense, horrific in reflection upon all the lives."

—JAMES WINE, AMERICAN POET,
WRITER, AND FILMMAKER

THE PENDULUM

A Granddaughter's Search for
Her Family's Forbidden Nazi Past

JULIE LINDAHL

ROWMAN & LITTLEFIELD
Lanham • Boulder • New York • London

For the angels of hope

Umacha Hashem dim'a me'al kol panim
God will wipe the tears from all faces
—Isaiah 25:8

Published by Rowman & Littlefield
An imprint of The Rowman & Littlefield Publishing Group, Inc.
4501 Forbes Boulevard, Suite 200, Lanham, Maryland 20706
www.rowman.com

Unit A, Whitacre Mews, 26-34 Stannary Street, London SE11 4AB, United Kingdom

Distributed by NATIONAL BOOK NETWORK

British Library Cataloguing in Publication Information Available

Library of Congress Cataloging-in-Publication Data
Names: Lindahl, Julie Catterson, author.
Title: The pendulum : a granddaughter's search for her family's forbidden Nazi past / Julie Lindahl.
Description: Lanham, MD : Rowman & Littlefield, [2018] | Includes bibliographical references.
Identifiers: LCCN 2018027691 (print) | LCCN 2018028013 (ebook) | ISBN 9781538111949 (ebook) | ISBN 9781538111932 (cloth : alk. paper)
Subjects: LCSH: Lindahl, Julie Catterson. | Lindahl, Julie Catterson—Family. | Women—Sweden—Biography. | Grandchildren of war criminals—Germany—Biography. | Holocaust, Jewish (1939–1945)—Atrocities.
Classification: LCC CT1328.L385 (ebook) | LCC CT1328.L385 A3 2018 (print) | DDC 940.53/18092 [B]—dc23
LC record available at https://lccn.loc.gov/2018027691

Cover illustration by Alice Wellinger, whose Austrian grandparents fled the Nazis. They left Europe for South America in 1940, traveling through Hamburg as Lindahl's grandparents did twenty years later. Wellinger's mother and aunt were born in Colombia, and Wellinger herself now lives in Austria. The image was first published in the Spring 2017 issue of *Wellesley Magazine* along with Lindahl's long article "The Hidden Truth."

Contents

Contents

Prologue

If I looked back would I, like Lot's wife, turn into a pillar of salt? Would I become brittle and crumble at the sight of devastation as I looked over my shoulder? Or perhaps like Orpheus, who looked back to ensure that his love, Eurydice, was following him out of the Underworld, might I lose all that I held most dear? Whether the law of God's angels or Hades, the dictate was the same: do not look back upon the story of your own—the story of the dead—lest calamity befall you.

Day to day, most of us live unaware of the extent to which we are influenced by the legends of our own cultures, important stories rich in learning, as long as we do not allow them to become propaganda. By the time I was in my early twenties and had started to become conscious that the story of my own family was troubled, I was fully immersed in the propaganda of our culture's legends. To pursue the answers to my questions risked the unimaginable, which only dared to reveal itself in the many fearful nightmares that fade in daylight. Yet, like the art we remember because it uncloaks our emotions, the nightmares left permanent traces. In them I had become the cause of suffering among those I loved, the object of their wrath, and, as a consequence, endured an expulsion from the safe structures that I had once known. Somewhere at the root of all this fear was the legacy of human evolution, which made the family—"the tribe"—the basic unit of safety. It follows that to question it must be to bring ourselves down.

There are many strands to disentangle in this narrative, and, to a great extent, that is what these years of exploration have been about. What is it that we will see if we look back, and why must looking back be punished with severity? Will we really bring down our families by doing so? While these are questions asked by the descendant of a perpetrator, my conversations with Holocaust survivors and their descendants have revealed that there are some dilemmas that we share, in particular the burdens of guilt and shame.

The urge to cut loose from the past has always been great. History can seem a burden that we must unshackle ourselves from in order to march confidently forward into a bright new future. Dear friends often entreated me not to dwell in it, not least as some of them had experienced World War II and the Holocaust, and knew the horror and the loss all too well. The desire to protect the young from our sordid past, and to keep them inside the boundaries of our figurative beautiful gardens, is strong. As a mother I know this instinct well. I have met people who believe they will be defined by an undesirable past if they speak about it, and others for whom the degree of pain evoked by memory threatens insanity. I sympathize with all these instances, particularly when it comes to the victims, who have experienced firsthand the evil that humans can wreak. I don't use the term *evil* lightly, and I have often objected to calling any person, no matter what they have done, "evil," because it can become a label that we use to absolve ourselves from trying to understand the human condition. There is no doubt in my mind, however, that there are acts of evil.

The experience of my half century has been that it is impossible to draw a line under history, particularly our family histories. At some point, each of us senses that what is behind us is also a part of us, and if we choose never to look back, we live in denial of ourselves, the very definition of suffering. Why uphold this state of things if it causes so much pain? The answer I found was that if we did not, we would have to face the source of our shame.

When a generation responsible for evil deeds rejects its own guilt, it creeps insidiously into the hearts and minds of the next generation and transforms itself into shame; an evil deed in itself, because it unjustly condemns the bearer to carry the burden of crimes they did not commit. To agree to live in this dark room without signposts, and to believe that you must stay there in order to protect those who came before you, is an astoundingly common and counterproductive instinct. Isolation breeds mistrust, which, in turn, asphyxiates the family relationships we prize most.

Shame will unrepentantly creep into the next generation, and, like a chameleon, take new forms, unless someone breaks the dictate and looks back.

There cannot be enough conversations between the families of the victims and the perpetrators. Descendants of survivors have described to me how the guilt of their parents or grandparents for surviving while loved ones were sent to the gas chambers, faced a firing squad, or died of starvation and disease lurks in their families unless faced and remembered. War and violence haunt universally. In the dark room there are no "sides."

A modest wise man, who had been recruited into the SS as a youth, once summarized my experience succinctly for me. "It is where we do not seek truth that ungoverned guilt does its unholy mischief," he said. I have since taken one of his terms to my own by renaming it unclaimed guilt. While truth can be elusive, often staring at us from outside the rain-spattered window of our own perception, the failure to believe that it exists and that we can and should try to know more clearly what has taken place is the seed of self-destruction. I know what it is to succumb to the false idea that there is no real truth, only perception, in order to guard my own treasured hopes and beliefs. We are now experiencing this disease in the form of "alternative facts." It opens a black hole into which the fall is endless.

Why then must looking back at the story of our own be punished so severely, or why at least do we fear it? In my own case, which I am certain is not unique, it is because to look back is the same as pulling the edifice out from under a precarious structure for handling guilt and shame that has been built up meticulously over a long period of time. Once the edifice is gone, guilt and shame have no home except in their origin, otherwise known as truth. Even if finding truth has its own complications, we will most certainly catch glimpses of it if we look back with open eyes. There in the past we will inevitably see human nature as it is, contradictory in every facet—glorious, grotesque, and everything in between. Our fear is that to comprehend this totality will blind us, or turn us to salt, or cause those who mean something to us to vanish from our lives and end in pain.

As the refugees from war and violence have sought shelter in countries outside their own during these past years, my thoughts go to their families. The societies that have received them are neither naïve nor wrong to have taken them in. To treat people who have come from Armageddon with the same decency as we would hope for ourselves in their situation, is an act of basic humanity. However, our naiveté lies potentially in failing to understand that while the outer war is over for the newcomers, the inner war begins. Whether related to victims, perpetrators, or both—these families must be supported in facing their own pasts, and the will to do it must be encouraged. It is a task of greatest importance for whole societies in order to prevent anger and indignation from rising out of the embers, not just in one generation, but in several.

But can't everything be solved without raking through the past, through the power of forgiveness? Our legends seem to tell us that it is so, and during my journey I encountered many who believed this to be true, and whom I cannot fault for it. The idea raised new questions for me, including forgiveness for what, by whom, and to whom? The burden of shame motivated me to seek forgiveness for deeds I had not committed myself, a fruitless and exhausting rat race. This was patiently explained to me by a man in his eighties, a child victim of my grandfather's deeds. It was a rare act of selflessness that I will never forget, and that put within my reach something that I could attain: a sense of responsibility for pointing out the necessity to our humanity of looking back.

I have often heard the argument that it is wrong to judge people who lived in another time. How do I know that I wouldn't have done the same thing? They must be forgiven, just as I would hope to be. As I traveled through the Polish countryside and met people whose lives were irreparably damaged by the racial scourge of the Nazis, I understood that it was not up to me to forgive my grandparents; rather it was up to the people they had wronged. Some forgave, others did not. Forgiveness must be left to them as a personal choice that I will never judge.

As for myself, I could only forgive those who had hurt me: mainly the generation that preceded me. As I retraced their footsteps, over the scalding coals of their parents' unclaimed guilt and began to grasp why they brushed over the details of their childhood stories, sympathy and forgiveness became easier. All children want to love their parents, and the choices they faced were soul-scorching: to cut off that love and to banish aging parents from their world, or to risk defending their unrepentant parents' ideology in order to maintain the bonds. Had I not looked over my shoulder, forgiveness would have been impossible.

There is no doubt that I will need to seek forgiveness for the wrongs that I have done to my own children. The heedless sapping of the earth's resources caused by the brazen hyperconsumerism of my generation will no doubt be our greatest wrongdoing. Did we have choices? Yes, we did. Did we make them? Yes, we did.

When I look back at my grandparents' story and their time, I see the blinding power of greed and the contagion of tribalism. In our time, I see these grisly henchmen of manmade disaster flexing their muscles once again, as simultaneous forces of change and the inevitable fear and dissatisfaction that accompany them provide a window of opportunity.

A former Nazi living deep in the interior of Brazil reminded me of the threat that people saw in the Bolshevik revolution. It represented a world of values alien and abhorrent to the West, and created a sense of desperation in a postwar environment when both the victors and the vanquished of the Great War were at their most vulnerable. "Red" street violence endowed images of the lancing of innocent Germans and other Europeans by hellish Bolshevik terrorists with effectiveness. Above all, these drove fear into the hearts of people, paving the way for the acceptance of ideas and measures that previously would have remained at the margins.

Lebensraum, the promise of living space offered to the people by Germany's new rulers, who claimed they were throwing out the establishment for the good of the common people, was a smokescreen for increasing their own resources and power in collaboration with old business elites. Hitler likely believed in his own diatribe, but the justification of greed in the idea of Lebensraum—the right of the German people to take whatever land and resources they needed in order to prevail in the eternal struggle against their enemies—was a central tenet of *Mein Kampf* all the same. It captured my grandfather's imagination and he remained possessed by it throughout his life. Aside from some early improvements, which I was reminded of by my grandmother whenever she attempted to mount a defense of the Reich and her own sympathies, the common people ultimately suffered in an economy that became ever more depleted by militarization and eventually war.

In order to convince the masses to buy into their scheme, and in the belief that politics could not be won by logical argument, the new leaders appealed to deep-seated tribal emotions, which they themselves shared. Blood and Soil—the idea that the source of the nation's renewal from the degenerate state it had fallen into was German farmers and their genetic stock, who must be given the country back and beyond—was another carrot my grandparents devoured hungrily. It followed that all other tribes or types that did not fit with the imaginary ideal must be expelled.

Continued gains for the two henchmen—greed and tribalism— depended on deepening the exhaustion and fear of the people. The onslaught of propaganda through the new media of radio, and the daily examples of law being determined on a whim, fulfilled this purpose. Apart from the loss of human life, trust and truth were the greatest casualties.

Today I cannot help but hear the echoes, and they form me. Above all, I ask myself what we must do to change our legends. If more looked back with open eyes, particularly into their own families, I have no doubt that fewer people would fall prey to the illusion of greatness that has been the source of so much division and bloodshed. It would be a critical ingredient in the "vaccination" that one of my dear friends, a survivor of several Nazi concentration camps, has sought to create for youngsters by speaking with them about the fateful experience of his own youth.

In *Night*, his account of surviving Auschwitz, Elie Wiesel says that "to forget the dead would be akin to killing them a second time." For the descendants of the perpetrators, I have long sensed that there is a violence we commit when we choose to look away from the deeds of our forebears. It haunts us, depresses us, and twists our families until such time as we stop murdering the past repeatedly by our neglect.

As I finished this book on the last day of 2017, the pendulum came to a standstill for me on this thought. While asking questions is imperative for expanding our sense of humanity, on this one point, I have ceased to ask questions. In the stillness I found clarity, and in the clarity there is love of family, friends, and strangers.

Drottningholm, Sweden

PART I

"QUIET IS BEST"

Chapter 1

Sweden, 2015

THE SPRING SUN STREAMED IN THROUGH THE WINDOWS AND WAN-dered like a spirit into the hallway of photographs. In a black-and-white series of summers long past, naked boys played on a raft in the very same lake as the one outside the window. The boys' expressions were wild-eyed and excited, uninhibited by the photographer or the constraints of iden-tity created by clothing. The snaps were of my husband's childhood with his cousins, in this cottage by the water flanked by the woods.

At the end of the succession of boyhood images was the photograph of a two-year-old girl with blond hair in a pageboy cut. She wore a traditional German dress, a dirndl, consisting of a white blouse with laced sleeves tucked into a snug-fitting bodice with a braid across the chest. From a distance, one would have thought both the child and the photograph to be older than they really were; more like an early-twentieth-century snapshot of a ten-year-old. A closer look revealed a restrained mouth, uncommon in a child so young. The desperate eyes longed to please the adults and to know their hearts all at the same time, casting an impossibility over the photograph that frequently alienated me.

I was Jülchen then, a German diminutive of my birth name. Jülchen in the hallway was like a question mark I kept trying not to notice, at the same time as I had hung her up myself and resisted daily taking her down for reasons I could not explain. This curious photograph clashed with the unremarkable legend of my early childhood in Brazil, in which I was apparently happy and pudgy, and stood up exceptionally straight as soon as I found my legs.

"You kept casting off your sapatos and running off on those firm little legs of yours!" they said, describing my persistent efforts to free my feet from shoes.

Like all other adults, those around me relished the comic relief that the unfettered behavior of toddlers can bring. The album on the shelf in my study at the end of the hallway across from Jülchen had been assembled by them as confirmation of this legend. There was no mistaking that the rich collection of cherished memories had been gathered with the sincere wish that I would remember my early childhood with fondness. The captions were driven by the imperative, common in such albums, to interpret the images correctly. Mostly I ignored the prepared script, preferring simply to watch the actors.

Sure enough, there were the pictures of the child with the sand-encrusted bare feet and the floppy hat on the beach. There was the talk on the plastic toy telephone with the big handheld receiver in a crib populated with dolls and stuffed animals, which gave the child a feeling of familiarity. There was the face that promised to grow into a mixed likeness of its parents' faces, caught in every mood together with relatives who doted over the preciousness of the firstborn.

For all this normalcy, there were a striking number of photographs of Jülchen in the dirndl; not just one dirndl, but different ones throughout the early years. She seemed to be wearing them particularly when her German grandparents, who also lived in Brazil, visited. At some point, the child became tired of this constraining clothing and sat on her mother's lap, half-clothed, with only the lace knee socks and lacquered shoes remaining.

Each time I leafed through the album, I stopped at a photograph where commentary became hesitant and the script had no content. The pregnant pause around this photo drew my attention to it like none of the other images in the album. Jülchen sat waving her spoon in the air above her meal next to a well-groomed man in his sixties with strict short-cropped sides and longer hair on top, customary for men of his generation, and dark glasses. He had finished his meal, and leaned over in the child's direction, placing his good arm around her and letting the stump at the end of the other arm rest on the table. He avoided direct eye contact with the photographer, who would never quite catch him behind the sunglasses, the constant guards of his personality.

This was my Opa, my German grandfather, whom I could not remember with my senses, only through a few scant photographs, because he remained in Brazil, a world we left behind when I was three years old. Quickly, he faded into nothingness, passing away when I was nine. I was as unaware of his death as of his life. It wasn't uncommon that relatives faded in families, occasionally reappearing in the hazy daydreams and nostalgic conversation that turned them into stereotypes. The difference with Opa was that his fading was not only total, it was mandatory.

His presence in my early childhood album had to do with protocol, something like a relative who was allowed to turn up just this once in his capacity as a grandparent. His fading to nothing attracted my attention from early days for many reasons beyond the album. The most powerful of those lay deep within me, in Jülchen's furrowed eyebrows in the frame in the hallway. From the very beginning I, Jülchen, was convinced that I had done something quite wrong. This wasn't like stealing a spoonful of cookie dough from the batter or peeking at the Christmas presents before it was time. It couldn't even compare to something much more serious such as stealing or lying about important things. This wrong was so profound that one could only be silent and bear it, because to speak about it would be a monstrosity. Worst of all, to bring it up would be to destroy the beautiful legend that the adults had so painstakingly woven; and because Jülchen loved the adults more than anything, she would simply have to bear the shame and be the guilty one.

Looking out my cottage window into the ebony nights of winter, I discovered how rich the darkness was in learning. I couldn't blame most people for rejecting it, and either longing for light or leaving for sunnier places. Darkness was frightening and disorienting. Yet I was drawn to it, without reservation, because it was already a part of me, something familiar that I must walk into and know fully. So it was that in this form-lessness, guided only by instinct, my search began.

CHAPTER 2

West Germany, 1989

OMA, MY GERMAN GRANDMOTHER, STOOD IN THE OPEN DOORWAY TO her apartment. As the elevator door opened, she stretched out her arms and, without saying a word, beckoned me to come toward her. Soon the underside of her thumbs stroked my hands affectionately, and I observed her fine, long fingers. They were elegant, not of the sort that had been stunted and roughened by hard work. The antique ring with the thin gold band on her left ring finger captured my attention, as it always did when she held my hands like this. It was one of the few things that remained from her husband, my Opa, a figure of distant history, who had long since disappeared from our lives.

"My dearest Jülchen," she said warmly. "Well? You are looking very slim these days. Very slim indeed," she added, avoiding getting into what I knew was a delicate subject. "I've made some warm lunch—trout with potatoes and steamed vegetables, and your favorite berry soup with vanilla sauce for dessert."

I hadn't seen Oma since the autumn of 1988, when my year-long scholarship in Germany began. Now it was spring and we had a lot of catching up to do. It was characteristic of her to discuss the composition of the meal before one got in the door. Food and digestion were prioritized above all other subjects. This had something to do with the fact that she had survived two world wars and lived on farms where a direct approach to the basic needs of all living things governed. Oma's lithe hands were difficult to reconcile with her farming life, but this wasn't a contradiction I spent much time considering. It was simply there, as were the many other facets of my grandmother I'd never tried to piece together.

"Hello, Oma," I said, kissing her on the cheek. Despite her near-eight decades, her face was soft as the skin of a peach. She often complained about the bleached spots on her forehead, a reaction to the merciless Brazilian sun. But that had been years ago, and in the shaded cool of her apartment in this temperate German town, one barely noticed them. She wore her usual unpretentious ensemble: an off-white blouse buttoned at the collar and the wrists; a tweed skirt that fitted generously over her wide, child-bearing hips and covered her knees; button-up stockings, and sturdy orthopedic shoes. Her gray waves were arranged in a tidy short cut, having long since relinquished the low bun at the nape of the neck. She had looked like this for as long as I could remember and even before, in her photo albums of the distant past, which no one else in the family wanted to leaf through.

For all her physical sensitivity and calm elegance, Oma could be brash. She wasn't open to the idea that there might be right ways of doing things that were not her own. Juxtaposed with her inexhaustible curiosity about the world, particularly in books, was a rigid sense of order, which was the insurance that her way remained superior.

I didn't question my grandmother. Perhaps it was because I didn't think that the young had the right to confront someone at her stage of life, but there was more to it. She had expressed such caring and gentleness toward me that I let her rigidities pass. It was curious that without having lived with us, Oma seemed to know exactly what I had been through. In the shape of her eyes, she was also distinctly the mother of my mother, the mother of M, and therefore offered me the glimmer of hope, which I savored every minute I experienced it, that M did in fact love me.

As I came into the small living room with the oversized armchairs, I remembered the many times I had visited this place as a young child. As always, the table was elegantly set for the meal, with a smaller tablecloth overlaid like a diamond on a larger one, and the gold-rimmed plates framed by sterling silver cutlery with the familiar crest engraved at the foot of each piece.

These items were what remained of a turbulent family history that no one wished to discuss. Raising it was like breaking a taboo, which, when temporarily breached, elicited an angry exchange of words between Oma and her daughters. M's words were always the sharpest, and when she wielded them everyone fell silent. It was as though she had wrenched opened a tomb and raised the dead. On the occasions when Father was with us, he intervened by suggesting a stroll in the park. Father walked a great deal. All my sister and I wished to do was to escape this room where the atmosphere had gone bad. Once, when we managed to get away, we sat in the room next door and my brash little sister drew expletives on her face with a black crayon. It was her rebellion against the pretending.

Today the air of Oma's apartment was peaceful. The four walls were a fortress to noise, and although one could hear the faint buzz of the street through the plants—the guards at the windowsill—all the furnishings of Oma's place, down to the pastel green carpet, collaborated in her mission to achieve a quiet space in life. The only furnishing in her apartment allowed to make noise from time to time was her tape recorder from which she played her extensive collection of audio books. Oma had been an avid reader, but now there were only a few remnants of that enthusiastic library, which she had managed to save from the termites in Brazil, propped up in the shelf. A nervous twitch interfered with her sight as soon as she looked at the written word, and instead she listened to her favorite stories, as recorded by some of Germany's best acting voices.

Once I had washed my hands, I helped her to carry the pots and serving plates from the kitchen to the sitting room and we sat down to the meal.

"Now, make sure you take enough," she said, eyeing my portions like a hawk. "You're young—my word, just twenty-one years old—you've got your whole life ahead of you and you must eat. Do you menstruate normally?" she asked, squeezing in an embarrassing question, which I understood to be a part of her obsession with biological health.

"Yes, Oma, everything is fine," I said, chewing my food awkwardly and feeling like a prize mare, as eagerly she watched each forkful that entered my mouth.

Eventually, she settled into the food on her own plate, which she devoured with a concentration that our generation no longer possessed.

Her plate was soon empty and she had begun to reach for the serving spoons again. "Come, come," she beckoned for my plate. "We cannot have any of this left over—it's all got to be eaten up." I didn't see why we could never save the leftover food. To Oma it was always better inside one's digestive system, rather than saved in a box in the refrigerator. The truth was that I wanted to go for a run in the spring sunshine, but it was the wrong time for this in Oma's schedule, and therefore I surrendered to her insistence that we empty all the pots.

When dessert was done, Oma settled back into her armchair with a toothpick and reached for her shaded glasses. The afternoon sun had reached her corner of the room, and even the mildest rays prompted her to shield her eyes.

"Terrible, this blasted flickering of the eyes!" She cursed her condition, which countless conventional and unconventional treatments had failed to cure. Oma had done everything, including drink her own urine, which she claimed had been one of Mahatma Gandhi's standard practices. I didn't recall that Gandhi had lived in exceptionally good health, but I guessed her logic was that he stood for peace and that somehow drinking urine would grant her greater tranquility.

"Oh, let's talk about something else!" she said, jamming her gray glasses onto her face in frustration. "Have you noticed all of the wonderful spring buds opening outside?" She pointed to the blooming cherry blossoms in the courtyard outside her window. "Nature is the strangest and most wonderful thing. It clears out the weak and supports everything strong and vital. We humans haven't respected that principle and Nature is punishing us for it. Just look around! We offend her laws all the time!"

In Oma's world, Nature was a strange god that was neither moral nor immoral. It simply was. I hadn't been raised with religion, but sometimes it bothered me that Oma's god offered no ethical guidance.

"Yes, I've seen that tree," I said, trying not to be unnerved by the absence of morality in Oma's spiritual outlook. "What is it that shouldn't be alive? What laws do you mean we have offended?" I could not help asking.

"Well, that is quite plain," she said matter-of-factly. "Just look at the AIDS epidemic. You don't think *that* is a coincidence, do you? Those people are bound to die, because what they are doing is unnatural. In any case, the world's population is growing far too fast, and AIDS is nature's way of correcting the situation."

I was conscious that I was nodding, and it bothered me. Sometimes Oma could sound so scientific that it masked the content of what she was saying.

"Just think of all those poor people who are born with deformations! What torture for them to have to keep on living! We should be merciful and put them out of their misery!" This series of exclamations was like a firing squad. I'd been very sick as a child and wondered whether this put me into the category of the weak. Besides, my large, flat feet had given rise to great consternation. They were an unsightly defect that had compelled us to visit a podiatrist and have metal insteps manufactured. "Good heavens, the child must only be allowed to wear health shoes lest she becomes crippled!" Oma had exclaimed. I remembered staring down at my long, wide feet with the low arch and wondering why they posed such problems for everyone but me. At the same time, I felt deeply, impossibly flawed as I lurched around in ugly health shoes for the elderly, and obediently did my prescribed exercises that chafed at a pubescent child's dignity.

Oma's scientific discourse was full of contradictions, and I struggled to excuse her on the grounds of age. Yet her eyes were so clear when she spoke that I wondered whether this was the right thing to do. I looked away from her, back at the cherry blossoms outside the window, and hoped we could quickly get past this conversation.

"Now, tell me, what are you studying?" she asked, despite the fact that I had explained it to her many times. This had nothing to do with her memory, which was clear as a well-polished mirror. Instead, it had to with the fact that what was history to me was life to her. She couldn't recall my academic terminology, instead capturing history in the simple and eloquent language of her memory.

"International affairs," I replied. "We're studying the Cold War." Oma temporarily removed her toothpick from her mouth and waved it around like a tiny saber.

"War, war . . . people will never stop fighting. Man has an evil inside of him that he will never be freed of. There will always be wars." There was a tone of bitterness that was blissfully interrupted when she shoved the toothpick back in between her teeth. Her head shook nervously as she continued picking.

As a young person with the future ahead of me, I had difficulty accepting Oma's thesis. Yet I didn't get in her way, as I regarded listening to her as something like opening a living history book. Besides, the continued division of her country for over forty years had fostered a deep-seated cynicism about the science of international affairs that, as a student, I treated with such reverence.

"You can read all about it in here," she said, patting her well-leafed copy of *War and Peace*, one of the few books that remained in her collection. "Bloodthirsty princes battled with one another for no better purpose than the ridiculous glory of spilling blood. How many young men believed them and returned, if they did at all, without arms and legs! Terrible, *ter-ri-ble*! But no one speaks about that anymore. It's all about us and the so-called awful things that we Germans did. But, let me tell you, it was nothing compared to what people did to one another back then!"

She tapped her hand on the cover of the book, as though it was her most reliable piece of evidence in a grand defense.

Oma's logic was convoluted, and, for this very reason, I avoided going down this hopeless avenue that she so often chose. She was my grandmother and had always been good to me. I wanted to stay in that space, to continue to receive the benefits of being her granddaughter, and not become entangled in this fruitless argument.

"I have some great new friends at the university," I said, attempting to shift the discussion.

"Oho! Now that's very nice—a dashing young man, perhaps?" Lifting her head, she set the toothpick aside in the pink glass ashtray on the side table to her right. I lied and shook my head. There was someone, but I didn't want to say anything about it in order to avoid returning to the embarrassing subject of my fertility. My efforts to create a diversion had rapidly come to a dead end, and Oma was free to continue with her catharsis, which now took a disturbing turn.

"And what do they say about that business with the Jews at your university? I am sure they tell you all sorts of lies. Let me tell you straight, from someone who was there, that nothing like this *ever* happened. It was all a lie by the media, so that we Germans would feel that we had to keep our heads down." She bowed her head in submission, eyes and voice lowered, as both hands surrendered, palms down, on the table. After a moment's silence, she lifted her head and tapped the table disdainfully. "Germans were responsible for everything bad, but no one ever talks about the good that we did, and doesn't *everyone* seem to want to come and live here!"

Her eyelids suddenly began to flicker uncontrollably behind the shaded spectacles, and she leaned back on the head rest of her armchair. "Oh, my eyes! I have tried everything—inoculations from the doctor and all manner of treatments—but nothing helps. It's an illness of the nerves, you understand; to do with everything we have been through. It was all too much." She raised her head slightly and shook her finger. "But the Holocaust, I can assure you, *did not happen.*"

Each of those last three words was said slowly and deliberately. On previous occasions when Oma had defended the Third Reich, I let her utterances pass as momentary lapses of temper and signs of aging. Perhaps then I would never have to see them again, which meant that I could avoid being faced with the prospect that there was another side of my grandmother that didn't at all match the gentle person I loved.

"It's all just invented nonsense," she continued. "We had beautiful times, you know."

Today I was so ashamed that I didn't know what to say. I should stand up in outrage in defense of the millions, but I didn't because there in that chair was a lonely old woman I didn't feel I had the right to judge. She was exhausted by her nervous condition, which worsened the further she ventured down the slippery path of her argument.

"I think you should lie down, Oma," I said. "I will do the dishes." As I sponged the suds over the plates, I felt anxiety rising from within. Why hadn't I reacted? Was it really just because Oma was old or was it because I had heard these arguments before and didn't want to take them on, or, even worse, had been influenced by them?

Interaction with Jews had always been mentioned in hushed tones, as though it was something one really shouldn't be doing but must live with. As a new undergraduate in the United States, I barely knew any Jews and often wondered what it was about them that could be so threatening. I decided to find out by responding to a work notice posted on my dormitory bulletin board, for a waitress to serve at a large family Thanksgiving dinner at a home in the surrounding town. The name of the family indicated that it was Jewish. As I served each family member slices of turkey from a silver tray, the matriarch burst out: "But you are too thin! You must sit down and eat, dear." The others at the table took one look at me and concurred.

"Sit down, dear! It's Thanksgiving. You must eat." I blushed as the kind Jewish family overwhelmed me with its generosity. That evening I returned to my dormitory with a paycheck, feeling full and ashamed that I had allowed my mind to harbor such bizarre attitudes.

It was precisely because shame was a familiar companion that it was easier to choose than the uncertainty of what would happen if I confronted Oma. Surely, such a well-read and curious person must be inwardly aware of the folly of her words.

I rinsed the plates and patted them dry with the kitchen towel. Nothing must be left on Oma's kitchen counter. Everything had to be shiny clean and put away. As I wiped, I wondered why she had said these things to me at all, particularly if it was, as I assumed, that inwardly she didn't believe in her own words. Did she have something to defend? I ran through the facts. Her husband had been a farmer in occupied Poland, nothing more. M happened to have been born there, nothing more. Opa had moved to Brazil because it offered good farming prospects, nothing more.

⌒⌒

By the time I returned from my run in the park, Oma had risen from her afternoon nap. She sat in her armchair, one elbow resting on the table and the other arm stabilizing the upright lower arm. Between her index finger and thumb, she clasped a string dangling an arrow-like metallic object that swung gently in narrow counterclockwise ellipses. I moved closer but she could not hear me, as she had switched off her unruly hearing aid so as not to interrupt the solemn judgment of the pendulum. On the surface of the table, a few inches under the tiny pointed nugget, was a black-and-white passport-sized photograph of a young man. The image was creased, as though it had been on many journeys, but one could see that the young man was square-jawed and handsome—perhaps in his midtwenties—and was dressed neatly in a jacket, shirt, and tie. His eyes, nose, and lips bore family similarities.

I placed my hand on Oma's back and stroked it. She responded well to the calming effect of touch and was never shocked when I came up from behind her like this. "Jülchen, my dearest," she said. "I would recognize those fine hands of your father's anywhere. They are just like his, you know. Precise copies."

"What are you doing, Oma?" I asked.

"This is your uncle," she said, grasping the photograph of the young man with her aged hand. "There." She held it up as though I might miss it.

"Yes, I know, Oma," I said, recognizing who this must be, although I had never seen a picture of Uncle Harty before.

"I keep trying, but it always goes counterclockwise," she said as she stroked the photograph with the underside of her thumb.

Like all of Oma's other ideas, her contentions about science were not to be challenged, and therefore I asked in the most nonjudgmental tone I could muster: "And, what does that mean?" She held my hand and stroked it gently with her free thumb, as she brought the image of Uncle Harty closer to her face.

"It means that he is dead." She gasped, as though her lungs were out of air. "They fought. How they fought, Harty and his father. The rage—it was terrible. One day he was just gone. Harty was angry and goodness knows what happened to him in that bad business he got into on the Paraguayan border. I have nightmares of his dead body being torn apart by the wild dogs in that place. It was terribly dangerous there, with the narcotics trade, the bandits and all."

I crouched down at the table and picked up the silk string to which the pointed brass nugget was attached, and held it over my hand. It swung undecidedly back and forth, not moving in one direction or the other. "It doesn't work for me, Oma. Are you sure you can trust it?" This question lured her out of sorrow to the defense of her truth-teller.

"Of course it works perfectly! Especially for sensitive people like us, but you must be still. You can take that little thing anywhere and it will tell you if something is good or bad, true or false. I always have it with me when I go grocery shopping. No scoundrel is ever going to sell me a piece of old meat!" She looked at me as though I was the most naïve creature in the world. "You must have one. Let's see whether I can find an extra."

I wished Oma wouldn't bother with finding a spare pendulum for me. Instinctively, I didn't want to have an object like that in my life. Surely I should be able to figure out whether something was true or false, good or bad, without that sort of help. Oma seemed to need it because life had thrown too many ambiguities and awful questions at her. It provided reinforcement to a person who at times seemed to have lost faith in her fellow human beings. As she claimed she didn't believe in God, he couldn't help her either. In fact, she was quite damning about God, a tendency that I thought might have pushed her to hedge her bets with another religion. The Order of the Pendulum became ever more important the closer she came to the end of her life.

Uncle Harty was as shrouded a figure as Opa. I didn't like to pry into a past that seemed so loaded, but since Oma herself had raised the subject of Harty and Opa, I thought I might take the opportunity. "What did Uncle Harty and Opa fight about?" I asked. She was only too willing to share the story with me, because no one else in the family wanted to hear it.

"Your Opa needed Harty to run the estates in Brazil. Harty could speak the language, but your Opa refused to learn it. They didn't get along." She shook her head and her shoulders sank. "We had such opportunities, but everything came to ruin because their natures clashed, and there was nothing either of them could do about it. Each human being inherits their nature from somewhere in the family—certain characteristics just drop down—and there is absolutely nothing anyone can do to change it."

I nodded, but felt trapped by the certainty with which my grandmother, who had seen so much of life, reached this daunting conclusion. Were we all so hopelessly predetermined? What nature did I possess that could not be changed?

"Harty was a good-natured boy and was liked by everyone," she continued. "He was a talented equestrian and after the war went riding at the best school in Schleswig-Holstein. Your mother went with him, you know. He was the son in the family, but it was your mother, not Harty, that was your Opa's favorite. She should have been a boy, he always said."

Oma chuckled at the images evoked by her own story. As M came into the conversation, I became conscious that whatever questions I asked Oma about the past and the family, all of them were driven by one motivation: to understand her better. Whether Oma was conscious of this or not, she always filled in a few more pieces of the puzzle each time that we spoke.

I remembered M's divided reaction on the few occasions we had been around horses. She got very close to them, held their heads and petted them, as though she understood them in a way that none of the rest of us ever could. She stroked the saddle and reveled in the smell of soft polished leather that was so much a part of the equestrian sphere. Yet all this pleasure in a world she was clearly familiar with was sullied by something the rest of us could not understand. Perhaps it was the permanent loss of Uncle Harty, who had also been a keen rider. Given what Oma had just shared with me, I thought it strange that I had rarely seen M ride. Instead, she watched us, her children, with a critical gaze as we struggled to stay in the saddle. All this time it was my impression that we could never live up to the glory of the equestrian past she had known, but maybe her look was just one of sadness at the loss of a beloved brother. I would never know, because it was impossible to ask her such things.

Oma could see my concentration, and what she deemed to be an impossible effort to understand a person's nature. She took my hand into hers once again and said, "I know you have had a difficult time, but you must not be so hard on your mother. Do you know that when she was little she told me that when I died she wanted to go with me? What an unusual thing for such a little child to say!"

At first, I too thought it odd that M, who had apparently been her father's favorite, would prefer to die with her mother rather than remain on this earth without her. This was the first I had ever heard of M's thoughts about dying, which she had otherwise always shunned as resistance to Father's constant preoccupation with the subject. Then it struck me that as a child I too had wanted to go with a parent at death. I had been desperately afraid of what life would be like without Father. My thoughts returned to M. What had she been afraid of?

Oma continued: "There is nothing she can do about the way she is, or that any of us can do about the way we are. When nature decides, we are helpless, and she is just like her father. It is incredible, really. A replica." Oma sighed and decided it was time to get away from this slippery topic.

There was a certain violence about this type of comparison that happened all the time in families. It was like stuffing someone in a box and leaving them there to suffocate. I too had been told that I was just like my father. The soft hands, the flawed feet, the impracticality. But I wasn't Father. What of me?

Despite my inner objections, I continued to listen avidly in hopes of learning more about Opa. I recalled the picture of myself, a white-blond toddler in Brazil, sitting next to this man with the dark sunglasses. Although he didn't smile, the child hoped that he was happy to have her there on his good arm. According to the family, the other lower arm had been shot off after the war in a hunting accident. Whenever this dramatic incident was explained, it was done quickly and without detail.

"Well, now look at you! What energy you have, running through the whole park, while I have been lying around like an old sleepyhead! I'm afraid the air is all wrong for me today. I cannot tolerate weather change at all. The air pressure makes me terribly dizzy." She leaned against the wall as she made her way to the kitchen.

"I can help you, Oma," I said, feeling bad that my grandmother felt obliged to serve me. She shooed me away.

"You must wash and change, and we will have some tea and cake. You don't take coffee, do you? I must say, I admire your abstinence from coffee. I couldn't do without it, at least in the mornings to wake me from my nightmares."

I often wondered how Oma could continue to have nightmares after living in such a peaceful, stable place for so many years. I had once asked her what these nightmares were about and her only reply was: "Oh child, all the foolish things we did! We lost everything."

CHAPTER 3

The United Kingdom, 1990

I SQUINTED AS I AWOKE TO THE BRIGHT MORNING LIGHT STREAMING IN through the window in my student quarters at Oxford, where I had commenced my master's degree after the scholarship year in Germany. The draft from the autumn wind that penetrated this ancient building through its many crevices made me grateful to be under the patchwork quilt my sister had sewn for me when I had first left for college six years ago.

In the early days of being away, the patchwork brought on a deep sadness, as it reminded me of my younger sibling, my closest companion in all the years of being transplanted from one country to the next. Whatever alien street we found ourselves on during those years, we had walked down it hand-in-hand, knowing that the other would never let go and would understand one's freakish, sometimes angry, reactions to imposed rootlessness. Many of those were etched in hard script on the pages of my childhood diary, which I had put away in a storage box, because it reminded me of the convulsive life we had lived, each of us in some way vomiting up our inner dislocation each time we moved. Beyond this, the words were a reminder of a strange sort of feeling I had carried around with me but could not explain. It was like being blindfolded from the beginning and having to accept that the room I lived in was a place called shame.

At Oxford I longed to leave that room behind and live free and perfectly in a new world. I pulled the patchwork up to my nose, resistant to the prospect of leaving my warm bed, and thought of the letter I would write to Father and M. I wrote to my parents once a week on a Sunday, clad in the elaborately patterned sweaters that M had knitted for me in the heat of the tropics. I saw them as another sign of M's affection for me, at the same time as they reminded me of how hard she had been forced to work early in life. She had mentioned it now and then in frustration, but like so many things that could not be discussed because they caused pain, the subject simply got left in a heap that festered in my guilt room.

I rose from my floor mattress and looked out the window under the roof with the weatherworn shingles, attempting to ignore the wicked draft in favor of the magnificent scene. Even as by now I had experienced them for several seasons, the changing colors of the autumn were new to me each year. The leaves that had fallen at the foot of the ancient tree across the street flew down the narrow cobblestoned road, like busy mortals passing under the noble architecture and spires that reached for eternity.

As much as I wanted to look to the future, I could not help being drawn to the past. During the previous autumn, on this same day one year ago, the Berlin Wall had fallen. I had watched the television in disbelief, as people from the East, hanging out the windows of their Trabants, crossed over to embrace their western countrymen. During the weeks that ensued I continued to watch as the "wall woodpeckers" took to the grotesque cement barrier that had held Europe and the world frozen in lies. I wept as freedom washed like a tidal wave over this previously unpassable boundary. During the year I had spent in Germany on a scholarship, the Wall had defined my studies. Now it was gone, and, as I sat in my drafty students' quarters warmed by one of M's sweaters, I could feel there was something very personal about this event; it wasn't just another headline in the news.

Suddenly, the dormant history behind the Iron Curtain had begun to mill with life. Borders became fluid, and with this fluidity came questions. Where was the rightful German border? Where was the rightful Polish border? Was the existing disputed border legitimate? I became obsessed with these questions, as though defending someone without knowing why. M was born in this disputed region during World War II. Did this make M German or Polish? What were my grandparents doing there?

My academic adviser didn't appear to be fazed by current events. Within the four walls of his dark mahogany study with the many books lining his shelves, the turbulence of the historical watershed seemed to be for others. Tucked away in the corner of the dark leather couch, in his black don's robes, he listened to my essays about different periods of history and mildly approved or corrected.

When it came to twentieth-century Germany, my passions flew in a way that was unexpected and not in keeping with the even manner of my professor. My presentation about the Hitler phenomenon obsessed me like no other, and I worked on it night and day, trying to understand how it could have happened. At the same time, I felt awkward and ridiculous about my passion for this subject, and sometimes thought I shouldn't touch it at all. To minimize the outward impression of feeling, I chose a thesis topic that sounded disciplined and academic. Yet under the dull surface of the title I knew that the disorder of high emotion was so close to my heart that it was doubtful I could say anything objective about it. *The Legitimacy of the Oder-Neisse Boundary.* I felt the color rise in my face as I attempted to explain the topic to my professor. He looked at me through the dark frames of his glasses in puzzlement, uncertain whether he should mildly endorse or correct me.

Once he told me to proceed, I began by devouring a three-book series that explored the plight of German refugees from the East after World War II. As I read about their terrible struggle and the atrocities inflicted upon them, I felt strangely reassured. M's family had been refugees and therefore they were victims, forced to flee before the advancing Russian army, with its grotesque appetite for rape and revenge. I looked for M in the striking cover image of one of the volumes, in which women and children returned on foot with their few belongings to a devastated nation.

There was still the problematic question of why M's family had been in the East in the first place. This wasn't their original home. As my studies progressed, a picture I preferred to deny began to form. What if Opa had been one of the invaders?

At night I awoke and saw the image of myself in the dirndl in Brazil faced by M, who stared at me with forbidding eyes. The moonlight streamed into the window and accentuated the form of the potted cactus she had sent me. According to M, cacti could withstand the most incompetent of gardeners. I observed the tiny bulb that had begun to protrude out the side of the plant and showed promise of blooming into a flower. Was I simply incompetent, or was there something to my imaginings? It was exasperating not to have anyone to ask.

Then I remembered that there was no need for the Sunday letter, because Father was scheduled to arrive for a two-day visit starting on Monday. The prospect filled me with happiness even if it didn't solve my current problem. It seemed as impossible to ask Father about the past as anyone else in the family.

My heart pulsed with the joy of seeing the most gentle and affectionate person I knew. As I met Father again, I remembered how important it was to respect his strong sense of privacy. I had never once felt that he had lied to me, but from his frequently worried appearance, I knew there were things he felt he could not discuss. We were so close that I could feel the struggle of his perpetually troubled soul.

"Are you very tired?" I asked, avoiding all discussion of what was bothering him.

"No, dear," he said. "I'll just put my bags down at the hotel, wash, and then take you out for lunch." Father never expected anyone to take him out for anything. He simply gave and gave, making me forget about everything else when he was there. The fact that I'd have to manage a meal had completely escaped me, but with my new sense of freedom things were changing on that front too, even if my reflexes still compelled me to keep a strict regimen.

No sooner had we sat down to lunch at a hotel in the center of town than Father launched into his worries. "I don't understand your sister," he said. He took a sip of water, his lips parched after the many hours of drinks on the flight. "Doesn't she have everything she needs? Why does she goof off all the time? Drives your mother and me crazy! Goodness knows what she is up to at university."

I didn't like to acknowledge the hard side of Father I saw emerging whenever he spoke of my sister. He used anything from clumsy colloquialisms to sharply critical language that didn't fit with the considerate person I knew. Quickly, I put the idea of asking about my grandfather out of my mind. The last thing I wanted was to bring out more of that side of Father I didn't want to see.

"She will be fine, Father. She is strong." I tried to lighten his burden, yet despised the suppression of truth that I felt increasingly forced to with Father. My little sister wasn't well, and her "goofing off" was a rebellion I often sympathized with as a result of our common childhood experience.

"Let's talk about something else," I said, forcing a strained smile. I loved Father, and I didn't want to open up old wounds. Outside, the leaves sailed through the air like wafers of gold in the autumn sun. Their flight was effortless and beautiful, just as I wanted our time together to be.

"Of course!" He smiled back. "So, what are you going to do next? You're almost done with your degree." I hesitated, as I knew he was eager to hear of a sensible plan, one that would take me away from the danger of ever wanting for anything. Father knew what it was to be poor, and therefore it was cruel not to have a good answer. I mumbled something about further studies, taking a few courses in economics to please him, but my thoughts were so preoccupied with the borderland where M was born and with who my grandfather was, that none of it could possibly sound coherent. I didn't want to tell him that I had filled out an application to do a PhD, and now as he sat before me I resolved to drop it because it would only entangle me further in that taboo subject that had exhausted my nerves and resulted in less-than-optimal exam results.

"But where is it all leading?" he said anxiously. I felt the pressure of Father's trust: behind my otherwise top grades there must be an intelligent career plan.

"Oh, I will eventually apply to . . ." I rattled off a series of impressive-sounding companies to quell his concerns, but all I saw before me was an insurmountable wall. The past seemed to prevent the future from unfolding. There were things I needed to know in order to move forward. If not entirely satisfactory, my answer seemed acceptable to Father, and we enjoyed the rest of the afternoon in the way that I had hoped.

On the bus ride back to my flat, Father could not help but take up his worries again. "Why do you think your sister does all these things?" He seemed desperate, like a man groping in the dark for answers. I disliked seeing him like this and turned away to look out the window of the bus. Sleet had replaced the golden leaves and struck the windows in an early sign that it would be a cold winter.

"I don't know, Father," I lied, reluctant to take up this battered, old topic once again. "Maybe she just needs time."

The wine had temporarily emboldened me at lunch, and I felt confident that before the day was out I could ask Father about Opa without any repercussions. Now those effects had worn off and the pessimism had set in. Father's visits were so short, and I would have to ask him soon if I was going to ask at all.

"Father, I've been reading a lot about what happened during and after WWII. What did Opa do during the war? He did end up in a remote place in Brazil, after all, didn't he?"

Father responded abruptly. "If there is one thing you must never do, it is to raise that subject again," he said, his voice shaking. "Do you understand?" He cast a look of disappointment at me I had never experienced from him before.

My heart plummeted. Out of the corner of my eye, I saw Father's soft hands tremble as he struggled to fold them on his lap. He looked away, his eyes seeking escape down the aisle of the bus. If only I could reverse time and take it back. The question must never be raised again.

CHAPTER 4

Germany, 1997

I HAD COME TO SEE OMA WITH MY FUTURE HUSBAND BEFORE OUR planned wedding during the coming summer. She was the first in the family to meet him; a deliberate move on my part, as I had wanted him to feel welcome in the family. It had been eight years since the year of study in Germany, and although my life had been turbulent, Oma and I had kept in close contact. She didn't judge my personal life, including one failed marriage that was already behind me. The main thing, she thought, was to have at least twenty good years in a marriage, which, she admitted, was more than her life experience had offered.

"Now then!" she said, greeting me from her armchair in the room adjacent to the entrance as she heard me coming through the front door. "What have you two lovebirds been up to?"

"It's just me, Oma," I replied, as I hung up my jacket and removed my shoes before entering the fine room where she sat looking regal with her arms extended on the wide armrests. "He wanted us to have some time alone, and he can't understand most of what you say anyway," I explained.

"I know," she replied. "It's unfortunate that we can't all understand one another's languages, but one can sense he is a thoughtful and charming person." A warm feeling went through me. Oma had always been supportive and strikingly modern for her years.

"The most important thing is that you are happy. Are you?" she continued. I didn't know what to say in response to her question. Happiness was a mystery to me, something I watched other people experience from behind a double-glazed window. This had nothing to do with my betrothed. He knew this side of me and was prepared to meet me in whatever room I stood. Perhaps love was not the same as happiness. "Forget all the rest," Oma insisted. "Believe me, happiness is the only thing that is important."

I was glad that we could easily communicate with one another in Oma's language. For years I was the only one of her many grandchildren with whom she could easily converse without a language barrier. She abstained from correcting my every sentence, and forged on in the conversation, providing the example of her literary High German as a guide.

As a child I didn't recall being encouraged to learn German, even when we lived in Germany for eighteen months. There was a love-hate relationship about German culture that permeated our home, just as a child can simultaneously love and detest her parents. We sailed through all the different countries we encountered on an island of German tradition, even though Father's side of the family was American. All our Christmases and several other traditions were formed by it, and on the fifth of December, the eve of St. Nicholas, I eagerly polished my shoe and placed it at the foot of my bed so that on the following morning I would find chocolate rather than a stick in it.

From an early age, it seemed perfectly logical to me that I should learn the language and so at the age of eight I implored my best friend, whose parents were German, to speak only German to me at our International School. As a university student in Frankfurt I had upgraded my command of the language, but it was the conversations with Oma that kept my knowledge of German alive.

"Look what I've brought with me." I said, and held up the box from Oma's favorite cake shop.

"Oh no!" she said with a devilish look in her eyes. "Now what have you done? Bought your old grandmother a thick slice of black forest cherry cake? Get it on the table, I say."

Oma was becoming stiffer in the joints, and each time I saw her she had a little more difficulty getting up out of the armchair. With a grumble of the alert mind at the ailing body, she rose and made her way to the coffee machine. She measured the ground beans, just as precisely as she measured all other ingredients. She often said it was because her body could not tolerate too much of anything that she had lived such a long and healthy life. As a chubby young girl, I had watched her painstakingly grate half an apple over her freshly made muesli, which she insisted must be prepared by soaking overnight to ensure smooth passage through the digestive system once consumed.

The exception to this healthful regimen was the slice of cake in the afternoons, which I had managed to avoid eating during all my years of struggling with food. This dark pact with deep feelings of inferiority and inadequacy was beginning to lose its power in the gentle light of affection and praise that my new fiancé had shone on my life. Even if I didn't get through the whole slice, I put it on my plate and told myself that I would enjoy afternoon coffee with Oma.

"Now, do we have everything here?" Oma's eagle eye scanned the table for any possible shortcomings in our coffee service. It was easy to see that she had spent some time in the hotel business after the war. "Take! Take!" she urged, eager to have a slice of the tall, multilayered cream cake herself. I lifted a fork of cake to my lips and tried not to feel self-conscious. After all, it was only cake and not a threat to my integrity.

As the small piece with cream sandwiched in between the chocolate layers dissolved on my tongue, the large painting on the facing wall caught my attention. The picture had been there for as long as I could remember, I just hadn't looked at it carefully until now. In an ornate gold-enameled frame was an oil painting of a vast wheat field. In the foreground were figures of strong men in white muslin shirts forking bales of wheat into a horse-drawn wagon. Their task was far from done. The wheat field stretched as far as the eye could see, and the struggle seemed endless. "It's one of the few pieces that survived from the early days. Your grandfather commissioned it and liked it very much," Oma said, lifting her cup to infuse another piece of cake with the flavor of well-brewed afternoon coffee.

"It's a grand picture," I said.

"Of course, your Opa wanted only the best of quality and oh how he worked! Watch out you don't become like him, you hear?" This was a half-joke that referred to my obsessive work habits. "The other families went on nice holidays to the sea or the mountains for a few days, but not us! It would have been very nice to take a little rest every now and then, but not your grandfather! After just a few hours off he became restless and lost his temper."

Her voice lowered and she began to scratch at her shiny cotton napkin, which she had folded and replaced on the table. "Ach!" she exclaimed, slumping in her armchair, the air going out of her and her voice shifting into a lower gear. "He got top marks in his merchant exams, but that profession was not for him. He wanted out—onto the land. There!" she said, pointing at the painting on the wall. "And didn't we just create those places over the years. One after the other." She shook her head and then exclaimed with a sort of resentment I thought I recognized: "Fantastic places!" She paused and collected herself. "He started with a small plot and a few straight rows of trees he planted himself, and traded eggs in the city. Everything was so proper. He built a chicken coop and kept it in immaculate order." She waved a finger high in the air, to represent a sort of standard that was unobtainable for the rest of us. "He was so industrious. Everything he touched had to become the best!"

As Oma's story infiltrated the picture, it began to assume the mantle of tragedy. The golden-haired men in the muslin shirts on the vast field were a utopia that had slipped through her fingers. "Is that a picture of a place where you lived?" I asked. She laughed bitterly and shook her head. "Oh no, my dear Jülchen, that is all that we lost. What fools we were! We built up beautiful places in Germany and then came the war. Your grandfather decided to sell everything we had because he thought he could get more and better in the East. Always more and better!" Her raised voice made me feel uncomfortable. "Then we built up our new life in Poland. We lent our gifted touch to one place after the other." She made a hand motion that looked like the distribution of alms. "The Poles should thank us for it! We found dirty and disorganized places and left them shipshape. Your grandfather saw to it that everything was so well organized, and then the war was over and we had to get out. *Out!* We had to leave almost everything behind."

Oma's hard voice signaled that we were back in that realm of history where wild dogs governed; where one only dared pass with head bowed in submission. Once again, I felt the heat of guilt coming over me for not reacting strongly, but I was used to it. Oma's outlandish statements about Slavs were not new to me. She had always insisted that the people from the East were dirty and disorderly. With the fall of the Berlin Wall and the breakdown of the old Soviet Union, these people had begun to stream into the town where she lived. They were becoming hotel owners and even the wealthiest of clients. With them, the East had come to occupy her town and the events of history had been reversed. I chose not to remind her of these realities, eager not to offend, but more important, not to create a diversion from her fascinating monologue. I had never heard the whole story and it intrigued me, as I had never stopped wondering about who my grandfather really was.

"Do you have pictures of any of these places?" I asked, hoping that photographs would generate a new string of memories.

"There," she said, looking drained from reliving the nightmares of her past. I opened the cabinet and removed some of the older-looking albums.

"Did these make it back from Poland and Brazil intact?"

"Yes, it's quite incredible with everything else that got broken and lost," she said.

I opened one of the albums and the empty placeholders gaped amid the remaining photographs. "Some of the photographs are gone," I said.

"Oh yes, that was probably one of your aunts fishing around," she said, as though to scold a mischievous child. "They say they are going to dispose of them when I am gone."

"Why would they do that?" I asked, feeling desperate at the thought.

"Oh, goodness knows. It's just old stuff they don't want to know about."

I perched myself on Oma's footstool, in front of her armchair so that she could guide me through the albums. "Yes, there we are, that was after the war. What happy years those were at my sister's farm. Unlike many, we always had enough to eat. The children had a wonderful time. Look! There they are playing in the river during the summer. Yes, those were happy days. Their father was gone a great deal. He was more than occupied by figuring out how to make a living, selling meat he and my brother-in-law had slaughtered in the black market. It wasn't allowed, of course, but everyone did it."

A new page opened up to a photograph of Oma and Opa posing with their five young children. There was an air of excitement and opportunity in the picture, as though the family could see a future emerging out of the rubble of war. Opa was well groomed, with short-cropped sides and an elegantly tailored jacket with wide lapels. The smoothly shaven skin accentuated a square jaw and a long nose that pointed affectionately downward at one of the children; the one with M's unmistakable sad eyes. "There's little Hilda," recalled Oma, of the apple-cheeked toddler perched on her lap in the picture. "The birth took place at my sister's farm just after the war ended."

Suddenly, it dawned on me that during the treacherous end-phase of the war Oma had been with child, and had been responsible for the four other young lives she had already brought into the world. "You mean you fled Poland midwinter with four young children and you were pregnant?"

"Yes, but we were young and could manage."

"How did you leave?" I urged her on, suddenly feeling unreserved sympathy for Oma, M, and all the others.

"In a horse-drawn carriage, and then special buses organized for SS families. We were offered underground bunker apartments in Berlin, but I said no and we went on to my sister's farm in the countryside. It was safer there."

Just as Oma had aroused my most compassionate feelings, they got caught in the term "SS." I wasn't an expert, but there was something deeply sadistic, like a thorn that refused to release the flesh, in this infamous abbreviation for Nazism's elite. I swallowed Oma's words and reassured myself that she was not an SS wife; she and her children had merely been offered transport and accommodation reserved for the SS; Opa had been a farmer and he had nothing to do with all of that.

"Look! Don't the girls look smart in their dirndls?" She pointed at a picture of three attractive young women lovingly gathered around a panting German shepherd. The tallest of the women was a chalk blonde and the two others were brunettes. "That was at a hunting house in northern Germany, which your grandfather eventually managed to get a hold of after the war. We moved away from my sister's and he was determined to turn it into the most elegant of hotels. We had the very best of regular clients, you know! Only the best, and that place is where these came from." She smoothed her right index finger down the length of a spoon on the table. For as long as I could remember, whenever I visited Oma's apartment, we ate with this cutlery with the stag engraved into the grip.

"Oh, and how we had to work. Work, work, work! Until everything was beautiful and fine, and then it was time to leave again. What idiocy! What fools we were!"

"But why did you leave Germany if everything was so good, Oma?" The question just slipped off the tongue without thought.

"Oh, you know, friends from Brazil, good clients of ours, mentioned it to us, and your uncle and Opa became obsessed. As usual, I just followed along with what the men said. It isn't at all what you think, you know." I wasn't sure what to think. I was born in Brazil, and that was all I knew. "It was already 1960, long after the war was over. Your Opa was always driven by his desire for more and better. *Nothing* to do with what everyone says. But then we got there and, oh, it was so primitive. It was right out in the Mato Grosso, in the interior!" She raised her voice as though I had sentenced her to this fate. "I couldn't tolerate the blistering sun. My skin is still bleached from it, you see." She brushed her hand over her forehead. "That was a dangerous place! We should never have gone there, but your Opa was insistent.

"Look, there he is taking a little afternoon coffee just before we crossed the great river into the interior. Ten kilometers wide it was!" She pointed at a photograph of a man with thinning hair, slicked back at the crown with sides cropped. The uniform and the hunting gear I had seen in older photographs had been exchanged for a loose-fitting, light-colored suit. The eyes were hidden behind dark glasses and a small cup of strong coffee was held to the lips. The elegant matching Panama hat rested on the makeshift wooden bar of what looked like a dwelling in a shantytown. Opa looked remarkably calm for a man on his way into a dangerous wilderness.

"He already had diabetes by then, just like his father before him. It was all nonsense, the whole thing! And then he lost it all. Everything gone because he refused to learn the local language. He needed Harty to run the business side of things, but the two of them fought night and day, and at some point Harty picked up and left. Just like that, and then it was all over. Oh, what we lost."

Oma slumped back into her armchair looking deflated. She had opened up so many questions, but I didn't want to press her any further this afternoon. I closed the album and stared up at the oil painting. It was a dream that had turned into a nightmare. Why did Oma keep this painting on her wall if it reminded her of all that had been lost? Why not a painting of an innocent flower, or a still life with fruit? This room I thought I knew so well was suddenly full of things I didn't know at all. There were photographs that had always been there in albums and boxes that I had never seen. There was the cutlery with the elegant insignia on it, and the painting in the ornate golden frame that attempted to say so much more but had been silenced.

—◦—

On the following afternoon, I returned to Oma. My fiancé thought it important that I continue the exchange with her. He seemed to know more about me than I did, and unselfishly encouraged me to take time with my grandmother.

When I entered, Oma was not in her usual chair. Instead, I found her sitting on the edge of her bed in her undergarments. She was silent, her head bowed, her shoulders hunched over. Her silhouette against the window was not the strong, upright figure I had known, rather it was a woman who had suffered acute depression for many years following her return from the wilderness. The cheerful, affectionate, and curious figure of my memory appeared to have collapsed under the weight of things that were too hard to bear. I assumed that our conversation the previous day had been the cause and immediately was consumed by guilt.

I walked over to her and stroked her back. "Are you all right?" I asked.

"Oh my dear Jülchen, I have had such nightmares. I don't have the depression anymore, but those beastly nightmares won't leave me in peace." She continued to look down, slumped over the stocking-covered feet she had tucked into her slippers.

"Do you want your bathrobe?" I asked.

"Oh no," she said. "It's time to heave this old body up from afternoon rest and put on some proper clothes." I reached for the silk blouse that hung over the end of her bed, and waited, holding her skirt as she threaded her arms into the sleeves. Oma looked elegant, even in her undergarments. The fine-spun cotton with the delicate finishing of lace and the silk stockings attached to garters looked remarkably stylish on this woman who was halfway through her eighth decade.

I helped her rise from the bed, and soon she straightened up, regained her composure, and led us both into the kitchen. "Let's brew some tea today, shall we?" she said rhetorically, counting each dried leaf before dropping it into the teapot, and putting the kettle on to boil. "Oh, and I see I am all out of buttermilk. When I get like this my stomach goes all bad, and a little cup of buttermilk before bedtime is a great help. Your mother was given buttermilk as a little baby soon after she was born in Posen, you know. My breast milk would not come for her. Terrible! How the child cried." Oma's mind had the habit of randomly fishing out the rarest of memories from the sea of history she had lived in.

"I can buy you some buttermilk this afternoon, Oma. It's no problem."

"Shopping for food in the afternoons?" she asked, puzzled. "One shops in the mornings before all the freshest produce is gone. I will buy what I need then." There were distinct habits and rules that came from a time I didn't know, and there was no use in arguing about them.

As we sat down to tea and biscuits, Oma pursued the thought that had crept out of her subconscious in the kitchen. "All that childbearing! It was so painful—five children—can you imagine? But in those times one was obliged to have many." She popped one of the tiny biscuits into her mouth, and her head wobbled as she chewed, until she washed the biscuit down with a stabilizing sip of tea.

"Well, you don't know anything about that yet," she said, demonstrating that the wobbling didn't get in the way of her concentration. Oma was right. I didn't know anything about childbearing yet, and I doubted I ever would. Ingrained in me was the idea, in fact the terror, that I wasn't the sort.

"Then there were all the miscarriages. Oh it was terrible! I had complications in Brazil too and there wasn't the right medical care. It all led to an awful situation later on. They had to take it all out, you know. *Everything* out!" I could feel the pain as she flicked her hand swiftly across her lower abdomen. "Then came the depression. You have no idea how bad that can be. If you haven't lived through it, you can't understand. Some don't get through it at all. Each day life seems less bearable." She lowered her head in the same way that she did when she spoke of the unjust burden on Germans.

The heat of shame spread over me. I could feel it creeping over my skin, into my mouth, down my throat, and into my heart and lungs. Its creeping was a reflection of myself: the one who didn't understand, yet was the descendant of all this suffering.

"Our life together was not nice." Her voice cracked at the end of the sentence. "It was hard and cruel, and I was afraid. As soon as he came into the house all of us froze and when he was gone everyone could breathe again. He couldn't handle the servants at all. Then there were those young dolls he satisfied himself with—couldn't keep his hands off other women. Our life together became painful, especially when he drank, and I didn't want any more. But he just kept coming at me against my will. Men have their needs and cravings." She stared at me solemnly, as though this was something that I too would have to learn to accept. I recognized the sad eyes so well. They were M's and my own.

I was struck by Oma's slim calves and ankles, which were just like M's. They seemed so thin and helpless, sticks that could easily collapse when the brutes of history struck. "Why did you stay with him, Oma?" The tears threatened to well over my lower lashes. She heaved a sigh full of regret.

"That was what one did, but at the very end I didn't. I left and eventually went home. He'd found a little dark thing, a mulata, to spend his days with. And when I arrived the depression was there waiting for me."

CHAPTER 5

Germany, 2010

IT WAS THE LAST DAY OF MY VISIT WITH OMA BEFORE THE ONWARD journey. Many years had passed since the encounter on the bus with Father in Oxford.

"Take care of my grandchildren," he had shouted, waving goodbye, with the last reserves of a body emaciated by disease.

He didn't want me to watch him die, and so we never saw one another again. Behind the mask of tears that I wore for months after his passing, I repeated this promise to him. It became like a chant that took me into a trance where I saw the ominous shadow the past had cast over us. I fell into the dark confines of depression, and on some days found it impossible to rise. Shame had wound its cunning tendrils around me and my family, and asphyxiated us slowly. In the darkness, I remembered the difficulties I had experienced with breathing as a child. It all began to make perfect sense. In order to take care of my children I had to take care of myself, and the only way to do that was to cut away the tendrils and go to their roots.

"Take time to attend to this," my husband said, as he sat by my bedside stroking my back in the morning light I no longer noticed.

I shook my head, not because I disagreed with him, but because I knew that in order to fulfill my last promise to Father, I would have to break the one I had made to myself and to him years ago, never to look into the past.

Today, as I sat in Oma's living room, Father had become another figure of history inside a photo frame. The pots clanked loudly in the narrow kitchen, which Auntie Best had taken over as her mother's caregiver. Oma was two years shy of a century but her voice retained its volume and her mind its sharpness.

"Oh, what a noise!" Oma complained, irritated by the clanking pots in the kitchen. "Shut the door! We can't hear a thing!"

Her lack of gratitude for Auntie Best embarrassed me, particularly as she insisted I sit still and continue our conversation, rather than help my hard-working aunt whom she treated as her foot servant. This haughty and insensitive person bothered me—she didn't match the caring grandmother I had known over so many years through our telephone conversations and visits. As I sat across from her, trying to be considerate of the fact that my grandmother had become a centenarian, I struggled in vain to reconcile these two personas.

Auntie Best, who was herself retired, handled Oma's haughtiness in a fashion that appeared robust, but in the end always did her bidding. As she entered the room with a stack of plates and utensils, I was reminded of how little she resembled Oma. She was petite and dark complexioned, with wide, thick hands that had most certainly worked hard. She organized each task, no matter how great or small, with faith in minute planning and precision as if they were the most reliable flood barrier against the storm surges of life.

Auntie Best, who had no children of her own that we knew of, was caring itself, and when my sister and I were very young we expressed our longing to nestle permanently in this quality of hers, away from our own erratic lives. Auntie Best had never forgotten this, and as she placed the dishes on the table, only to be scolded by her own mother, I realized that her caring was like a dandelion. Despite thin nourishment it had learned to become strong and hardy all by itself.

"Not those!" Oma scolded, her fingers brushing the surface of the finely laundered tablecloth in disapproval. "There," she pointed imperiously toward the side table. "Take the plates from there." Her commanding voice was the antithesis of all fairness and patience. As punishment, her head began to nod and the uncontrollable blinking started once again. It was a cruel thought, but there had to be some consequences of her ill behavior toward my favorite aunt.

35

"Yes Mutti, that is fine. Of course, I will fix that," said Auntie Best, raising her voice slightly to indicate that she didn't appreciate being addressed in this manner, and returning to the kitchen once again. It was like this between Oma and her daughters. Tempers flared for a brief moment and then retreated, as no one wanted to bring the source of the anger back to life. A thick blanket had mindfully been pulled over it, and although sometimes the limbs twitched, they were eventually ignored for fear that the body would have to be exposed.

"Now let's talk about something more interesting," said Oma, her face softening and her eyes calming as her attention turned to me. I was relieved to see that face again and to ignore the corpse in the room, at least for the moment. My onward journey from Oma's might take me to it, but for now I was glad to rest in the familiar peach hues of her face as she spoke.

After months of struggling with the idea, I had come to the conclusion that I must learn about Opa. As none of the family would ever be willing or able to tell me the whole truth, I had decided to go to the German Federal Archives and find it myself. The guilt of not sharing my plans would have to be borne for the time being. Oma was old, had suffered from depression, and Auntie Best had been her caregiver. According to an experienced archivist I had spoken to, it was unlikely I would find anything, and therefore I concluded there was no sense in unnecessarily upsetting anyone.

As I looked at Oma, I felt awkward about not sharing my plans. Above all, I faced the feeling for the first time—which had been standing there all my life, staring at me stone-faced like a guard at the gates—that I didn't have a right to this history. My reflexes forced me back to Oma's way, if only temporarily. The corpse must remain under the blanket and we must talk about other subjects.

"The beautiful flower and herb books you gave me as a child come in handy these days. Remember them, Oma?"

"Oh those, yes," she said, at first absentmindedly. "That place you have up there: that is what we lost!" she exclaimed. Those words she had uttered a decade ago, when she and Auntie Best had visited my adopted home in the countryside in Europe's last wilderness far up north, were branded into my memory. At first, I thought she was referring to her farms in the East, but soon I realized she meant space for living in general; and who didn't want that? I myself had been drawn to my island home in Sweden by its abundance of space and lack of people. But her fleeting comment assumed a certain heaviness when I recalled that Lebensraum had been one of the popular political slogans of her time. These watchwords of Nazism crept into the present like small ogres, intent upon flagging something that no one wanted to see.

"Nature is so masterfully clever: it weeds out all that is weak and only allows for the best and the very strongest to survive." The idea of nature as a cruel but just god, and the self-righteous way that she expressed it repeatedly, clashed with the tender touch of her hands, the affection that I had felt streaming from them during all my years, and the beauty that she saw in the fine detail of the smallest petal. Her words persecuted me, because I felt flawed. How could she pass such a judgment upon all the delicate, sorrowful creatures I thought she had felt such a communion with as a sufferer of depression?

Outside, the church bells rang like provocateurs. "What rubbish the Church feeds people!" Oma snapped. When she said the Church she meant the Catholic Church, an institution that to her mind was the opposite of all that nature had intended, and that annoyingly surrounded her with its many spires. The mere thought of the pope awoke in her a deep-seated wrath that could not be sufficiently explained by present-day developments. "How can that criminal continue to encourage poor people to reproduce themselves in such numbers? We have far too many people on this earth already! It's insanity!" This was followed by the line that always frightened me, because she said it with a vengeance that was quite personal. "Why, he should be shot!"

I didn't find a number of the teachings of the Catholic Church to be of relevance to the modern day, but the hard and unrelenting quality of Oma's judgment upon the pope and my failure to question her about it left me feeling feeble and confused. Her soft face hardened when she said these things, and then she was not at all the person I thought I knew.

—◆—

Two days later my suitcase stumbled over the unevenness in the pavement as I made my way down a wide empty street on the southern outskirts of

Berlin. The cold rain hung heavy in the air, making the pressure of feeling lost all the more intense. As I stopped to read the street sign, my troubled heart battled with my will. Wasn't this a betrayal of the family? Yet my feet were determined to find the way. They simply had to.

Just as I was about to pull out my map of Berlin, a petite auburn-haired woman with dark-rimmed spectacles stopped and asked whether she could help. I had just one day to spend in the German Federal Archives and was glad for any assistance that could speed my journey there. "Ah, the Bundesarchiv," she said, nodding. "Why don't you come with me? I'm on my way there." The soft wrinkles around her eyes suggested she was in middle age. With her battered leather briefcase in hand, she looked like someone who spent time in archives and knew her way around them.

A few minutes into our walk I asked her what her line of research was. She looked up at me briefly as though considering whether it was safe to say, and then faced the road again. "I'm a journalist based in Argentina. During the past decades I've interviewed some of the last surviving Nazis who fled there after the war. I come here often." Her openness lightened the burden of my soul. When exposed to the light, the darkest secrets scuttled away like weak and toothless scoundrels. It struck me that there was something natural and intended in our meeting, which transformed the gray and alienating street into a place that now welcomed me.

"Why are you here?" she asked, eyeing my suitcase. I wasn't sure what to say. Should I tell her—this stranger in the street whom I had met just minutes ago?

"I'm here to learn about my grandfather. I was born in Brazil." If she didn't pick it up, I wouldn't explain further.

"Ah!" She nodded, making the connection straight away. "Quite right," she added, endorsing my decision as though she knew my story already.

I had expected doubt or indifference at the very least, but this was a blast of fresh air. "Have you ordered the files already?" A look of ignorance came over my face. I hadn't done anything, except to check opening and closing times. "It's all right," she said, helping me out of my embarrassment. "If they have anything—and that is a big *if*—you can order it today and most likely have a look at it in the morning. The fact that so much was destroyed at the end of the war frequently makes this type of research a thankless task." From the worried look on my face, she surmised that I didn't have another day. My flight was scheduled to leave that same evening. "Don't worry," she said. "Let's get you into the archives first and then take the next step."

In the locker room, where we stored our bags and coats, she gave me a few more tips and pointed in the direction of the entrance to the archives. "Good luck! I'll watch out for you and we can talk when you're done."

"What's your name?" I asked, realizing that we had become friends without the usual introductions.

"Gaby Weber," she replied and extended her hand. "Your name is on the label of your suitcase, so I already know yours. Now go, and don't lose any more time!" Her keen sense of observation could be unnerving, but I had no reason to suspect anything other than that she genuinely wanted me to find what I was looking for.

❦

The disapproving glance of the archivist at the front desk provoked my bad conscience about prying into my family history. I pictured walking away, thanking Gaby for her kindness and returning home. The archivist interrupted these thoughts and pointed at the arsenal of colored slips on the counter. "Fill in the relevant ones," she said. I stared at all the colors and felt disillusioned. If I didn't state clearly why I was here at this moment, I would most certainly excuse myself and walk out the door.

"I am looking for information about a particular *person*," I said, still afraid to impart the relationship between myself and this person.

"Not possible unless you are family," she replied curtly.

"I *am* family," I shot back, my voice shaking noticeably.

She sighed, recognizing my type. "Please wait," she said sternly, and vanished into a back room.

Another opportunity to leave presented itself and then passed, as a fresh-faced young man emerged from the back room and took me aside to a corner where we wouldn't disturb the other researchers. We sat across from one another, and he folded his hands as he leaned forward across the table so that he could keep his voice down. "You want to know about a family member, I understand?"

"Yes, my grandfather," I said, convinced that no one in here would take me seriously. "I was born in Brazil and I believe I was never told the real reasons for my mother's family's presence there. You must understand that not knowing has produced a very complex family situation," I added, realizing that in the dispassionate world of the archives I was taking a great emotional risk. Once the words were out, I felt considerably better. "Complex" was fair, and once again I marveled at the way that the past lost its virulence when it was exposed.

"I understand," he said, the sharp blue outlines of his irises softening. This was the second stranger in one day who seemed prepared to listen. "We can have a look and I can provide you with copies of whatever we find, but I have to ask you not to share the documents themselves with anyone else. Do you understand?" Immediately I said yes, because I couldn't imagine who else would want to see them.

"Very well," he said. "Please write down the name of your grandfather and his date of birth." A feeling of hopelessness came over me. I didn't know when Opa was born. "Never mind," said the archivist, recognizing the problem. "Just write down his name."

Theroux, as he was called, stood up energetically and typed my grandfather's name into the search engine on the workstation behind him. My heart pounded, hoping that nothing would come up. "There we are," Theroux said, satisfied that he had found a lead. "There is only one record in our archives under that name. Same middle name as the one you provided. Could this be him?" I looked at the year of birth and realized that it would be a very great coincidence if this person was not my grandfather.

"Yes, it could," I replied solemnly. "What sort of documents are these?" Each question forced its way through my doubts about wanting to know.

"They are *Ahnenerbe* and a few other papers—hard to tell exactly until we have a look at them. Most likely they contain information about your grandmother too. I'll have them copied and sent to you. There are about one hundred pages."

Oma? Why would Oma be in these papers? Theroux and I sat down once again at the table. I folded my hands in a desperate effort to stop them from shaking. "Mr. Theroux, what does this say about my grandfather? Was he in the SS, for example?" Theroux suddenly realized I didn't understand the meaning of the word *Ahnenerbe*.

"Yes, most definitely," he said, with the dispassionate responsibility of a professional archivist. "Without a shadow of a doubt," he added, acknowledging the weight of our discovery. "Ahnenerbe was an organizational part of the SS. Now please fill in these short forms so I can get the copies to you."

I lifted my pen and tried to make out what information the various lines required, but my vision was blurry and my hand unable to form a single letter of my own name. Theroux noticed and removed a pen from his shirt pocket. "I can take care of this," he offered. "Just give me your details and then you'll need to sign."

As I walked out the archive doors, I imagined opening the documents and finding they were not about my grandparents. There were other faces in them that had nothing to do with me. It was all wrong, but in my heart I knew it wasn't. Of course it was true. These people were my very own.

Gaby stuck her head out of the locker room. "Coffee?" She smiled. I nodded with a numb look on my face. As we sat at the small table in the locker room, Gaby restrained her journalistic instincts and didn't pose any questions. I took a sip of the weak brew in the small plastic cup that burned my fingers.

"He says he has found one hundred pages on a person with the same name with around the right year of birth. My grandmother is in the documents too. They are mostly Ahnenerbe documents, and I've got no idea what that means. I just don't know what to think. The archivist says this most definitely means he was SS."

"Yes, without a shadow of a doubt." Gaby nodded, repeating Theroux's words exactly.

"He is sending me copies of the documents, but I have no idea what to do then." Gaby recognized my hesitation about facing the many questions raised by my discovery, and the possibility that I might give up at any moment.

"You have just learned that your grandfather was in the elite. You cannot let that go, and you must pursue the matter as far and as best you can."

The dark rims that framed her eyes were intense, like microscopes. Under them, she could see that the very cells I was made of were formed by the history in the documents, and that I must understand their makeup in order to be able to live with myself. Quickly, she wrote down some leads; names and numbers of people she thought could help.

The day seemed unreal, because the ground I had trusted all my life was falling away from under my feet. I longed for security and stability, and excused myself to call my husband. "He was SS," I said, choking up over the phone in a corner of the hallway outside the locker room.

"What?" my husband replied in shock. I said it again in a more even voice, noticing how easy it was to slip into abominable self-pity.

When our conversation ended, I knew that I could no longer hide outside the archive doors. Gaby, Theroux, my husband and, most of all, my very own will had made sure they had been forever opened.

Later on I learned that the one person who happened to be on that street in Berlin and offer her guidance on that fateful day was the same person who had fought tirelessly to prevent the declassification deadline on the German National Intelligence Services files about Adolf Eichmann from being extended. Lurking in the soul of our meeting was the belief that history belonged to the people, not locked away in forbidden government vaults.

———

After I left the archives, my instincts took me back to the Wall that no longer existed, except in pieces that were now regarded as grim memorabilia or works of art. It wasn't practical to traipse around this sprawling city pulling a suitcase, but I didn't care. It had become an unconscious extension of me that I dragged around, like my heavy and unwieldy life.

Under the Brandenburg Gate, the tourists hungrily recorded every moment with their cameras and mobile telephones. In their midst was a woman who stood silent with her suitcase in a time warp; a granddaughter for whom the war had neither a beginning nor an end.

The after-tremors shook me and, in many ways, were more disturbing than the moment of discovery itself. The keystones fell out and the greater structures collapsed. Everything permanent became fleeting; everything real, a mirage. My old family were strangers or, even worse, opponents on the other side of the dividing line we called truth.

I seemed to be in one location and then suddenly in another, not knowing how to take myself anywhere. Signs pointed in the direction of different sites, but there was no sign that could point me in the right direction. Right-left, right-wrong—it was impossible to know where to turn. The transitions from one place to another were swallowed by the enormity of what I had just learned.

I sat on the ground, against one of the cement slabs in the Holocaust Memorial not far from the Brandenburg Gate. The chill of the stone penetrated my coat like a punishment. At least I had been able to release the burden of my suitcase, which rested against another of the slabs. Were we in a block of prison cells or in a graveyard? Perhaps both, because for millions, being imprisoned was the same as a death sentence.

What was I to do? I waited for the gray slabs to mete out their sentence, but strangely they refused. Instead, I could feel them crowding in around me, surrounding me with the sorrow and sympathy of fellow inmates. I wanted to ask for forgiveness, but this seemed pointless, and instead I wept before them, laying my soul bare as the gray stone.

When I reemerged, I found a tourist examining me like a museum exhibit. The camera dangled around his neck in a rare unused moment. Mute seconds passed, and then he continued on his way through the maze. The only thing to do was to accept my bareness.

—◦—

As time passed, I found that self-imposed nakedness could lead to instant trust between strangers. After the first meetings with Gaby and Theroux, many other torchbearers appeared to illuminate my way. They helped me to see into those one hundred pages from the archives, understand the detail, and read between the lines. To look at a document was one thing, but to slot it into the puzzle of history so that the fit was right was quite another.

During the early mornings of the summer gone by, I had sat outside my cottage at the water's edge devouring history books with the hunger of my student days. Somewhere on those pages was the answer to what had happened to my family—to Opa, Oma, M, and her siblings—but it was scattered like code in the different accounts, and difficult to put together without other trained decipherers.

One of those books presented the deceitful game the Hitler regime had played in order to craft the pretext for the invasion of Poland in September 1939. I looked at the back cover and saw a friendly, youthful face. Did it matter if, among the many emotionally torn grandchildren who felt forced to face what their grandparents had done, the author didn't take me seriously?

I hammered out an email, but wasn't satisfied. It omitted my true motives, which had to do with my family and the complex way in which the past had affected our relationships. My fear was that someone so learned might be alienated by the nonacademic nature of such personal details. He could just as well reject them as having no place in the study of history, and suggest that I save my sad story for the therapist's couch. On the other hand, the account was incomplete without all that I knew and had lived with, so I replaced sentences that I had previously deleted, heaved a deep breath, and pressed Send. With that one action, I tossed the most troubled part of myself out into the world for scrutiny. While self-imposed nakedness could yield trust, it was also frightening because people could either identify with it or reject it as vulgar and undignified.

The phone interrupted my thoughts.

"I just received your e-mail," said the high-spirited voice of Jochen Böhler, the author of the book.

Barely ten minutes had passed since I had sent the email.

"Thank you so much for calling me," I fumbled. "I hadn't expected you to respond so soon. I really appreciate it."

"There is no better time to start than the present!" he said with an energy that banished all my reservations. "So, let's get going."

A half hour later, I put down the receiver, walked outside into the sunlight, and received its warmth on my bare face, which by now had become used to the dampness of tears. Beyond taking my story seriously, Jochen had provided a road map of where to go next.

Chapter 6

Germany, 2012

THE EMOTIONLESS VOICE OF THE GPS LED ME DOWN THE DESERTED two-lane road that once had been the main route north out of Hamburg toward the Danish border. "Continue for twelve kilometers," said Greta, a name I had given to the GPS so that I would not be without a travel companion.

On this cold, wet December evening I made my way to the hunting house and inn that Opa and Oma had settled in with their children some years after the war. I had been there before, over twenty years ago, as a university student. The staff had treated me with aloofness then, and I didn't know whether I could expect anything different today. I remembered the heat of shame as I had sat in the restaurant of the inn as a twenty-one-year-old, my face flushed red as I sensed the many eyes of the inn mocking me. It was like being an outcast without knowing why.

This time, I had notified the mayor, a retiree in the sleepy community where the inn was a notable establishment. I told him that I would be happy to meet anyone with memories they could share. "Happy" was of course an exaggeration. The research was like an anesthesia that stemmed the pain of agony, which set in whenever I reflected upon my latest findings.

As I looked at the story that was forming, it was impossible not to arrive at certain damning conclusions. The worst of these was that my nearest had not told the truth about something, the magnitude of which was so great and so serious, that it was hard not to feel the sting of deceit.

In a briefcase in the passenger seat next to me were the one hundred pages Theroux had copied and sent. Each page was full of many small shards that cut as I attempted to piece them together into a comprehensible narrative. The handwriting of my grandmother's pages was familiar. It was the same as in the many birthday cards she had sent to me over the years. Still, I found it impossible to match the woman who had filled in these forms for racial qualification as an SS spouse with my grandmother, a woman with whom I shared so many interests.

The details in the documents qualified my grandparents for membership in Hitler's elite. There were birth dates, places of birth and residence, details concerning children, and a family tree going back to 1800 intended to uphold the illusion of racial purity. What was my own flesh and blood doing in these documents? There must be some mistake.

The photographs delivered the final blow to my embattled hope. Shot from every angle in order to ascertain their apparent racial superiority, these images undermined my heart's vain struggle. Oma smiled widely, almost provocatively, at the camera. Her full figure was indicative of a woman in her childbearing years.

The photographs of Opa were taken some years apart. The earlier ones revealed a defiant young rebel, his crossed arms and impudent chin making him perfect material for the SS. The tailored tweed jacket, the jodhpurs, and the polished high-cut leather boots were typical of his Hamburg middle-class origins, which aspired to the likes of the British landed gentry. The facial features were strikingly familiar.

In the later photographs, the lapels of Opa's jacket were wide and proud, with ample room for two gleaming pins. His body was slightly turned so that the right lapel, where the pins were fastened, caught the onlooker's attention. The insignia of the party and the SS were unmistakable. From the defiant prewar photographs to the dutiful wartime images, something had happened. The impatience and anger had been packaged by the uniform.

He had joined the party in 1931 before the takeover of power; membership in the reservist mounted SS followed three years later. Throughout the war, Opa and Oma had resided with their family in western Poland where they, as members of a new elite, spearheaded the creation of the Reich's model blond province, the Warthegau. This was the cruel heart of Nazism's racial experiment. The order of the day in this place was violence, and into this M had been born.

"Turn left in 200 meters," the GPS warned.

As I pulled into the parking lot, Greta stated the obvious. I had reached my destination. It was dark and I could not make out the entire property, but I could see the illuminated castle-like house. It was unsettling to be back in this place where I had once felt such rejection, and which evoked such high emotion in Oma and her daughters.

The prospect of checking in at the reception desk seemed daunting. The staff must already know why I was here. In rural northern Germany, which had been an early stronghold for the Nazi Party, anyone asking questions about this period of history could be treated with suspicion. In the small towns scattered across the flat landscape, news of a curious granddaughter traveled like wildfire and many withdrew, like snails into their shells.

My grandfather and his family had not gone unnoticed in the annals of this region. In the same folder with the thick stack of pages from the Berlin archives were two copied pages from the published chronicles of this area, shared with me by the mayor's office. I reread them countless times, hoping against hope that they might not be so bad if I returned to them again.

On one of these two copied pages about the history of the inn, the following claims jumped out of an otherwise mundane account of a village and its buildings through history: Opa had left Germany suddenly for Brazil due to his National Socialist past. As Sonderführer or Special Führer for Landed Estates in East Prussia and Poland he had tortured, shot, and caused the death of many. When Adolf Eichmann was arrested, Opa fled.

This account had been provided by a Knight of the Iron Cross by the name of Baum, who had served with Opa in the East and worked in the local textile factory after the war. Baum, a respected member of his community, had vowed never to stand under the same roof with my grandfather because of his acts of barbarity in the East.

For several nights after reading this, I dreamed of a child walking through a war-ravaged landscape bled colorless. She was firmly focused on the road ahead and avoided the sight of bodies piled up like sacks on either side of a narrow path. Each time I awoke, this image haunted me and I wondered whether I had dreamed of myself or of M.

⟶ ⟵

Nervously, I awaited the arrival of the mayor, who, the staff at the reception assured me, was on his way. A table had been booked for us in the restaurant, which was filled with the smell of red spiced cabbage emanating from the kitchen. There was no particular reason it should smell as familiar as it did, and so I played with the thought that there might be sensual experiences that dwelled in the collective memory of a family. Perhaps there was a type of instinctive knowledge that trickled through the generations. It could be spiced red cabbage, but it could also be violence.

The hotel's front door swung open and two men in raincoats nodded a familiar greeting to the staff at the reception. A heavyset, bald man wearing spectacles emerged from the back room and rushed forward to greet them. "Welcome, Herr Mayor, Herr Schuhmeister, always pleased to receive you here," said the inn owner stiffly, helping them with their sleet-covered coats.

"Thank you very much. Now where's our visitor?" replied the mayor, who appeared to be in a constant rush despite the fact that he was retired. With eyes lowered and a slight action of the hand, the inn owner alerted them to the fact that I was standing nearby. The mayor presented himself in a businesslike manner, keeping his thin leather portfolio close to his side. Schuhmeister, a contemporary of the mayor's, smiled widely and searched my eyes, as though to find traces of something long lost. He pressed my hand tightly as he shook it.

"Shall we?" said the mayor, breaking the grip of Schuhmeister's stare and ushering me into the dining room. The dark beams of the restaurant hung over me like guards over an impostor. I recognized them from the family photographs.

As we sat down to the immaculately set table and unfolded our napkins, the engraved stag on the silver cutlery gleamed in the candlelight.

I had been eating with the same cutlery in Oma's apartment ever since I could remember. "Is something the matter?" asked the mayor.

"No," I said, realizing that it was impossible to explain how surreal it was to be in this room. "It's just that I recognize this symbol." I lifted the dessert spoon and examined the engraving more closely.

This triggered a flood of storytelling by the mayor and Schuhmeister. It wasn't long before the latter had revealed that he had once fallen in love with one of Opa's beautiful daughters, all of whom were always dressed in orderly dirndls and forced to work in the hotel. Schuhmeister described the oppression that the women of the house had lived under, which he claimed he had tried to alleviate at great risk to himself.

"The lady of the house dared not raise her head and was very quiet." He paused, realizing he was referring to my grandmother. The times I had seen Oma bowing her head and lowering her voice flashed before me; reflexes whenever she spoke of her husband.

"I smuggled the girls out at night for a ride in my father's car when the old devil had gone to bed next to his revolver." The mayor grinned as Schuhmeister told his tale of heroic deeds. "He could have been your father, you know." Schuhmeister cast a look at me I didn't like. "All so well built and everything in the right place," he commented, raising an eyebrow and observing my dress for the evening. I blushed as I realized that for some reason I couldn't explain I had chosen clothes—a ruffled blouse, tight vest, and skirt—that could be construed as dirndl-like.

Just as we were getting onto the hopeless track of broken romance, a blank look came over Schuhmeister's face. "One day the girls told me they would have to leave. They simply had to depart at once." Schuhmeister played uneasily with his dessert spoon.

"Yes, well, that was quite a shame," the mayor interjected. "Now you can see how blindly in love he was." Further revelations didn't seem necessary.

The mayor looked around to see who else was in the restaurant before his next action. A couple sat on the other side of the room absorbed in each other's company. The mayor reached for his leather portfolio and lowered his voice.

"I have some documents that may be of interest to you," he said, his voice a snippet above a whisper. "There are some people in these parts who remember your grandfather and his family. The memories are strong, you understand. I have recorded some of the things they told me, and there are some other local records showing dates of arrival and departure in this town that could be of interest to you."

He placed the papers on the table and quickly consumed his dessert, eager to be done with dinner. "Thank you," I said, realizing the mayor would prefer it if we didn't discuss the material in public view.

Schuhmeister consumed his dessert slowly, hoping to prolong the meal, but neither the mayor nor I obliged. Soon the two men were gone and I was left with the bill.

Back in my hotel room, I put on the complimentary Christmas music, which had been placed next to the CD player on my night table. The sound of the German carols filled my room with the memory of M's Christmases. She put so much effort into keeping traditions alive that must have been passed on to her in this very house.

I lay down on the bed, opened the folder, and read its contents. On each page were the confessions of villagers who remembered. Collectively, they formed a picture of a paranoid tyrant who kept his revolver by his side. As a result, the family hadn't mixed much with the local community, and Opa maintained strong connections to his former SS network. On days when the parking lot was filled with Mercedes, and the inn was closed to the public for exclusive hunting weekends, the locals knew.

The townspeople were without doubt about Opa's motives for suddenly departing for Brazil in 1960. During that year, the property with its extensive forest was suddenly put up for sale at a fraction of its worth. Prospective buyers suspected there must be something wrong with the place. Opa's shot-off lower left arm was a subject of much speculation, but none of the bizarre rumors seemed to make any sense. I began to wonder what the villagers' motives were. The weight of the confessions was immobilizing, so that turning off the Christmas music or the lights was too difficult. The image of Father's shaking hands on the bus in Oxford passed before me, and I thought I understood why he had tried to protect me from all this.

I awoke two hours later; the music had stopped. Without thinking, I pushed the Start button and the first track played again. It filled the high-ceilinged room with M's favorite carol. Sorrow for her and for her sisters filled my heart. Perhaps they had been in this very room cleaning it and pulling down the covers for Opa's comrades. What must they have thought when they had been to school and perhaps seen the images of emaciated bodies piled high in the camps? I fell asleep with their anger and confusion, and awoke each time the music stopped to press the Start button and force myself through the nightmare again, all because I wanted to understand.

The first rays of morning light cut through the heavy curtains like swords. After a broken night I was surprisingly alert, and pulled on my sneakers so that I could head outside and see the whole property. It was magnificent, with the surrounding forest caressing the castle-like inn. Closer to the road was the two-story house the family had lived in. I wondered from which window the sisters had lowered their escape ladder at night. They had been defenseless, their eldest brother gone to learn to be an estate manager.

The wet leaves from the night's sleet sank like a sponge under my feet and the cold rainwater seeped into my shoes. I wasn't sure about this place, this town and its people, but the story portrayed in the gathered confessions passed on to me by the mayor could not be entirely untrue. What else could have moved a couple in their fifties, who had been through the upheaval of war and who were not in the best of health, to leave for a dangerous wilderness on another continent? What had it taken for them to send their only son ahead, and why had he agreed to do it?

The reading and research assignments I had already been given by my friends in academia provided credible explanations, but the heart wanted to forget those facts until the mind said it was no longer possible. By the time Adolf Eichmann was captured in May 1960, the unofficial amnesty of the 1950s made possible by the exigencies of the Cold War was over. While Adenauer's Christian Democratic Union had campaigned on "a quick and just denazification"—a contradiction in terms that served the desire of the general population to draw a line under history—a decade later the chancellor could no longer resist the pressure from outside the Federal Republic to bring at least some of the many perpetrators who walked free to trial.

The heartbreaking images of ghostlike beings discovered in camps featured in Alain Resnais's film, *Night and Fog*, a winner at Cannes in 1956, gripped the world and made the unthinkable deeds of the war ever more widely known. The Cold War itself became a force that pushed against the dam that Adenauer had built in order to focus on the postwar rebuilding and avoid giving what he regarded as unnecessary attention to the past. In his perspective, excessive reflection could only undermine an emerging yet delicate confidence in the future among his countrymen. The East German regime took political advantage of the West's failure to come to terms with the atrocities of the Third Reich, accused it of continued fascism, and threatened unsavory revelations about public figures. Government offices, including courts, and other key positions in society were filled with people who bore undeniable responsibility for what had taken place during the war years. In 1955 West Germany gained full judicial sovereignty from the Allies, and the decision fell into the chancellor's hands. The dam had broken and Adenauer submitted to the calls for greater justice. "Your Opa was a big fan of Adenauer!" Oma had declared. I wondered what he thought now.

In 1958 Germans listened with grim interest as the circuit court of Ulm charged ten men with the murder of over 5,000 Jewish men, women, and children in the former Lithuanian-German border zone. The sentences included between three and fifteen years in prison, and the withdrawal of civil rights for a commensurate number of years. It was the first trial of Nazi perpetrators to take place in a German court, and paved the way for the establishment of a war crimes prosecution office in Ludwigsburg in December 1958, which created a legal basis for the federal prosecution of Nazi crimes.

Between Eichmann's capture and the beginning of his trial during the following year, the Federal Republic made a flurry of arrests. The fifty-four-year-old Eichmann's argument about following orders fell on deaf ears, and Opa, a contemporary of the accused, must have felt the figurative noose tightening. The capture of Eichmann sent shock waves through former-SS circles. Who would be caught in his incalculably sticky web of revelations, and who could be trusted in a climate where former comrades would most certainly choose to save themselves over loyalty?

As the morning's gray light penetrated the spaces between the trees, I was reminded not to settle for simple explanations. Why hadn't Opa changed his name, and why head for Brazil when Eichmann was captured just next door in Argentina? The truth seemed such a slight and fleeting thing, I began to wonder whether it really existed.

Later that morning, I drove to the tiny town that was the site of an estate Opa had acquired in 1937. I knocked on the doors of the orderly farmhouses scattered across the flat landscape, but was advised to keep driving and look out for a grander place. A friendly woman who ran a boutique in a handcrafting barn pointed to a driveway that appeared to be a dead end. A few steps away from a large wooden plaque bearing the engraved name of the estate was a brick mansion covered in red creeping vines.

"We children threw stones at the windows and thought the place was suspicious," the boutique owner admitted. "We never really thought much about why we threw them. It was just a place nobody liked. A widow lives there now—just lost her husband. Try knocking on the door."

Long orderly barns, where the horses had once been kept, flanked the mansion. Even in the depressing gray with the raindrops beginning to fall, I could appreciate the grand vision.

Sheltered under my umbrella from the accelerating rain, I knocked on the front door, ready to be turned away. "Good day," said a tiny woman with the purple-blue lips of a chain smoker.

"I've been driving around this area looking for the place where my grandparents used to live and I believe it is here," I said, and removed an old photograph of the place that I had been keeping in my pocket. She glanced at it and welcomed me in.

"It was in a shambles when we took it over," she said, with the hollow eyes of a new widow. "The Baader-Meinhof people made a mess of it. They had their printing press here, you know."

We sat down at the sturdy table in the middle of the grand reception hall, where there was a half-drunk cup of coffee, an open pack of cigarettes, and an ashtray heaped with butts. The widow fetched a book about the local area and turned to the page about the property.

"At the turn of the century the kaiser established a horse-training station for the imperial cavalry across the whole area, and this was its center," she said proudly. She continued to elaborate on this golden era, as though to keep a haven of safety, far away from the dangerous threshold of the 1930s, which my presence would inevitably force her to.

"Do you know anything about the prewar or wartime occupants of this house?" I asked.

"No, I'm afraid I don't know anything about that," she said, and nervously snatched the open pack of cigarettes. I guessed the widow was from M's generation.

The elaborate wooden paneling all around us had witnessed a grim and turbulent history: the rigidity of the imperial cavalry, the hubris of the mounted SS, and a postwar terrorist group incensed by all that had come before. Little wonder that children had thrown stones at the house.

CHAPTER 7

Germany, 2012

"So, tell us more," said Oma, her ancient eyes still sparkling with the curiosity of youth. "What adventures did you get up to in Hamburg? What were you doing there?"

I had decided not to keep my visit to her old home a secret, and instead presented her with a Christmas arrangement I had purchased at the handcrafting boutique. With the many impressions of Hamburg still unsorted, I chose to avoid answering Oma's question directly.

"Have you noticed where the arrangement comes from?" I pointed at the label that hung from one of the silver-sprayed pine cones.

Auntie Best, who still had perfect vision, reached for the label to read it. Oma pushed her hand away, suggesting it was not for her. Despite the fact that she had arrived at an age where the vain objects of life should have become irrelevant, Oma's lust for fine things and her often-abrasive curiosity remained strong.

"Give me my glasses," she demanded haughtily. I reached for her spectacles, feeling pity for my enslaved aunt. Oma leaned over and read the label out loud. Her nervous disorder didn't seem to bother her when curiosity took over. "Why! Your aunt was born there before the war," she exclaimed.

"Yes, I know," I said, uncertain as to how I was going to handle this conversation, but aware of the growing feeling that I had the right to this history and therefore the right to decide.

"Your grandfather made that place so fine. It didn't have a scratch on it when we were done fixing it up. I'm sure it's all fallen into ruins now. No one could run these places the way we did." How could she know? It bothered me that Oma assumed everything fell apart without her and Opa.

"The Baader-Meinhof gang occupied it for a few years, but the place has been renovated and the house is in good order," I said. This dramatic revelation didn't make any impact on Oma at all. The ghosts of 1939, the year my aunt was born, had already surrounded her.

Auntie Best attempted to shift her mother's attention by lighting the candle in the arrangement. It had become her function in life to divert Oma from facing her own history. While I could not blame my best aunt, who did everything with the finest intentions, it felt absurd for us to carry on within the confines of a story that each of us knew was a lie.

"There, that's very pretty," said Auntie Best, sitting upright in her chair and attempting to ignore the intimations of the past. Perhaps I had assumed too much. What could my aunt really know? She had been no more than a toddler during the war, and her generation did not speak with their parents about the past. Rumors flew here and there, but history was mostly a no-man's land. Between Oma's advanced age, Auntie Best's potential ignorance, and my own inherited guilt, hope seemed to be waning that the important questions would ever be addressed between us.

"I can see why Opa went for that place, with all its past connections to the kaiser and his horses. Opa liked horses, didn't he?" I couldn't bear the deadlock any longer and decided that somehow we had to break it.

Auntie Best stood up to busy herself with one of her many chores. The word "horses" had clearly triggered discomfort. Oma sat back in her arm chair and grasped its generous arms. "Horses?" she ridiculed. "We never had anything to do with horses."

"But Opa liked riding. You said so yourself."

"You've got things very mixed up, child," said Oma, who seemed a thousand miles away from me. "Your grandfather had nothing to do with horses."

I rose to see whether I could make myself useful in the kitchen. Even if my aunt disapproved of my questions, she would never reprimand me. She had begun to busy herself about the evening meal, which must never be served after five o'clock, lest it make Oma's night more unsettled than it usually was. "How can I help?" I asked.

"Leave aside those questions now," said Auntie Best, looking oppressed. "She just gets all worked up."

The haughty voice called from the living room. "Why don't you come back in here and let your aunt take care of that!" The tone filled me with an aversion I had never previously felt toward my grandmother.

"Go on now," said Auntie Best nervously. "I can take care of these things." I longed to remain in the kitchen, but did as she asked.

Since Oma had called me back into the boxing ring, I decided to face her with the question that the documents had already answered. It might make Auntie Best's job harder, but acknowledging facts must surely be better for all of us.

As I sat down across from Oma's armchair, she had already launched into memories of Poland. "We lived a beautiful life there," she said, looking dreamily at the painting of the men in the golden field on the facing wall. "But we had to work to make it so." Her tone changed abruptly and she looked sternly at me. "Those lazy Poles just let everything fall into disrepair and had no idea what an honest day's work was until we arrived and organized things. They were always off holidaying at the Riviera instead, neglecting their own land. We brought order, and they learned how to work!"

For the first time, I found it impossible simply to listen, and interrupted her monologue. "Oma, he was in the SS, wasn't he?"

"SS!" she scoffed. "No, no," she continued, dismissing my suggestion as so outlandish that it was undeserving of attention. Instead, she continued her tale of the unclean and lazy inhabitants of the land that she and her husband had left in a better state than they had found it.

I slumped in my chair. The blow of being lied to was nauseating, and my head was immediately gripped by the most painful headache. Whether or not Oma noticed my reaction, she felt compelled to come to Opa's defense. "Had he not done as they told him, they would have strung him up, you know! That was just the way it was. You had to do what you were told!" My head nodded unthinkingly, racked by pain. These were not the insane mutterings of an old lady. There was a logic to it all. Oma had made a desperate effort to justify a lie, and this time Auntie Best didn't come to her rescue.

—◦—

That evening at a local café Auntie Best ordered a quarter carafe of red wine. She sipped awkwardly as I stirred my sparkling apple juice. She didn't like drinking alone, but I encouraged her to order it because she needed some reward after another harrowing day in the service of her mother.

Her eyes were filled with the worry that I might revisit the question I had raised with Oma, and I felt moved to alleviate her concerns.

"There was someone I met in Hamburg who remembers one of you sisters as his sweetheart."

Auntie Best's eyes lit up. She had lived alone all her life, but liked to recall some of her flings, which she always hastened to add had been quite proper.

"Now, who might that have been?" She smiled. "I know!" she said, like an eager schoolgirl. "It was Kurt Schuhmeister! But how did you meet him?"

Word of Schuhmeister was clearly a lift, and I was determined to keep things going in this direction, even if it meant not sharing the whole story just now.

"It's a small community up there and he was very forthright with his story when he learned who I was," I replied.

Auntie Best's account of the nighttime escapes with her sisters from a tyrannical father aided by Schuhmeister matched the story I had heard up north. I gained confidence that the accounts that had been shared with me during my visit had substance to them. She relived the joy of escaping the inn, and subverting the existing autocratic order with her sisters and Schuhmeister, their knight in shining armor.

Suddenly, the usually stable weather of Auntie Best's humor changed, and her eyes turned downward. She took another sip and tried to swallow the memories. The last thing I wanted was to upset my best aunt, but it occurred to me that her sadness most likely had very little to do with me. Whether we were joking or not, all of us were carrying on within the dark confines of a terrible lie, and this was bound to be upsetting.

"Who was he, Auntie Best? Who was Opa?"

My aunt continued to stare downward, circling her finger around the base of her wineglass.

"I never had any problems with Vati, you know. He was always quite correct, and although we had to work hard at the inn, we got most things we wanted."

She heaved another sigh, wishing that the mild prelude of what she had to say didn't have to be over.

Though the skies were clear and quiet outside, a storm raged over us as I listened, and my beloved aunt explained things that her tender heart should never have had to bear. Aunt Gise, her older sister, had always been the last to finish up in the inn at night. She was very pretty—blond and blue-eyed—and so Opa had *touched* her. Besides this, Oma's life with him had been terrible and had left her in an awful state. He drank and couldn't keep his hands off other women.

The storm of this story raged until Auntie Best stopped speaking, and all that was left were the ruins of youth destroyed. I wished that she could get angry—really angry for once—but instead her eyes became a fearful red that from this day forth would always color the eyes of the pretty girls in the dirndls in those black-and-white photographs whenever I looked at them.

I tried to lighten the burden of confession by saying that I already knew how things had been between Oma and her husband. She had told me herself years ago. Auntie Best wiped her eyes with relief, but it was time to retreat back into the confines of the family's pact. "Now we shouldn't stir all this up any more," she said. "We should let Vati rest in peace."

———

That night, alone in my hotel room, I heard the hard footsteps and felt the fear. Before me, I could see the figure of Gise moving gracefully behind the illuminated windows of the inn, checking that everything was in order for the guests' breakfast on the following morning. Her head turned and her heartbeat raced as she heard her father entering the room. I tried to imagine what happened next, but it defied my imagination.

As I lay sleepless, many things became clear to me. Opa had taken the violence of war home with him and unleashed it on his own family. For them, the war had never ended, and perhaps this was the reason I felt it alive in my own life, so many decades later. Each of the women had her own way of dealing with the disgrace, but in the end all fell victim to the common fate of hurt women and children, which was to protect the offender. All sorts of myths had been spun around Aunt Gise, which had the collective effect of laying the blame on her, but today I understood them as a tragic effort to cope with the unthinkable.

The records from the mayor showed that Aunt Gise had left home at the tender age of seventeen and soon after left for the other side of the Atlantic. The pieces had begun to fall into place. The only one who remained a mystery to me was Oma. How could she continue to live with such a man, taking the risk of exposing herself and her children to his whim in the isolated wilderness that eventually became their home?

In my dreams I stood on the narrow road flanked by the bodies and screamed with rage at the man in the black uniform. He mocked me with his impassive look, arms folded, feet astride. He would never be brought to justice, or so he thought, because he was dead.

"I have set up my own special court on behalf of the other children!" I shouted. "In this court what you have done will be heard in their cries, and by its sound you will be damned. Shame *will* eventually find its rightful place!"

CHAPTER 8

Poland, 2012

As I stood waiting in the reception area of the Institute of National Remembrance in Poznań, my ever-present worry seemed strangely far away. Two years after my first discoveries at the Bundesarchiv, I was about to be provided new classified documents about my grandfather from the Polish authorities.

In the hallway ahead, I tried to see whether the people walking in and out of the doors had the look of devastation in their eyes. Most came to learn of personal betrayals and injustices during the Communist period, and then there was the small handful of people like me.

Daily I awoke in the shadow of guilt at the offense I was committing against my family; and daily my husband and the army of friends I had met along the way pulled me out of that morass using the power of their compassion.

"We are handling you as a Polish citizen," said the official at the Polish Consulate in Stockholm after he reviewed my application. I couldn't determine whether this kindness, delivered with a sympathetic smile, was a response to the fact that M had been born in Poland or commiseration with my case in general.

Afterward, I sat in my car in the parking lot outside the consulate and clutched the steering wheel. All my contact with Poles in the long and complex process of applying for classified documents was like the unselfish application of a rare balm on gaping wounds. Theirs seemed to be a culture that understood the pain of the human condition and did not attempt to dismiss it.

Two sisters, Mira and Agnieszka, had prepared my application in Polish and arranged contact with the IPN. They told me about their father, a member of the resistance movement against the Germans, who learned to speak the language of the enemy from a young German woman who deplored the Nazis. This young woman had put her life at risk to equip the Polish Underground with one of its most fearsome weapons: language. The sisters reminded me not to get trapped in assumptions and stereotypes, and laughed at their father's constant nagging to know the language of one's neighbors.

New friends emerged when the challenges seemed particularly insurmountable. Without official proof of Opa's death, my application to the Polish authorities could not be processed. I imagined a piece of yellowed paper that would decompose before I found it. The Brazilian consulate had stated in no uncertain terms that it couldn't help, so I sat at my desk at home, closed my eyes, and thought of who in the world could. An American professor provided a link to a graduate student in São Paulo. Within a few weeks there were four of us: Nicole and Enzo in São Paulo, and his daughter Katia who lived in Stockholm. A lively exchange of information concerning the possible location of the death certificate developed between us. There were many moments of hopelessness during the months of searching.

After six months, the message arrived from Nicole, the young graduate student in our ad hoc research group. "Death Certificate Success!" she announced. Another door had just opened.

The last people to prepare me for the journey to Poland were Jens and his wife, Katinka, who lived in a beautiful valley in the Austrian Alps. With his wife and daughters by his side, Jens had spent the last decade attempting to reconcile the picture of the beloved father he once knew with the viper of history he had discovered through many years of research. Werner Ventzki had stirred thousands of German men to murder in his role as a Reich Speaker, and had overseen the notorious Łodz ghetto, the second largest in Europe.

The son spoke of the existential nightmare of a German child born in occupied Poland. Like M, he was child number four, revered by the SS as a sign that the Aryan world order was being born, whatever the setbacks of the war. His even demeanor was interrupted by a shudder when he thought of the occult ceremonies that took place in honor of the fourth child. A dagger with the insignia of the SS was passed over the infant swaddled in cloth imprinted with the swastika and other pagan symbols. Daily he struggled with the question of how his parents could bring him into the world just outside the ghetto wall, in full knowledge of their complicity in the murder of Jewish children on the other side. On several occasions, he had faced the anger and grief of the victims' descendants in Łodz. Reconciling the two images of his father seemed an impossible task, and he expected to continue until the end of his days never fully able to answer the elusive question of "why."

"Perhaps we're not supposed to be able to answer it," I said. "And maybe that is what will always keep us engaged in these questions." The truth was that now I was so close to knowing, I wasn't sure I wanted to know.

"You are doing important work," Jens urged, noticing the doubt written across my face. "Just continue."

With this army of the committed standing invisibly behind me, I shook Robert Nowicki's hand. "Welcome to the IPN," he said, his energetic smile beaming down from a great height. Instead of the gray-suited and solemn-looking official of my imaginings, here was Robert, an energetic font of humor and curiosity.

"I'm sorry about all the confusion," I said, fumbling for words. In my nervousness I had muddled the dates of our meeting and arrived a day later than expected.

"So, well, that is the life, isn't it?" he chirped in his charming English, which was delivered in Polish sentence construction.

He ushered me through the next set of doors to a table with two chairs at the back of a room where there were other researchers examining documents. "Please sit down here," he said quietly. He placed a number of forms in Polish before me and said he'd be back in a few minutes. The Xs marked where I should sign.

I returned to the chilling moments before I'd seen Opa's name appear on Theroux's screen at the Bundesarchiv. Was it really better to know, and what did I mean to achieve by knowing? I hid behind these questions, nestling in the familiar excuses I had heard throughout my life: it was his nature; it was the times; it was anything but him and he should be allowed to rest in peace. Weren't we all simply victims of history and circumstance? I glanced around the reading room at the other researchers and felt like a coward, or, even worse, a self-styled victim.

Robert pulled out the chair next to me and placed three sets of bound photocopied documents on the table. Opa's name was spelled in a Polish variation on the covers. On one of them was a photograph that was the same as the one that had rolled down my screen more than a year ago.

"You need to sign here before I can release these to you," he reminded me. I picked up the pen and signed three times. In the space between each signature was the possibility of turning around and giving up. "These are photocopies and you are free to look at them here or take them," he said.

"What sort of documents are these?" I asked.

"They are accounts from the people to the local courts in 1946. Your grandfather's extradition to Poland for trial was requested." Robert slid one of the documents across the table toward himself and opened it. He leafed through pages crammed with eyewitness accounts recorded by one of the few typewriters that had survived the destruction. "See here." He pointed to three German names in a list. Opa's was the second name.

"I never heard anything about my grandfather being put on trial," I said, feeling the anger of betrayal rising once again.

"It's not such a big surprise," Robert replied. "Many cases we sent to Germany got 'lost.'"

"What do these documents say he did?" I asked, knowing that the institute's policy was not to provide translation services. Robert slid the other two documents toward us and paged through them with a look of disgust that didn't match his otherwise sunny demeanor. "It says he beat people very badly, was a terror to the people, called them pigs and dogs. Documents were recorded at two courts in different places in Poland.

"There is a document missing—here, you can see, noted 1969." I looked at him questioningly. "Local archives were sometimes not very good at sending everything to us." He looked more carefully at the note again. "Could be about Sondergericht."

"What does that mean?" I asked, and felt foolish about requesting explanation of a language I thought was one of my own.

"Special court under Nazis for killing Poles," he replied. "Maybe your grandfather was involved in one in this area. Not so unlikely." Robert closed the document and looked at me searchingly. "You are welcome to look at these here or take them."

He closed the door, leaving me alone with the pages of testimonials in Polish. As I leafed through the documents, the momentum of anger lost some of its force. I scrutinized the many German names that had been underlined and circled, interspersed with the letters "SS" and "SA." Then there were the names of the eyewitnesses I had difficulty pronouncing. The acute accents, overdots, tails, and strokes of Polish script were innumerable hurdles to knowing. I would have to go back to Mira and Agnieszka, but could I really ask them to pick their way through these testimonies to repulsive brutality?

Soon, Robert was next to me again, asking for something I could barely hear through the haze that overwhelmed me. He patted me on the shoulder, piled the documents together, and led me out of the reading room. For the half hour in the staff kitchen, Robert listened patiently as the unplanned monologue of why I was here poured forth.

"Families where there is silence and lying are not happy—it was the same thing in the Communist time," he said. Robert had a way of putting things that was refreshingly straightforward. "It is a special case," he said. "Maybe we get one every five or six years, and less all the time. What will you do now?" The ever-present curiosity danced in his eyes.

"Drive into the countryside tomorrow and see whether I can find these places," I said to my own surprise, fanning through the many pages of Polish text.

"I could go with you," Robert offered eagerly. "But first I must ask my wife if it is okay. She looks after our son. Tomorrow is weekend."

That evening I received a message from Robert. "Everything is fine— at what time will you come? Please pick me up at home. Here is address."

On the following morning, Robert forced his tall frame into the passenger seat of the compact rental car and unfolded a detailed map of west-central Poland, Wielkopolska. His sturdy hiking shoes suggested that he was ready for challenging terrain. I felt ill-prepared in my white linen summer clothes and sandals, which I had slipped on unthinkingly in the already stifling heat of the summer morning.

"Well, so how are you today?" Robert said smiling, his superpowered battery charged and ready to go. "I have been thinking that we should go to this village first." He pointed to a location on the map about an hour east, northwest of the city of Konin, to a place called Wilczyn, which the Nazis had renamed Wolfsburgen during their brief reign. "We will try to find estates of your grandparents—documents say there were three in this area—and maybe some eyewitnesses." A stone dropped in my stomach. Would any of them still be alive, and how would we find them?

"Okay, let's go!" said Robert eagerly. I stepped on the pedal and the car leapt forward, hurling the two of us toward the windshield, before I stepped on the brake and brought it to an abrupt standstill. "Well, at least we know the brakes work!" Robert joked. As I started up the engine again and we drove on, I realized I had a partner who wasn't easily fazed.

"We are getting close to the first place," Robert said, about an hour into our journey. A few farmhouses, some of them derelict, dotted the flat countryside. Opa and Oma must have felt at home here, the landscape similar to their home in Schleswig-Holstein, only more sparsely popu-lated and with more space for living. Oma's words, "Oh, what we lost," echoed hauntingly across the flat fields of rye, which laid the villages bare and made them vulnerable to the invader.

During our travels, Robert didn't allow time to wallow in morbid thoughts. "Stop the car!" he exclaimed, and then walked into the brush or a ditch and discovered a landmark that had remained hidden from sight for years. Brick barns were one of his specialties, and he could easily identify the age of buildings from the appearance of their bricks, or the information in the engravings. We drove on and he told me how much he loved this sort of fieldwork, which he experienced as a release from documents and protocol.

"It is the real history," he said, exhilarated by everything around us.

"How do you feel about Germans?" I asked.

"I have been to Germany, and I enjoyed myself there." He smiled, taking all the drama out of my question. I felt freakishly stuck in history.

"Maybe it's this one," he said, pointing to the right side of the road, where a brick wall separated a well-kept mansion with a park in front of it. Farther away were some large barns that looked as though they hadn't been reconstructed since the war. "Drive in and I will ask," said Robert. I sensed history coming dangerously close, and didn't feel prepared to meet the descendants of persons my grandfather had tormented or even killed; but was there any way to prepare?

A middle-aged woman with dyed auburn hair and an apron over her skirt stepped out of the mansion onto the terrace. She held her hand like a visor over her eyes to shield them from the sun.

As I sat waiting for Robert to make a brief inquiry, the car quickly heated up. Nothing seemed brief in Polish, and it was cowardly to sit in the car, so I decided to join the conversation. As I approached and extended my hand, Robert looked uncharacteristically coy. "Can I tell her who you are?"

"Yes, of course," I said, realizing that it was now or never. As he explained, the woman's eyes shifted from Robert's to mine. They were filled with worry.

"She is asking if you are here to take back this place for your family," Robert translated. I shook my head, horrified.

"Oh no," I said, history creeping into my throat like a disease. "Please assure her that we have no such interests!"

Robert continued to explain, and soon we learned that Opa had lived on the neighboring estate, most of which had been torn down. Another of the Germans had taken over this place during the war, and, as for several of the properties, land rights and legal ownership remained a gray area.

On the neighboring estate, we pulled up in front of a house, parts of which had clearly been amputated. There were a few lone trees that had once formed the park, a German model for buffering the mansion from the rougher world of barns and farmland beyond. I remembered the parks I'd seen in Opa's mansions around Hamburg. The design similarities were striking and chilling.

Robert stopped some of the villagers passing by and soon returned with new information. "We can meet the son of Romański," he said. "See, here"—he pointed to one of the names in the documents I had been provided by the institute. I froze. Romański had been a teenager during the war and would remember, as long as he was still in good health.

As we stood at the doorway of Romański's dilapidated house, Robert whispered apologetically. "They are poor," he said. An elderly woman opened the door and nodded a greeting, which suggested she had been expecting us. The threadbare wall-to-wall carpet emitted a strong smell under each footstep, but it was the echo of Oma's words that brought on the nausea.

"The Poles lived in dirt and filth—we had to clean the place up." The thought made me angry at myself and then at her. It was poverty, not carelessness, that forced people to such conditions.

In the middle of the small dark room sat the son of Romański, a sick old man sunk in an armchair with springs that screeched when he moved. Through his unbuttoned shirt I could see there was nothing left but skin and bone. His protruding eyes stared with the white heat of fever and outrage. He shook Robert's hand, but avoided mine.

Opa's name was exchanged several times in a Polish version I had by now got used to. Romański spoke clearly in a strong voice that did not match his withered physique. He spoke in the shortest sentences I had heard in Polish so far. "He remembers your grandfather. His father worked for him. He remembers from when he was a child. He doesn't want to say any more. I think we should not ask him." It was unusual for Robert to give up so quickly, and I wondered whether he was trying to protect me from hard words.

Robert nodded and thanked the couple. Although I suspected Romański didn't want it, I extended my hand to say goodbye. It was the only thing that mattered to me. He stared at it hesitatingly, strands of his full head of gray hair falling over his deathly white forehead. Terrible moments passed, and then I felt the clasp of the swollen, callused hand that had known so much misery and hardship. I nodded a farewell and Romański searched my eyes, confused.

———

We visited a second estate, which I recognized from photographs. The remnants of a great wall built around the mansion and the park were still visible. In the middle was an opening, which I recognized as the passage between family life around the mansion and the scenes of brutality in the working fields beyond the wall. A gigantic brick barn stood like an ancient ruin, with half the bricks broken and heaped in an imposing pile. Opa had once stood there admiring his horses and stroking their muzzles, as they peeped out of the arched openings.

"Over here!" shouted Robert, who was on all fours in the lower level of a smaller dilapidated barn on the opposite side of the courtyard. "This was for animals in winter, but look at all the old stuffs left here. Maybe it is from time of your grandparents." In one corner was an orderly gathering of items, one of them a heavy wooden cupboard of the sort Oma had always admired: assembled by a skilled craftsman, without a single nail being hammered into the wood.

At the gutted house we met a trio of squatters, who played cards under a cloud of smoke and drank from bottles of clear liquid. An unshaven man in rags approached us timidly. "He wants to know whether you have come to claim this place," said Robert, and quickly followed up with a reply. The man revealed his toothless smile and returned to the card game. "This whole area is very poor," Robert explained. "What can you expect after five years of occupation and decades of collectivization?"

As we drove on, Robert spotted a farmer driving a tractor in a distant field. "Stop the car—I will ask him," he said. Robert ran across the field with the well-worn papers in hand. The tractor came to an immediate halt and, after a short conversation, the farmer pointed in the same direction we had been driving. Robert nodded, waved his thanks, and sprinted back. "We can meet someone who knew your grandfather," he panted, dusting some traces of soil off the wrinkled papers and pointing at the name Kiśnewski. "He is very old, but it is worth a try. Drive straight ahead."

With each meeting so far, my enthusiasm for our investigations had waned. We had learned very little at a high emotional cost to impoverished elderly people in ill health. Robert's continued enthusiasm was the only thing standing between me and quitting, and so I stepped on the accelerator.

As we pulled up in front of Kiśnewski's home, two young people in their teens caught sight of us from the long stairwell outside the entrance to the house where they were fixing a bicycle. Not far from them, perched on a tree stump, sat a ninety-year-old man with thick, arthritic hands carving a piece of wood. He ignored us as Robert spoke with the youngsters, Kiśnewski's great-grandchildren. I looked more closely at the old man, who was absorbed in his own world, his sunken mouth devoid of teeth, making an unconscious chewing motion.

Kiśnewski's great-granddaughter greeted me cheerfully, and summoned the old man into the house, helping him off the log and up the stairs. "He cannot hear very well," said Robert. "We will speak with him inside." I didn't like the situation already.

Kiśnewski sat across the table from us, unperturbed and continuing to chew, as Robert explained our reasons for visiting. "He doesn't hear us," said Robert. The young woman repeated Robert's words in Kiśnewski's good ear, and he began speaking under his breath, as though talking to himself. "He is very old," Robert said, disappointed. "But I will try with your grandfather's name." Robert repeated the name twice, and the old man leaned his head toward us, placing his thick hand behind his ear in order to catch the sound.

Without warning, his great-granddaughter began to shout the name repeatedly into his ear. It seemed to me a whipping—like the lashes Opa had meted out to Kiśnewski and others like him. "Stop"! I said desperately, but it was too late. Kiśnewski became distant, as though in another time. His eyes lit up with fear and he shouted the name, covering his head with his arms to protect himself from imaginary blows coming from above. "What is happening?" I asked, realizing that we might be losing Kiśnewski to history.

Robert had himself become entranced and repeated the old man's words in truncated English phrases. "Some people are lined up against a wall to be shot . . . they try to escape . . . he is hiding in a barn watching . . . he is afraid."

"We must stop! Stop this!" I pleaded with Robert, reaching for the old man's hands to draw him out of the time warp we had sent him into.

Kiśnewski's great-granddaughter took hold of the old man's arms and calmed him. Soon he was back at the tree stump, carving the piece of wood, restored to his former state of calm. "Please tell her thank you and I am sorry," I said to Robert. The young woman nodded and shook my hand.

"Okay," she said, reassuring us that it was all right.

The meetings with Romański and Kiśnewski left a bitter taste. I had come to the conclusion that my search was entirely selfish and that we should not continue. Robert, on the other hand, was resolved to keep on. He was ecstatic that we had managed to meet eyewitnesses, and still hoped for one who would be able to tell us more. Perhaps he believed we were not just looking back at history, but that we were also shaping it with our meetings and handshakes. It seemed a grandiose thought—we were nobodies in the course of history—but what if the people we met passed the story of our meetings onto others, and the others to even more?

"There is at least one more eyewitness we can visit. The farmer told me about Mr. Januszewski." He pointed at the name in the documents.

Half an hour later, I waited in the car as Robert walked through the gate of a property with a single-story house and a beautiful garden. To the left of the entrance gate was a vegetable and herb plot. It was separate from the rest of the garden, where cherry trees and wildflowers filled the air with an intoxicating aroma. Under the shade of one of the trees was a bucket half filled with ripe red fruit. "Come inside," said Robert through the car window. "I think this will be good."

A stocky man in his eighties stepped outside the front door and waited in the shade of one of the trees. His clothes were well laundered and pressed, and although there were no signs of wealth, Januszewski and his family had created their own small piece of paradise with limited means. Under the shadows of the leaves it was difficult to see his face at first, but eventually the happy round visage with the long scar over the right eyebrow revealed itself. He shook my hand heartily and examined my appearance, as though looking for familiar traits. "Mr. Januszewski and his parents worked on one of your grandfather's estates," Robert explained. "He remembers your grandparents from his boyhood."

Januszewski welcomed us into a light and airy room where we sat at a large dining table overlooking the garden. He folded his hands and looked across at me with sympathy before speaking. Robert translated.

"He wants to tell you the *real* truth. It is not your fault. You have done nothing." The events of the day had left me so full of guilt that I could hardly take in Januszewski's kind opening words to me. Was this forgiveness?

"Your grandfather beat him when he did not take off his hat, but *only* with the hands—he beat *only* with the hands." Januszewski pointed above his eye. I looked at the scar. What hand could deliver such a blow?

"Your grandmother liked her garden very much. Many flowers. Gardener was beaten very bad many times. Blood everywhere. He almost died. Farm manager too when he tried to protect other workers. Your grandfather tricked workers so he could beat them. When they were sick he did not let them rest. Instead, he beat them and made them get out of bed. Always on white horse watching and making terror."

Robert continued to translate Januszewski's many detailed episodes. These included insights into the continuation of the terror by the Russians after the war. How much strength it must have taken to shed the ugly burdens of the past and create the pretty garden outside.

"People remember him. Not happy man." Januszewski shook his head at the memory of Opa. He had occupied this community for three years over seventy years ago and this boy, today an old man, remembered the personal qualities of his oppressor. Of all the cruel SS and SA types who had occupied this area at the same time, it was only this man who was remembered among locals for his "unhappiness." I thought of my own childhood experiences. Where did this deep sense of anger at the world begin?

Soon, two women, one elderly and the other my age, entered the room with trays of biscuits, cherries, and juice. "His wife and daughter," said Robert. I nodded an ashamed greeting. The women placed the trays on the table and the younger of the two asked Robert a question. A conversation ensued between Januszewski's daughter, Robert, and the old man, which I assumed was the explanation of our discussion. The women looked at me again, this time embracing me with their eyes. The younger of the two women placed her hand on my shoulder and pressed it tightly as she looked into my face with a smile as warm as the sun on the fruit trees.

Once the women had left, Januszewski urged us to try the cherries. I took one of them, which must have been very sweet, although afterward I could not remember what it tasted like. Januszewski spoke as Robert translated. "He says if you are like your grandmother you are an angel." I looked at Januszewski in disbelief. How could he find the generosity to say it after my grandfather had stolen his childhood? "She made sure they got medicine, treatment—from doctor—after beatings. Your grandfather didn't know." I couldn't understand it. How did this behavior fit with Oma's demeaning comments about Poles?

"Do you remember the children?" I asked, beginning to doubt that we were talking about my grandparents.

Januszewski looked down at his hands and searched his memory. "No, he remembers no children," Robert translated.

"Then maybe we're talking about different people," I said, relieved until Januszewski recalled the first names of both my grandparents. "Perhaps you didn't meet the children?" I asked.

"It's possible." Robert translated. "Polish children were not allowed to mix with German children."

As we said our farewells, Januszewski clasped my forearms tightly in his hands. "Be happy," he said. "It wasn't your fault."

While I waited for Robert, I stared blankly into the vegetable patch. Gardens had a way of framing one's thoughts, although just now mine were like furious particles hitting up against walls, refusing to settle down. What of Oma? She was the young angel of Januszewski's memory, who had risked her own safety and secretly called upon the local apothecary to treat her husband's victims; and she was the bitter elderly woman who beat those victims back down with her harsh words. Could these two people ever be one and the same?

In this cold confusion, I sensed two warm bodies on either side of me. Januszewski and his wife had come out of the house to say a last farewell. We stared silently at the vegetable patch together. I wanted to ask for forgiveness on behalf of my family, but he would have wondered what for. It was the garden he wanted me to see.

On the way home, the rain fell so hard that I could barely see the road. Robert was prepared to continue, but after nine hours, we decided to head home. Both of us had gone without eating more than a few cherries all day. I felt bad that the tall and energetic Robert, who had jogged through fields and crawled in dusty barns on my behalf, had gone without food. So I bought him dinner at the only place we could find in the heavy rain, a McDonald's just off a roundabout.

As Robert hungrily chomped his way through his second burger, he reflected on the day. "Well, anyway, I think we found a lot. I am satisfied. Are you?" Robert had taken this project personally, and all the time it was important to him that I was satisfied. What had I done to deserve such a friend?

"We will visit the other place next time. It is too far tonight. It will be dark and people will be afraid of us when we knock in the night with questions about Nazis." He contorted his face and we laughed. The last place my grandparents had occupied during the war was three hours south. I didn't know when next I could make it back to Poland, but I had already promised that I would return soon.

As we drove back, the windshield wipers cleared the chaos of my thoughts. So many things suggested that Januszewski was the son of the gardener, although I hadn't dared ask him. Yet, what I could be certain of was that this man who as a child had been slave labor to my grandfather and had watched his nearest having the life beaten out of them with regularity had seen to it that the descendant of his family's oppressor could walk free. Without question, it was the most selfless act I had ever witnessed.

That evening, my husband and teenage children waited for me at a café in the town square in Poznań. The evening sun shone through the heat of the day, which refused to lift. Parents watched as their small children played at the large fountain, fascinated by the trickling water.

Colorful musicians and street performers filled the air with playful sounds, and all around people ate, drank, and laughed. The buildings of the nineteenth-century square were tastefully reconstructed so that there was no evidence of war. The hospital where M was born, one of the very few buildings that had withstood the bombings, was just steps away from us down the street. Oma had boasted that it was a fine clinic for Germans only.

As I sat with my family I was silent. They related the events of their day, but I had difficulty keeping present in the conversation. In the square not far from us stood a young boy, not more than five years of age. In Opa's monstrous order, his doe-like dark brown eyes, bushy dark hair, and child's Polish would have condemned him to death or a childhood of misery. The fountain caught the boy's attention and he ran toward it, laughing and tempting his father to chase him. The joy and playfulness of this child gripped me. My family held me in their arms and, even if they didn't quite understand, saw the agony.

"I am so glad that child is laughing," was all I could manage to say.

—◦—

Upon my return home from Poland two envelopes waited in the mailbox. Both of them contained documents that complicated my determination to detest my grandfather for what he had done. The first of the documents, Opa's birth certificate, presented the obvious, but overlooked, fact that Opa had once been a child too. In the cage of my memory he had always been that old man with the dark sunglasses in whose lap I had sat as a blond-haired child. The mayor I met at the inn north of Hamburg found it in the city archives, copied it for me, and kindly translated the elegant Sütterlin script that was difficult for the untrained eye to read. It seemed that the businesslike mayor had taken my project for his own, because no matter how much one insisted upon drawing a line under history, it didn't really work.

In the margin of the first page was a long paragraph of swirling script that had been signed off by a Helené Schachne. The mayor's translation revealed that Frau Schachne was a midwife who had been present at Opa's birth. The infant had been left with her until he was three years old, when his father claimed him. Opa's parents came from different social classes, and in the strict hierarchy of Wilhelmine Germany their marriage, let alone parenthood together, was a violation of social norms.

I opened my albums to one of the few pictures of Opa's mother. According to the family she was raven-haired and wild. I looked into her pleasant face, which was framed by a dark bob, and at her fashionable drop-hip white summer dress. There was nothing about her that seemed wild in this photograph. If only these black-and-white images could speak. Like many family stories, hers had most likely been contorted, first by an era that could not condone her liaison with a man of lower birth, and then by one obsessed with the idea that non-Aryan features were a danger to society.

Not far from her in the same photograph, leaning awkwardly toward his mother to satisfy the photographer, was Opa. "He couldn't tolerate his mother," Oma had once said, shuddering at the memory of watching the two together.

I began to realize that Opa was the inheritor of social contortion manifested in desertion and inferiority. The new order would wipe this out, give him belonging and power. He would shift the weight of embarrassment from himself to his raven-haired mother. Suddenly, I thought I understood the unhappiness that Januszewski had noticed, and rested momentarily in the image of the deserted child, until the brutal perpetrator overtook him and defied all comprehension.

The evening light in my office shone hard on the second envelope. I opened it, and soon the wartime newspaper clippings of the bearer of the Iron Cross, Baum, who had publicly defamed Opa after the war, were strewn across my desk.

"He was Wehrmacht," the mayor said, referring to the belief that the traditional military retained its honor, in contrast to the morally bankrupt Waffen-SS.

The articles before me showed images of the same man in a Waffen-SS uniform being decorated by Adolf Hitler himself. Baum's collected letters written to a fellow comrade as a contribution to records concerning key battles of the Second World War portrayed a man concerned with military maneuvers and the morale of his men. It was easy to understand why the mayor, who was too young to have fought in the war, was under the impression that Baum was "a decent sort."

Why would Baum denounce a fellow comrade in the way that he did and why hadn't Opa fought back? Was it that Baum was a soldier and that Opa had tortured defenseless civilians, living a comfortable life far behind the front lines? Or was it that Baum had done his prison time after the war while Opa had escaped justice? What other reasons could there be for the denunciation?

After his release from prison in England, Baum worked in a prominent business, which employed most of the local population after the war. He was well liked, but Opa, who had shot at a neighbor for trespassing and who kept a revolver by his bedside, was not. Perhaps Opa had come to the conclusion that he couldn't win against this masterful wartime strategist, who knew the truth behind the benign-sounding claim that he'd been a farmer and was backed up by the local business owners. Instead, he fled in an overall climate of diminishing patience for those who remained unpunished.

My head spun. Oma must be able to shed light on the truth behind the documents scattered across my desk. "Yes, hello!" she shouted into the telephone, which she still regarded as a miracle of communication. "Well now, what are you up to, my dear?" she said in good spirits.

Hearing her voice was disarming after all that I had experienced in Poland. Was she really that angel of mercy Januszewski had described? If so, why had she lied to me? What light could she shed on anything if she couldn't tell me the truth? I realized in an instant that I wasn't ready to share my experiences, certainly not long-distance on the telephone through Oma's hearing aid.

"I have been in the garden—working in my garden today," I stuttered, disliking the fact that I too was lying.

"Oh, that is wonderful!" she said. "There is such peace in the garden. It is terrible I cannot do those things anymore. I am too old for just about everything, but let's not go into that. Tell me more about your garden."

During the hour that we spoke, I savored speaking with my grandmother about the beautiful things in our world, the peace of Januszewski's cherry orchard filtering into my thoughts. Opa seemed so far away in a terrible time we had left behind us. As I spoke, I switched off the harsh light that shone across the papers on my desk, leaving only the corner light to illuminate the room. Existence felt so much easier without all these thorny questions.

"Now I am very tired. I am sorry, my dear. Thank you for your beloved call," said Oma. We hung up.

CHAPTER 9

Germany, 2013

WITH EACH DAY THAT PASSED, THE BRONZE HORSE ON THE MANTEL-piece at home haunted me more. M had given the statue to me years ago—wrapped it in a cloth, stuffed it in a bag, and said that she had never liked it. As I crossed the Atlantic bearing this imposing object, I wondered why I had agreed to take it with me. I didn't have any special relationship with horses, or so I thought, until I gave the subject attention. Riding was something my sister and I were supposed to be able to do naturally, as though we had inherited the capacity to control these great animals through mother's milk. Each time I sat in the saddle—ridiculously straight, as though for some reason to impress upon others that I knew what I was doing—I felt the clash of wills. My desire not to be there conflicted with the force of my inheritance. I watched international dressage and jumping competitions with an interest that had no basis in my own skill or experience, and was rather driven by the idea that what happened in the riding rink was the pinnacle of high culture. It simply behooved us to watch and admire.

Today as I observed the horse, I asked myself why Opa had joined the mounted SS and what exactly the implications were. The family photo albums were replete with evidence of his love of horses and riding, but this wasn't a sufficient explanation. How had the colossal jump from the young man who loved horses to the oppressor with the whip on horseback taken place and why?

"See you tomorrow at the airport," came the message from Nele, my new friend from cyberspace whom I would meet in Hamburg on the following day to answer these questions. Nele Fahnenbruk was an expert on the mounted SS, with a particular focus on her native Schleswig-Holstein. The connection between us was immediate: I was the grand-daughter of one of the types she had devoted years to studying. Our plan was to visit the villages where Opa had lived before the war and to trace the impact of joining the SS on his life and the life of his family.

———

"I have to go out to Dondolino later today," said Nele, breaking the awk-wardness of meeting in person for the first time. We had been on the train from the airport into the city for the past ten minutes, but, with the many people around us, didn't feel comfortable with beginning to discuss our common subject. I had read her PhD thesis, which was dedicated to Dondolino, and guessed by the name that it must be a horse.

"Where do you keep him?" I asked, taking the risk.

"Oh, out at my mother's. I don't train him the way he is supposed to be trained in these parts. Some of our traditions in Germany are very screwed up," she said. I found her attitude refreshing after an upbringing in which everything German was best. The train began to clear out and we felt free to converse.

"So, what did your family do during the war?" It was an aphorism common in our line of work.

"Oh, they were Social Democrats, hounded by the Nazis. One of them was arrested."

She looked at the messages on her phone. "Oh God, not another one!" she exclaimed under her breath.

"What?" I asked, curious to know.

"The media," she replied. "They sniffed me out some time ago when I did a local radio program about my thesis topic and now they're like terriers. I don't want to talk to them again until my thesis is published."

"What are they after?" I asked, wondering what in particular could cause such intense interest.

"A lot of people are not going to be pleased with what I have to say, and so I have to do this properly," she replied, as though swallowing a bitter pill. The puzzled look on my face prompted her to explain.

"My thesis questions an institution regarded by many as the apex of high sporting culture in Germany. One could say that it has long been regarded as beyond scrutiny because of our successes in the riding ring. Many other sports have long made amends for their complicity in the Third Reich, renaming competitions and prizes to ensure they no longer bear the names of former Nazis, but in many riding associations in this country this has not happened."

A fire sparked in her eyes, urging me to see the flames that books and truth and people had been burned in. "These continuities, sustained by a sporting elite that insists upon tradition above all else, are indefensible, bizarre, and vulgar."

"Is that so?" I asked somewhat lamely, as another of the pillars of my childhood, the high culture of horses, collapsed into a heap.

"Yes," said Nele, incensed. "Did you know that the mounted SS were excused at Nuremberg on the grounds that these men were simply interested in riding sport, when in fact a number of their most prominent members were involved in the most nauseating chapters of the war in the East?" She tossed out a string of last names, some of which sounded vaguely familiar for reasons I wasn't sure of.

"How is that possible?" I asked.

"That's a very good question a few of us are scratching our heads over," she replied. "There are a lot of theories, including connections between members of the mounted SS and the royal houses of Europe, but the official line was that riding associations were forced to become a part of the new system under the Führer principle, meaning that all these men who were purely interested in sport automatically became SS. Allegedly, they had no say in the matter."

"What do you think of this official line?" I asked, the image of Opa as an innocent young man hugging a colt in my thoughts.

"It's an oversimplification and not true in many cases. There were choices to be made, and those were frequently made in favor of affluence."

Nele looked out the window. "The next stop is ours," she announced. "I won't have much time this afternoon, so let me share what we've got. I have managed to book a number of meetings with mayors in the various towns you named, but your grandfather's old riding association won't budge."

"Based on what you have just told me, I am not too surprised," I said.

Nele shook her head. "Yes, I checked with them previously and they have always been very tight-lipped because they don't want to alienate paying members by bringing up the unpleasant business of the past. This particular place keeps claiming it has got nothing to share, which in my experience means precisely the reverse."

"I sent them a query about my grandfather some time ago, but they never responded," I said, recalling that I had written to this particular association.

"Well, then, the red lights will be flashing over us when we turn up there!" Nele smiled provocatively.

"Do you really think it is worth a try?" I asked.

"Of course! Even if it is only for the satisfaction of saying we tried." The doors of the S-Bahn opened and Nele signaled it was time for us to exit.

＊＊＊

On the following day during the meetings with the mayors of various small towns, shame hung on the walls like an imposing old painting one didn't dare to take down. Momentarily, I was no longer its bearer, rather the one who had come to remove the old portrait so that we might speak freely. As a nation Germany had done more than any other to atone for its past, but in families and communities people continued to suffer with the burden of the unspoken.

As we drove away from our last meeting, Nele sighed and shook her head. She was impatient with her countrymen and our journey. Yet as we drove into the first estate, which Opa had taken over at the same time as he joined the SS in 1934, her mood changed.

"Looks like he didn't lose time cashing in on his privileges," she said with eyebrows raised. Just as in Oma's photographs, a massive tree still stood in the foreground of the mansion with the velvety lawn, which had oozed of ambition then as it did now. I parked the car and looked around us. Affiliation with the mounted SS had accelerated the class journey from humble city merchant with a cabbage patch in the countryside to grand estate owner.

"After this he purchased the imperial horse training station you haven't seen yet, and then went on to grander ambitions in Poland," I explained.

The property teemed with equestrians, some of them on horseback in the riding rings and others tending to their horses in the stalls. The place smacked of order, discipline, and quality, befitting an estate that had become an elite center for training national teams.

"My grandmother said he had nothing to do with horses, but of course this place could have changed throughout the years." It was an attempt to keep an open mind, but inside I could hear myself covering up my grandmother's lies. Nele grimaced as we hung over the fence around the practice ring and watched the horses being exercised according to conventions she regarded as painful and unnatural.

"Your grandmother didn't tell you the truth," she said, keeping her eyes on the tortured animals. "This has always been horse country and it's obvious that your grandfather's career was given a nice lift by the mounted SS. Of course she wouldn't want you to know this, but everyone knew it then. Look," she said, turning to me, impatient with my tiptoeing. "The mounted SS were Himmler's chosen knights who would restore Germany's honor and demonstrate its Aryan supremacy in the riding rings of Europe, and eventually in war. Power and influence came with the job."

"Only the best," I said, quietly—hopelessly—to myself.

"Yes, that is one way to put it," she replied, overhearing my remark.

I looked up into the grand tree that towered above us. "It's going to rain," I said.

"Shall I show you the next palace on the program? Don't want to be late for our meeting with the widow."

Nele's telephone rang in the car. She answered and then hung up after an abrupt exchange of words. "The widow has canceled. Disappointing but not surprising."

"Is there another time we can meet her?" I asked, hoping in vain that we had not lost another valuable contact to suspicion and shame.

"No, she's indefinitely unavailable." Nele spat out the words. "As soon as I got involved, she knew it had to do with the SS. Many in these parts aren't interested in revisiting this history. This whole area was a gathering point for former SS after the war. They felt comfortable and were among friends here."

We decided to turn back and make one last stop at the riding association where Opa had joined the SS. As Nele checked her telephone, I reflected on her words. I had heard it before: this area had been a melting pot for former SS after the war—a place where everyone and therefore no one had sinned, like the special weekends at the hunting hotel.

Nele put away her telephone and stared forward out the windshield. "That hunting hotel of your grandfather's reminds me of the story of another SS rider. Ever heard of Fritz Haerlin?" I hadn't. "He was a renowned dressage rider and former SS Hauptsturmführer who took over the Four Seasons Hotel in Hamburg from his family after the war. It was renowned for champagne evenings with old comrades who drank only from the finest cut crystal."

As a young student, I had gone to the Four Seasons, just to stand in the lobby and experience its fineness because my German family had spoken of it as though it had been a sort of mecca. This was another of the many throwbacks—those mental fixtures that I had never questioned openly but that chafed at my conscience. It landed on top of that toxic heap that included the Mercedes sports car I should buy M when I had made some money—Daimler Benz helped so many former SS after the war—and my flat feet, which I subsequently discovered had been regarded as an unfortunate Jewish trait. These sinister fragments of another time had stayed with us, all because we simply let them.

"When I was a child that place was a legend," I admitted to Nele.

"Not impossible that your grandfather could have known Haerlin."

"No. Not at all impossible," I replied, feeling as though cut by broken crystal.

We approached the riding association—the oldest and most tradition-steeped in the country—certain that we would be refused, just as we had been turned away by the widow.

"Is it really worth it?" I asked, recalling that Nele had been rejected repeatedly by them during her research.

"We can't give up now, can we?" She laughed, resigned to the awkwardness and disappointment of her chosen field.

"No, of course not," I replied, encouraged by her persistence.

Not far from the parking lot was an imposing riding arena. "This is the Hamburg Derby," said Nele as she looked into the entrance of the arena with the giant locked gate. "It's still used for national and international equestrian events. For the Nazis it was a perfect propaganda opportunity, because it was where the elite socialized. Your grandfather most certainly rode in the place at some point, since it is right next to his old riding association."

Nele ran her hand down the thick grooves of the old tree near the entrance. Some engraved plaques had been nailed to its thick trunk. "The original plaque that hung on this tree bore the name of the Derby's founder, a Jew murdered by the Nazis. They replaced it with a plaque engraved with the name of an SS rider." Nele pointed to another of the plaques. "They hung a new one up for the murdered founder in 1950," she said. "But how they can continue to honor an SS rider I don't know."

As I waited for Nele to inquire inside the riding association, a white cat wound its way around my right ankle. I stroked its back, and watched the staff attending to the horses of well-to-do Hamburg residents. Purring, the cat closed its eyes, relishing in the pleasure. Just as I had resolved that it was important not to see everything about these places in the daunting light of history, Nele walked out of the association building with the look of rejection. "They say they don't have time for such queries. It's obvious they would like it if we disappeared." Her face was flushed with frustration.

———

On the following morning, before the flight home, I decided to make one last visit to a farmer called Becker. One of the mayors had intimated that his family knew mine from prewar times.

Becker's friendly wife greeted me at the door. "Ah yes," she said as soon as we introduced ourselves. "We heard from the mayor that you were in these parts. Do come in!"

She ushered us into the room where Becker sat holding a cup of coffee that seemed too small for the thick fingers with damaged nails from many years of running the family farm. A bright look came over his face. He rose slowly and limped toward me. "Well, this is quite special," he said, shaking my hand for a very long time.

Soon after we settled down, Becker launched into his memories. "We never played together," said Becker.

"With whom?" I asked.

"Let's see now, it must have been your Uncle Hartmut. He lived in the grand mansion just down the road, and it would have been natural for us to play together, but we didn't mix."

"Why not?" I asked.

"Your grandfather moved in exclusive circles and my parents didn't believe in all that nonsense. My father always said to us, 'That Hitler is up to no good with all his warring talk,' and when my brother enrolled in the Waffen-SS, he said it was ridiculous. Why, my mother had to hide my father in a closet several times when the Gestapo came calling."

"Was my grandfather responsible for that?" I asked, feeling nauseous. Becker simply smiled, not wishing to offend. He exchanged some words with his wife in plattdeutsch, the dialect of northern German farmers Oma occasionally joked in.

His wife fetched an album, and I held my breath, ready to be shown something terrible as Becker opened the cover and leafed through to find the right page. There, occupying one page all to itself, was a photograph of a young black African man with a broad smile holding an equally happy blond-haired woman who looked similar to Becker's wife. "Our daughter and her husband," said Becker proudly. "He's training to become a farmer farther south, and doing a great job."

Becker and Nele had been profoundly shaped by their families' choices. Where did this leave me?

When I arrived home, Opa's denazification papers had arrived in the mail from the Lower Saxony archives. I wondered what other documents there might be about him that I still hadn't found. We lived in a time when secrets were ending, when information that previously appeared to have been swallowed by history had become more easily accessible if only one looked for it. All that stood between us and knowing was time and the will to, resources that could quickly run out.

I leafed through the pages, which were a declaration to the Allied military administration in 1947 of Opa's record in relation to Nazism. The extraditions of war criminals to the East for trial and hanging had ceased that summer, and it must have seemed safer to emerge. Like so many of these documents, this one was an effort to wash off the dirt of the Third Reich in order to move on. Opa had already set his sights on purchasing the hunting house in the north and turning it into an upmarket inn with help from a relative who had profited from Hitler's rearmament drive. The latter was not specifically mentioned in the document. What else was there to do? The world was in ruins and Opa had a large family to support.

Even if I could feel sympathy for the family's circumstances, reading this document with all I already knew was a farcical experience. Each claim collapsed under the weight of the knowledge I possessed. It was full of testimonies to his decent character and intentions, so-called Persilscheine, a cynical term for such character endorsements that referred to the washing detergent Persil.

Yet there was one testimony that stained the artificially bleached surface. The British occupying authority had itself sought out a statement from local government in Opa's prewar home, and received a reply that confirmed his immersion in elite SS circles before the war. Maybe it was this testimony, or the declaration of blond hair and blue eyes in his personal description that caught the Allies' attention. Opa had anything but a fair complexion, and I wondered why he would write such a thing, which was so obviously incorrect. Had the propaganda simply got to him so that he no longer knew how else to portray himself, or was this a snubbing of denazification, which so many regarded as an insult or a farce?

Whatever the reason, the Allies didn't buy his mild confession and put him into a Category III for "lesser offenders." The two categories above this were for "major offenders" and "offenders," persons whom the British military authority regarded as having been dealt with through the

Nuremberg trial. The Allies regarded Opa as an extremist who had joined the party before the takeover of power and the SS in its early days, and who needed to be defanged for the safety of society. His penalty was economically damning and socially denigrating for a man who, after eleven years of service in the SS, had believed in his destiny among the chosen. He could not demand a pension, which could be entirely withheld; was banned from holding any leadership position in a significant public or private undertaking, and from hiring or dismissing anyone in such a concern. In practical terms, this hobbled both one's current life and future plans. At the same time, Opa was lucky not to have been judged in the American zone farther south, where examination was more rigorous and classification not as lenient.

In September 1947, shortly after being informed of this classification, Oma pleaded on behalf of her husband, referring, in a letter addressed to the president of the regional government, to their large young family. A lawyer was hired to request a Category IV reclassification and to patch up the holes, perhaps in the realization that Opa was his own worst enemy. The lawyer portrayed moderate interests in the party and the SS, which were neither political nor ideological, rather driven solely by the desire for an improvement in the economic situation of the country.

The longest portion of the argument addressed Opa's engagement in the mounted SS, which had already been exempted from Nuremberg. Like all the other riders, he had only been interested in the sport; membership in the SS was a coincidence; ideologically he had remained indifferent throughout. He'd been a soldier briefly, and now was a refugee, terms that evoked feelings of heroism and pity. The "lowly" rank of Scharführer or squadron leader was offered up in the space available for rank, with the admission of two promotions that were unexplained. This caught my attention. How did his case compare with others, and why would he have felt threatened by the law if he had held an insignificant rank?

I looked to my bookshelves, which had changed character markedly since I had started the work. The studies in tyranny that I had swallowed as a master's student at Oxford had been removed from their boxes in storage and stood upright, next to the many newer works about every imaginable facet of the Third Reich. I scanned the shelves for the answers to my question and fell upon Jens's book, *Seine Schatten, Meine Bilder—His Shadows, My Pictures*—about emerging from the long shadow cast by his father, a devoted lifelong Nazi who lived by the three "As": anti-Semitic, anti-democratic, and anti-communist.

I scanned the table of contents and turned to the section titled "Mitläufer," meaning "follower." Here I was reminded that Jens's father, the Nazi mayor of Łodz, where people had been crammed into a dehumanizing holding space of disease and starvation before they were transported onward to the gas chambers, was assigned a Category IV—Mitläufer or follower—by the comparatively lenient British authorities responsible for overseeing denazification in northern Germany. He held the rank of Unterscharführer, or corporal—a rank under Opa—which contrasted with his notable role as mayor and as Reichsreder, a functional role in the SS in which he used his oratory skills to stir thousands of SS men into the frenzy required to fight Himmler's grisly racial war in the occupied territories. Two years before he died, he privately revealed his disappointment at only having been classified as a IV. Didn't they realize what he had accomplished?

Opa's denazification papers named the Reichsgesellchaft für Landbewirtschaftung, which had become an organizational vehicle for the Ministry of Agriculture to overtake the most extensive estates in occupied Poland and transform them into a breadbasket of the Reich. It was within this organization that he had occupied the functional role of Sonderführer, or Special Leader for Landed Estates in East Prussia and Poland that Baum had noted. He'd been a local farming leader and a regional farming leader and, I knew from his party card, had affected the lives of so many on estates throughout west-central Poland. Again, this neither featured in the lawyer's arguments, nor in the eventual classification, which focused on evidence of ideological commitment before the war. What had happened in the occupied territories between 1939 and 1945 was a gaping hole.

I returned to Jens's book, to the table of contents and to another section, titled "Die Ludwigsburger," a reference to the office for prosecuting Nazi war criminals in southern Germany. One of the reasons for Jens's father's peculiarly lenient fate was that the British occupying forces soon turned over most denazification cases to the regional German courts that lacked the jurisdiction to make classifications or pursue cases on the basis of deeds committed against non-Germans on foreign soil. They knew about his role as mayor and that he had served a brief prison sentence immediately after the war, but he was regarded as a Schreibtischnazi, a deskbound Nazi, who hadn't physically hurt anyone.

My thoughts went to the people I had met in Poland, who had worked as slave laborers on the estates my grandfather had occupied. They went to that scar over the right eye, the whippings and the beatings to unconsciousness, and the acts I still didn't know about and might never discover. Opa had not been a Schreibtischnazi. He had been the law on his estates, and his law was merciless. The gap in his denazification documents screamed of these very physical deeds, and he was no doubt frightened that the Allies might hear it.

Yet there was no time or will for considering any of it in the chaos, war-weariness, and mounting tension with Stalin's Russia in the immediate postwar years. In October 1948, Opa was dismissed as a Category V: "exonerated, no sanctions." It was the Cold War rather than Oma's impassioned letter or the lawyer's arguments that had lifted the sentence. Jens's father went on to work for the West German government in Bonn.

—————

Flustered by these documents, I picked up a photograph of Opa as a young man with his beloved horses and stared hard at it, demanding that he tell me the truth. The perky youth in the merchant's suit thirsted for life just as much as the wobbly legged foal he had purchased, and, in doing so, toyed with my frustration.

"What happened to you?" I asked in a shaky whisper at the bright-looking young man next to the foal. "What happened to both of you?" While I had heard the confessions of eyewitnesses, I still didn't have a clear picture of the consequences of Opa's engagement in the mounted SS.

In the denazification documents, Opa claimed that he had taken up his assignment in occupied Poland in November 1939. This clashed with Oma's insistence that he had left in September of that year. "I remember, because I had to get this after he left," she said, holding up her driver's license proudly. The document bore a stamp with the date 11 October 1939. "It still has the stamp of the swastika on it," she said, grinning like a child who had managed to hide something it wasn't supposed to have.

Since I already knew that so much of what was in the denazification documents was untrue, and Oma's memory was sharp as a scythe, I began to wonder why Opa would change the date. Was it just another snub of the Allies, like his fair complexion?

I emailed Jochen Böhler, my expert on the invasion of Poland. The response was immediate. "Germans from the Old Reich weren't busy farming in Poland in September 1939. Call me," he wrote. I picked up the phone immediately and we skipped the niceties, both of us eager to get to the point.

"As I told you, if he went in September, he wasn't doing any farming. Let me fill you in." He heaved a deep sigh, which was the sign of a heart that hadn't been numbed by narrow intellectual pursuit. "The early phase of the war during September was a time when the SS, particularly the mounted SS, let its inner beast loose on unarmed civilians. Propaganda had made these men hungry. At that time, some of Hamburg's best SS riders had been incorporated into policing squadrons, which followed on the heels of the Wehrmacht to establish so-called law and order in occupied Poland. They were given rather broad instructions by Hitler, which nevertheless had a devastating effect."

"And those were?" I asked anxiously, running my finger across the photo of the young man and the foal.

"To close hearts to empathy. . . . To proceed brutally. . . . The stronger has the right. . . . Greatest toughness. Not my words—quoting Hitler of course."

There was silence as Jochen waited for me to respond. "Are you still there?" he asked, realizing that this was potentially very bad news for me.

"Yes, anything else?" I felt like a patient forced to a terrible treatment in order to be cured.

"Well, yes." His voice halted, as though before a dark abyss. "The consequence was that these men unleashed a war so dirty that later analyses of what happened could only describe it as the decay of man. These squadrons set the tone of life in occupied Poland, and, according to those who knew them, were themselves never the same again."

The different snapshots of Opa passed before me: the young hopeful with the giddy foal, the angry young estate manager in the tweed jacket, the glassy-eyed occupier in the black uniform who took the war home with him.

"Do the lists of these men still exist?" I asked.

"Maybe," he said. "We can follow that up."

"If he was one of them, how did he go from being a mounted invader to an overseer of agricultural estates?" I clung to the hope that my family's old farming argument might still get me out of this mess.

Jochen promptly closed the door to this escape route. "Several of the mounted SS were estate managers, which is part of the reason they were so able on horseback. There are records of these men who were reassigned to agriculture directly after the invasion. Look, the Reich's plans for Leb-ensraum were unfolding, and there were opportunities for those with the most urgently needed skills. We cannot preclude that your grandfather might have been assigned to his task later on, but you say that he was an impatient hands-on sort, not interested in paperwork, who was eager for land. Well, this was the fastest way to get a hold of it."

"And what if he wasn't involved in the invasion? What if my grand-mother's memory has just gone bad and he really did leave in November?"

"That's not a pretty story either," said Jochen, closing the last door. "Let me send you a paper where you can read about the alternative."

The document was in my inbox before we hung up. Estates and farms were raided in the early hours of the morning. The inhabitants had min-utes to pack up, if they had not already fled into the freezing forests with a few belongings. If they attempted to return, they were usually shot. The new SS overlords called these places and the things in them their own, despite their views on the degeneracy of the conquered culture. Homes were stolen, people hounded and chased, and the remaining laborers beaten into submission, all from the back of a horse.

I put away the documents and photographs and went to bed, but found no peace in sleep. Instead, I heard the agonizing sound of the unmilked cows across the countryside, their owners either driven away or shot. This high-pitched sound of unbearable pain mutated into the sound of men, women, and children in villages being crushed under the deafening hooves. I struggled to picture what the rider was doing to them but my senses failed me.

On the following morning, I resolved that I must call Oma and talk to her about all of this. "Good morning, my dear Jülchen. How is it with you on this fine morning?" Her voice was weak and strained. "This dizziness is terrible, particularly in the mornings." Her voice deflated my determination, and my questions felt selfish. "I was dreaming of your Uncle Harty last night. He was such a fine little boy. I remember him playing in our very first home together. Fine place your grandfather fixed. How hard he worked to put it all in order."

Suddenly we were back at the mansion they had purchased in 1934, the horse-training center that Nele and I had visited. Oma didn't know I had been there, and I didn't want to go into that now, but the question of how Opa had got a hold of the place still bothered me and it seemed a benign question.

"Ach!" she replied dismissively. "There were just a bunch of old heath farmers squatting there. Disorderly types, who couldn't manage the place at all."

"Heath farmers?" I asked, wondering what she meant.

"Yes, they came from the Lüneburger Heath and thought they could farm the place. Well, never mind. It's all so long ago. We must hang up now, my dear, and speak another time. Thank you for your beloved call."

"Goodbye, Oma," I said, backing down from the moment of reckoning that must come some other time.

After putting down the receiver, I looked up the heath farmers and learned that they were persecuted as socialists by the regime. Did Oma know, didn't she, or was I just imagining things? I disliked the way that this work raised doubts and question marks over everything, with little hope that these might ever be resolved.

I wandered through the house, turning off the lights for the night, and stopped before the horse on the mantelpiece. I longed for it to step out of its stiff, bronze shell, graze free on the grass, and shoo the flies away with a gentle swish of its tail.

CHAPTER 10

Germany, 2013

It was midnight and soon night would pass into day, my last day with Oma. She had looked the same for a very long time, the snowy white waves of hair still framing a peach-skinned face. Yet she was over one hundred years old and each time I visited her, I assumed this time would be the last.

"What is for dessert?" she said, impatient for her after-lunch sweet. Even if no one else wanted dessert, Auntie Best was obliged to serve it. As she rose to do her mother's bidding, protesting that the last thing anyone needed after a large meal was dessert, Oma turned her attention back to me.

"It is not nice to become this old, dear Jülchen, and I certainly don't wish it upon you, but I am sure you will become even older." She looked out the window at the gray sky. "If only dear God would take me one night in my sleep, but then I awaken and am still here." Nervously, she scratched at the damask on the dining table. "God doesn't want me."

I couldn't comfort Oma in this matter. Through the years I had listened to her many feisty protests about the duping of people by religion, and thought it presumptuous of her to expect God to pay any attention to her at all. Opa's denazification papers had even used religion as a shield, claiming the christening of all their children as evidence of his spiritual distance from the party. It was a cynical game. Oma's schizophrenic attitude toward religion had taken its toll, because in the lifelong process of hedging her bets she didn't know who to trust.

The pendulum lay in the pink glass ashtray on the side table close to her, never far from her hand. If she held it over me today, it would most certainly go the wrong way. At the end of the day, my train would depart for the onward journey, which neither she nor Auntie Best knew anything of. I would travel to various archives in Germany, including the one at Ludwigsburg, from which war criminals had been pursued since the late 1950s. Increasingly, I began to wonder about the precise circumstances of Opa's departure in 1960, and what old and new networks had eased him into his new life. After Ludwigsburg, I would cross the border from Berlin to finish the work that Robert and I had begun during the previous summer in Poland. My journey would take me on the same route that Opa had taken in the autumn of 1939.

The time for charmed conversation with Oma was running out, but I didn't want to acknowledge it. During the past two days, we had continued to find other subjects of discussion over Auntie Best's meals, which were carefully prepared for a digestive tract unable to absorb the slightest excess. In the middle of the table was a black hole of suspicion that none of us was prepared to name.

I guessed that Oma and Auntie Best had begun to wonder about my voracious interest in Opa and the family's past. The suspicion and dishonesty went far beyond those of us gathered at this table. These attitudes had governed our family for decades, keeping an iron grip on our attentions and deforming our relationships.

Oma's eyes began to twitch and she scrambled for her tinted glasses, which fell on the floor. I picked them up and handed them to her. "Thank you, my dear," she said, putting them on.

If I told Oma what I knew would it bring her more or less nightmares? The last thing I wanted was for her to return to the depression, and to ruin Auntie Best's good work. Looking into the past was important to me, but did it serve any useful purpose for any of the others? What I saw as bringing out the truth might just as well be recklessness. It was like taking a sledgehammer to the thick walls that had been painstakingly built around the past.

I thanked Auntie Best for the meal, kissed Oma on the forehead, and returned to my hotel room. As I lay in bed that night, I summarized the arguments and determined that I would stand by the old rules of our family, leaving an old woman in peace. Yet it was precisely this last point that didn't make sense. With her nightmares, blinking, and depression, Oma appeared never to have found any peace, despite the outer silence she had surrounded herself in.

My husband called. "I can't sleep," he said.

"I can't either," I admitted.

"You must tell her," he said, sounding quite certain.

"But why?" I was desperate not to unravel the finely crafted arguments formulated during the past few hours.

"You must tell her about what you have learned, because if you don't she might pass away and you will never forgive yourself. You cannot play the same game of lying if you are to have any self-respect."

I knew exactly what he meant. All along I had pursued a story that I didn't feel I had the right to. Fear of facing the family and of breaking their taboo had followed me wherever I went and would continue to do so unless I told them the truth. I remembered all the tension-filled family gatherings in Oma's apartment over the years. Had we lived then, or had we merely danced around a lie?

I lay on top of the starched sheets and stared at the immaculate ceiling of the hotel room. Oma thought it peculiar that I should stay in this establishment, which was run by people from the East, and therefore, according to her, must be disorderly and dirty.

I slept restlessly for a few hours, and as the morning of the last day dawned, I made up my mind.

After we had consumed another gut-friendly lunch prepared by Auntie Best, I moved to sit on the footstool in front of my aged grandmother so that she could easily see and hear me. "How are you, Oma?" I asked, hoping that this was not one of her bad days.

"I'm feeling quite Catholic today!" she replied, joking in the dialect of her northern German origins. "That's what we used to say where I come from to describe not feeling very well."

Small traces of truth made themselves evident on the sharp blade of her humor. In Opa's prewar documents "Catholic" had deliberately been toned down to "god-believing" to adjust to the SS's distaste for religion, aside from its own strange hodgepodge of paganism and Hitler-deification. On September 1, 1941, the SS had brought the church bells of western Poland to a standstill, closing down all its churches and deporting its holy men. I couldn't get it out of my mind as Oma continued with her lambasting of the Church.

As she chatted, I took her hand into mine and said a little prayer to myself. "Blame must not enter this space," I repeated in my heart. Sensing that something important was about to happen, Auntie Best sat down in one of the armchairs so that she could see me. It was not her usual place, but one I often wished she would claim to enjoy life's small comforts.

"I don't know when we will see each other again," I said. Although Oma spoke daily about death, it came as a surprise to her when her own morbid thoughts echoed back. I had always avoided responding to her comments about dying, but today was not a day for avoidance.

"Since I know you don't believe that we'll meet in heaven, I think I had better say what is weighing on my heart," I said, realizing that I had already gone past the point of no return. Oma looked at me searchingly. "As you know, I have always wanted to understand M better. You have always insisted that she was just like her father."

"And how . . ." Oma added. Both women nodded their heads in affirmation, puzzled as to what I was about to say.

"You must understand that as you said this over so many years I wanted to know who he was. I was born in Brazil, M in occupied Poland. What was I to think?"

The silence was palpable and I knew that the moment had come to take the first cut. "I think it is time for us to acknowledge the truth between us without blaming anyone, which is that Opa was an avid National Socialist and a fanatical SS man." A final conclusion dropped out, which was unexpected but more important to me than any other. "The comparison is deeply unfair. M is her own person."

Not a window had been opened, but the air in the room was suddenly cooler. Oma's hands retreated to her lap, but didn't flinch. Instead, she straightened her posture so as to appear undiminished. "That is correct," she said, and at first I wondered exactly what she was referring to. "He looked very smart in his uniform too. They all looked dapper. You should have seen them. They were beautiful men. What people said about them is quite wrong. They were the best sort. People didn't have as bad a time in the labor camps as was said. That was just Jewish propaganda!"

There was no longer anything Oma could say that jolted me. The shock was in what she didn't say. In desperation, I envisioned myself scratching at a thin layer of dust on impenetrable ground. There had to be more. The remorse would surely come.

Auntie Best couldn't remain upright, and leaned forward on the table, supporting herself on folded arms. She looked like a frightened child, deserted by her unrepentant parent in the burning redness of shame and confusion. She was speechless, but what could she say? She had been a small child during the war, after which a blanket of silence had been cast over the crimes of her parents. In that moment I saw what had happened in our family: Shame had been left to the next generations. Those responsible had shunned responsibility, and the unrecognized victims were their children.

"So, what do they say about us in the documents? Are they coming to get me?" said Oma, looking defiant and terrified all at the same time. The pathos in these words moved me to calm her and I shook my head.

"No," I reassured her. "In fact, a young boy whom Opa hurt remembered you as an angel because you called the doctor."

She cut me off. "That is ridiculous! There was no doctor, only an apothecary." Was her reaction an insane fussing with irrelevant details, or an attempt to debunk my discoveries? I noticed a strong instinct in her to deny things that went against her husband. Although he was long dead, as was her dependence upon him for livelihood, the instinct to defend him was very much alive. I suspected she was still afraid of him, like a ghost that would never leave her, and thought I had gained a first glimpse into her nightmares.

"He didn't kill anyone!" she insisted. "I was with him *all* the time. Yes, he screamed like everyone else. He only beat them," she said, regaining her composure. "Those were the times! People did that type of thing and we just did the same as everyone else." My head drooped. I had never felt as distant from her as when she uttered that "we."

As she continued with her defense, it occurred to me that I might know things about Opa that she did not. She had been at home with her children in the early phases of the SS's dirty war. How could she know exactly what happened in the killing fields of men? It must have been unnerving to face her granddaughter who possibly knew more than she did. The struggle with these thoughts brought me to the disheartening conclusion that I would never know what went on in her head, because I could no longer trust anything she told me.

Oma spoke incessantly for two hours, forgetting her usual tiredness after lunch. Many stories were recycled. The sudden and unfortunate flight to Brazil still had nothing to do with the war. She offered one credible explanation—exhaustion with the onerous hotel business—and obliterated it in the next breath by insisting that it was the Cuban crisis and the associated heightened Soviet threat, which took place one year and eight months after their departure, that had forced them out of Europe. A Prussian baron named von der Kleist was their contact in Brazil. Scraps of information were tossed out that contradicted other scraps.

"I was in the NSV," she said proudly of her affiliation with the National Sozialistische Volkswohlfahrt, the National Socialist welfare agency. "They wanted to appoint me as leader, but I didn't like public speaking so I declined." She said it as though she should be proud that she had risen to a position of responsibility in this organization, which busied itself with spreading the corrupt idea of Aryan superiority and redistributing the belongings of people who had been sent to the ghettos and the gas chambers "to support the war effort." Opa's lawyer had used as evidence in Opa's defense that he hadn't been a member of the NSV. He omitted the fact that Oma had been an enthusiastic member.

Now she stopped and searched desperately for the next thought. "The human being has evil in him, and that is the reason there will always be struggle and conflict."

"What about Harty?" she asked nervously. "Did you find out any-thing about him in your 'searches'?" With the help of Fábio Koifman, a Brazilian immigration expert, who had become my friend from afar, I learned of the possibility that Uncle Harty had not died at the hands of bandits in a ditch in Brazil. Records showed that a person of the same name and birth year had settled in Florida, where he was buried. There was a three-day discrepancy in the birth dates, which made the search inconclusive. Contact with his family revealed that this Hartmut never spoke of his past to his new family.

I shared the information with Oma, hoping that I could at least pro-vide some solace amid the shock. Oma sat up tall in her armchair. "Yes, I know," she said bitterly. "If it is true, it provides me with great comfort."

I glanced at Auntie Best to see whether she was surprised, but it seemed that she too already knew. Why, if Oma and her daughters had known that Uncle Harty was alive, had they let him die in their minds? Was there something he knew they didn't want to hear—a reason for the rift between him and Opa they didn't want to discuss? The pain of it all was so great, I began to understand them.

The revelations so far were hard to digest, but none was as difficult to bear as the one still to come.

"Your poor father!" Oma said in a conniving tone. "Getting involved with our family was just too complex for him. He really couldn't handle it. Your grandfather had amassed land the size of the state of Baden-Württemberg, and that required resources. No small pickings, and it was never enough! Oh, what we lost!"

The callousness of her words shocked me. According to her, Father had been a pawn, a simpleton, not of the same superior class, not capable of the same comprehension, who shared my flat, inferior feet. Father's warm heart beat intensely inside me, and I knew that whatever he had done, he had done it for love. All of my being reached out to comfort Father's trembling hand, the one that had held Oma's on so many occa-sions and calmed her nerves. I shut my eyes, exhausted by the weight of Oma's cynicism and self-obsession.

Noticing my disengagement from her diatribe, she changed direc-tion. "In the morgue they dressed him up with shoes that were too big for him. It was odd to see. We should let your Opa rest in peace." Auntie Best nodded with relief that this ordeal might now be over.

After two hours in this surreal conversation, I was relieved that it was time to go. Realizing that we would never reach that common recognition and feeling of responsibility I had hoped for, I took her hands back into mine and stroked them with the deep pity I felt for this woman who could not be honest with herself.

"Goodbye, Oma," I said, kissing her forehead, which could not take the sun, and which today I understood had been forced into it, ironically to hide.

Auntie Best had no desire to comment on the afternoon's events as we walked together to the bus stop. It was as though the conversation had never existed. It wasn't fair to demand more of Auntie Best. She had done whatever she could to manage under circumstances that most would have found unacceptable. "Goodbye, my dear. Call when you get home," she said, and hugged me as she always did.

On the train, Oma's reactions replayed in my head like a broken record. Notably, her eyes had not flickered once during our conversation. I tried to dismiss her words about Father as the cynical utterings of a morally frustrated woman, but they were like a thorn in my side. I had felt so close to Father, but had I really known him?

— ◆ —

The Central Office of the Judicial Authorities for the Investigation of National Socialist Crimes, founded in 1958 in the wake of the Ulm trial of the same year, wasn't far from Oma's town. Primary documents that described the war in occupied Poland, which contrasted starkly with her own accounts, were openly available in archives both to the East and to the West, in close proximity of her quiet apartment. During all the years I had sat with her listening to her stories, the accounts of the eyewitnesses lay organized in the storage facilities of nearby archives.

The main building of the Central Office resembled a monastery. It was white, pared down, had a quiet courtyard, and wasn't easy to penetrate. What happened in this place was the culmination of changed sentiment toward handling the past during the late 1950s. Drawing a line under the Third Reich didn't work because, among other things, it created suspicion and an ethical quandary that challenged the foundations of the new democracy.

Inside, a young man in jeans whose kindness humanized the clinical white walls ushered me to an empty table in the reading room. Another researcher sat three rows ahead, bent over documents on top of a low pile of folders stacked neatly on her desk. The young man excused himself for a moment, like a nurse gone to collect the medicine, and then returned with the information that my prescheduled appointment with a senior member of the staff would take place immediately. I could return to the reading room later to review the documents, which I had reserved in advance of arriving.

A well-meaning but weary senior archivist sat behind his desk as the young man ushered me into his office and then left us. As we spoke, it struck me how understandable the weariness was. How many traumatized, obsessed family members had visited this office over the years? Even as the last living war criminals were in their nineties, it continued to be subjected to political pressures, which most frequently would never result in a trial for all manner of reasons unrelated to the nature of the crimes.

"Look, he isn't in our records, and if he isn't in our records—whatever filth he got up to—he didn't kill anyone." The words were uttered as caring advice with a strong tone of frustration at people like me who didn't give up because they had a hunch. For a moment I felt like a bloodhound rather than someone interested in truth and justice. Yet I stood my ground because my journey had already been too long, and I knew too much to give up at another minor hurdle. The timing of Opa's departure from Brazil and all I had learned about him left me convinced that one had to put this knee-jerk response down to fatigue.

"I see, but in that case I must ask you just one more question," I replied. "Do you have records of all the men in the Einsatzgruppen that participated in the invasion of Poland? I'm interested in the mounted squadrons, as you might have guessed."

The official heaved a sigh, still hoping I might give up, but realizing there was some point in asking about these mobile killing units that had followed the Wehrmacht into Poland. "No, we do not," he confessed. "It just wasn't possible."

"Thank you," I said, closing the discussion. It wasn't my intention to make trouble, but the official's reply renewed my determination to return to the documents and examine them meticulously.

Back in the reading room, the young archivist explained the form I should fill in to begin using the files, and hesitated at the line concerning "purpose of visit." "I think it's about your grandfather," he whispered, looking sympathetic and casting a glance at the other reader in the room to ensure he hadn't attracted attention. I took his demeanor as a kind effort to prevent me from having a mental breakdown. Several like me hadn't dared to visit this monastery of documented horrors without their psychiatrist accompanying them.

The young archivist disappeared for a moment and then returned with a trolley loaded with files. The other researcher smiled skeptically at my overambitious order. "You might want to have a look at the others tomorrow. They're still in the back room," he said, glancing at the clock. I nodded, feeling foolish enough as it was, and not wishing to add that I didn't have much time to spare tomorrow.

An hour and a half later, just as I was beginning to doubt my own judgment, I hit upon twenty-four testimonies of people who had been scattered to the four winds by the war, but who had submitted statements about events in their village, one of the places Opa had occupied. Their accounts delivered a unified picture.

A bearer of the Blood Order had established his reign of terror at the palace from which he had evicted the owners. The Blood Order was a distinction created by Adolf Hitler to recognize "old fighters" and the most dedicated Party faithful. This man had eventually murdered the palace owners by his own hand in a forested area, which became known as the site of nighttime executions by the SS and local Gestapo. I recognized the name of this notorious place from my previous trip to Poland.

The clock ticked ever more loudly, and the other reader left as closing time approached. I read faster. Fifty-two men had been named by the eyewitnesses, and their crimes meticulously described. Hidden close to the bottom of this imposing list was Opa, the forty-eighth man, "devil to the people," who beat and tortured those on his estates to unconsciousness and who had been the bearer of the Blood Order's close associate.

Although the relationship between these two men was new to me, I had seen and heard similar testimonies about Opa before. Each time I heard them was like another lash of the whip. To read it here in the prosecutor's office, where I had definitely been told that Opa was not in their records, brought the realization that although many had studied this war and its atrocities, so much of the details remained unresolved. There were reams of documents waiting patiently in archives and other public files, and the things that stood between us and greater knowing were our own fatigue, self-doubt, and impassivity.

Politely, I ignored the young archivist who stood at the doorway waiting to finish for the day. Of the fifty-two men in the list, not one was eventually brought to trial. The repeated conclusion by the prosecutor upon closing the query of the Polish government in 1977, one year after Opa's death in the interior of Brazil, was that the perpetrators could not be traced.

I didn't bother taking up the emergence of Opa in the documents with Ludwigsburg, figuring that this would be a fruitless effort since he was dead. Instead, I ordered photocopies of the most important documents and thanked the considerate young archivist.

As I walked into the town of Ludwigsburg, which like so many others had the generic look of a heavily bombed town rebuilt since the war, the words "could not be traced" overshadowed all other thoughts. How was it that so many men, some of them employed by the same state-run agricultural organization as Opa, were consistently untraceable?

I returned to my motel room on the edge of the city. It punished me with its frugality, which served as a reminder that my financial resources were wearing thin and that I couldn't carry on with this search forever. This bothered me intensely, because the information that I had just been party to in the Ludwigsburg archives turned my attention to postwar networks and continuities, which I had begun to think about since the trip with Nele. I began to consider the networks within the Reich Ministry of Agriculture and, in particular, Opa's employer in Poland, the Reichs-gesellschaft für Landbewirtschaftung.

———

"Are you there, Jens?" I asked via Skype chat. Jens had frequently mentioned that his father maintained his wartime networks as a bureaucrat in Bonn and throughout life.

"I'm here," came the split-second reply. Jens knew that I was in Ludwigsburg and might need to talk. "How is it going?" he asked, eager to hear my news. It was a comfort to hear his familiar voice.

"I just viewed a file today with the names of fifty-two men stationed in the same rural area of occupied Poland, including my grandfather, none of whom were prosecuted because they could not be found. Some of them worked under the Ministry of Agriculture, likely in the same organization as my grandfather."

"Interesting!" said Jens enthusiastically, and suddenly I didn't feel so foolish anymore.

"How could it be, Jens?" I asked, exasperated, and then broke off into another separate but possibly related thought. "I've been thinking about the fact that the person who ran the Reichsgesellschaft became a Minister in the Adenauer cabinet during the 1950s. Kraft was his name. Waldemar Kraft."

"Even more interesting!" said Jens. "Kraft was in my father's postwar pool of old comrades. Visited us in Poland during the war and at our place in Bonn on several occasions."

"Really?" I said, feeling reassured that Jens would not think my theory too far-fetched. "Tell me if my imagination is running wild, but could one of the explanations for so many unpleasant cases being dismissed be a concern about damaging the credibility of the government, particularly with the Soviet threat? Kraft doesn't seem to have been a fanatic himself, but as an SS Hauptsturmführer he did preside over an organization with torturers and murderers among its employees."

Various inquiries with the Bundesarchiv had revealed that very little documentation about the activities of the Reichsgesellschaft remained after the war. It was one of those organizations that seemed to have avoided scrutiny, partly for lack of information and perhaps because after the war its fanatics could operate under the cover of being engaged with farming. The most revealing facet of its modus operandi was that, as a result of a law passed by Himmler early in the war, estate managers were given the freedom to determine the law on the lands they managed. The German farmer, according to Himmler, was to become the "blood source of the Germanic-Nordic race" in the new lands and would thereby cure the "illness" that had befallen the German people. Filled with this propaganda, Himmler was confident they would make the "right" decisions.

"Your imagination is not running wild," Jens replied. "That is exactly the type of thing that could possibly have happened."

"All right, let me test the next piece on you," I said, feeling more confident. "Visiting dignitaries stayed only in the finest places when they toured the occupied territories, and my grandfather controlled some of the largest and finest estates in central-western Poland during the war. Later on, Kraft settled in Schleswig-Holstein and took up the rights of refugees from the East as a political cause. He would have frequently traveled past my grandfather's hunting hotel on his way up to Kiel. There weren't many places of such quality he could stop at on that road during the 1950s. What I am trying to say is that maybe unrepentant, overt fascists like my grandfather who were too closely linked to senior members of government—even if Kraft left the cabinet in 1956—became troublesome as time wore on. Maybe, aside from being unnerved by the new wave of trials, there was another 'push' to leave. Do you understand what I am trying to say, Jens?"

"I know what you are trying to say, and you are not mad," Jens reassured me. "A person like your grandfather would have been just too close to home. You know, my parents became members of the BHE, the league of expellees, the right-wing party Kraft chaired during the early fifties. You could find a lot of old Nazis in those circles, particularly in Schleswig-Holstein, during the fifties and sixties. They covered for one another, supported one another's public statements, and were united on one point: the Nazi era did a lot of good."

Jens paused to restore the balance that his voice often lost when he spoke of his father and the nest of cronies who had continued to thrive in the postwar government of the Federal Republic.

"Kraft was even on a list of people compiled by Dr. Werner Naumann who had tried to organize the overthrow of the new democracy and bring back fascism in the early fifties. Naumann had been Göbbels's state secretary during the Third Reich. Don't let anyone fool you. Kraft was among those who regarded the occupation as 'a beautiful time.' After serving as a soldier in the first war, he became the director of the German Farmer's Association for years—represented German farming interests in Poznan from 1925—and was no doubt an avid supporter of the push eastward. He just stayed behind a desk, and, yes, your grandfather may have been one of those people who revealed too much by his behavior alone."

Jens's words recalled those that had been repeated to me countless times by Oma during our conversations in her apartment. Now I understood what that beauty consisted of: the absence of accountability and a false freedom conferred upon the elite in the occupied territories to do what they liked, including letting their prejudices loose, unchecked.

I thanked Jens for listening and for his openness, and excused myself, feeling as if I were on a boat rocking dangerously in a turbulent sea. I knew all too well that I was living in the brittle world of theories, yet ones that had emerged out of watching very real known patterns.

I slept for an hour and then awoke, the adrenaline pumping, and glanced at my computer screen. An email had arrived from Fábio. He had identified documents concerning a Baron von der Kleist and his family, who might have been my grandfather's contact in Brazil. Von der Kleist had declared himself to be an estate manager, a profession that matched the interests of Opa and his son. Oma said the baron had been in Brazil since after the First World War, and therefore had nothing to do with the Reich. Yet the von der Kleist in the documents had arrived in Brazil twelve years before my family, in the maelstrom of refugees. If it was the same person as the one who had been Opa's Latin American contact, Oma had either lied or been lied to, and if it was the same person, he had certainly had sufficient time to become a helpful adviser with local knowledge.

Certain aspects of the documents made the usually cautious Fábio suspicious. "Why were they in Switzerland in 1948? It's a good question," he said. Von der Horst had left Europe from neutral Switzerland during that year and never turned back, taking up permanent residence in Brazil. According to his papers, his birthplace was in the old East Prussia. If this was a falsified document, it would not have been the first in which an SS man had claimed that his place of birth was in the East in order to qualify for refugee status. At least 120,000 SS men were issued Red Cross passports, facilitating their flight via known "rat lines" to Latin America after the war. Among former SS men Brazil was rumored as being a more favorable destination than Argentina; the ease of entry was explained by the perceived need for skilled Europeans in a growing economy.

A quick search confirmed the falsification. Von der Kleist declared his parents to be a well-known Prussian baronial couple, but this couple had no sons. Both Fábio and I had by now seen enough of such dense and disturbing information to know that one needed to take a step back and observe it from different perspectives before reaching any conclusions. While we accepted that in all likelihood we would never know the full truth, both of us sensed the evidence rising like a river about to flood.

Fábio signed off in his usual sympathetic manner with a phrase I thought I recognized.

"Com um abraço"—with a hug—he wrote.

CHAPTER 11

Poland, 2013

ROBERT AND I STOOD IN THE SAME FOREST MENTIONED IN THE DOCU-
ments at the Central Office. It was not far south of the town of Wilczyn
in central Poland where Opa had governed over two large estates early
in the war. Three prominent memorials stood alone, tucked away in a
deserted forest off the roadside in the middle of nowhere. Here, the
blinding headlights had been switched on. The victims had been told
to run and were shot in the back in flight amid tall trees that mourned
over the many other bodies that were already buried between their roots.
Neither of us could find anything to say, the sound of the leaves under our
feet a punishing reminder of all those who had run and fallen.

Concealment was by now a word that wound its way around almost
everything I observed. In an environment in which the smell of murder
hung in the air, the SS had played a game with its own people, in which
the innocent forests played a sinister role. The most important rule of
this game was that as long as it hadn't happened in plain sight, it hadn't
happened at all. The executions that had taken place in this forest were
rarely recorded, but people on their spacious new estates in the surrounding area knew. I recalled the photograph of Opa and Oma sharing what
appeared to be a tender moment in a forest clearing in these same parts
and felt deeply alienated.

We hadn't planned to make any further stops on our way down
into southwestern Poland where Opa and his family had spent the last
phase of the war, but another image from the photo albums had begun

to haunt me. A monk posed obediently with hands folded in front of a monastery with high towers, one of them under repair. There were also profile photos of the same man. I wasn't sure why and had asked Oma who this man was. "Oh, just an old uncle," she had said, keeping her reply uncharacteristically short.

I became so obsessed by the photograph that I researched the robes worn by this monk and found them to be those of the Camaldolese order. Robert had mentioned that not far from us and the estates where Opa had presided in these parts was a Camaldolese monastery.

"Can we stop at the monastery you mentioned, Robert?" I asked abruptly.

"Yes, of course, but it will take more time. Why do you want to go there?"

"Because of him," I said, pointing to the image of the monk on my computer screen. Robert veered off the main road onto a smaller path and within a half hour we had arrived. The grand structure pushed its way out of history and the photograph onto the hill, seemingly pleased to defy concealment. It was the same monastery as in the images.

"Why don't I go inside and ask about this picture?" Robert said.

"I don't think I'm allowed in anyway," I said.

I waited in the forest below the imposing hill and watched Robert walk up the path that cut through two grand walls on either side. This place must have seemed dangerous to the invaders. A Catholic fortress, strategically placed, was a proud symbol of national resistance. A great door opened and a tiny monk emerged. He and Robert exchanged words and Robert pointed down the hill at me. They exchanged a few more nods and the monk withdrew once again behind the door.

I became impatient as Robert took a rest stop behind a tree in the forest. What had the monk said to him?

"The brothers who were here during the war were sent to Dachau by the SS," Robert announced as he reemerged. "None of them survived."

I looked up the hill at the beautiful building, its spires whole once again. The photo in my album was most likely the last image of a man who only a few weeks later had gone to his death at the hands of the

SS. Oma's disdain for the Catholic Church and Opa's renunciation of Catholicism made perfect sense.

⎯⎯

The gravel crunched under the car tires as we drove into the groomed driveway of a baroque-style palace. It was the only major structure we could find in this picturesque village of Siemianice, or Schemmingen in Opa's day, in the southwestern corner of Poland. We needed help with directions to find the last place my grandfather and his family had lived in during the war, before fleeing the advancing Russian army.

As I waited for Robert to inquire at the main palace building, the striking property revealed itself. To the left of the driveway was a well-kept park with a cathedral-like stone church. Beyond the wall, which separated the residence from the farming estate, were a number of large, well-maintained prewar barns, one with pitch black doors meant for keeping carriages. Closer to the farmland in the distance were a few ruins, barns that hadn't been reconstructed. Nearly seven decades later, the scars of war still marked the landscape.

At the beginning of the vast stretch of green farmland, past the ruined brick structures, stood a white monument, curiously placed all on its own. As the rain began to fall, this statue of the Madonna gripped my imagination. A minute figure in the vast landscape, she was still its undisputed queen.

"You must come inside!" shouted Robert. "I think it was here."

"What do you mean?" I asked in disbelief.

"I think this was the place!" he repeated.

I had visited every estate that Opa had taken over since 1934, both in the Old Reich and in the occupied territories. Each was grander than the last, but this was beyond my wildest imagination. I mused at the thought that the hunting lodge he had purchased after the war, which had the look of a mock castle, was a sort of pouting over the loss of the palace before me. It was as though he had aspired to become the kaiser himself.

As the rain fell hard outside, the director of the forestry institute, which had taken over the building, called a number of the local inhabitants.

A young man in his early thirties, called Tomek, accompanied by his father, shook my hand heartily in the intensifying rain. We moved into one of the barns and exchanged stories.

"My grandfather was deported by the SS from here to a labor camp," he said. "We have had to work hard to get this land back since then, but it is ours now."

"What happened to your grandfather?" I asked, suspecting that, with a crack of his whip, Opa had determined the fate of yet another family.

"He survived, but he was already in his fifties when he came back. Almost too late to have a family, but he managed."

I struggled to form a response at first and then somehow found the words. "I am very glad your grandfather returned," I said, and Tomek laughed and patted my arm.

"My father says that your grandfather was a good farmer," he added. "He introduced a type of potato we have planted here ever since."

Tomek's father nodded with eyes eager to alleviate any guilt, but I already knew that there was truth to what he had to say. Others had attested to Opa's exceptional farming skills. What might he have become in another time?

"We have many things to show you," said Tomek, excited, treating me like an honored relative. "We will take my jeep."

The first stop was the Madonna in the field. "Last summer we put her back up again," Tomek said proudly. "It's a replica. Your grandfather struck down the original when he came here. It was one of the first things he did."

The minutes of basking in my grandfather's talent ended abruptly, and I was ashamed to be so closely related to a person who would do such a thing. At the same time, the fact that the Madonna stood here so quiet and mild, long after the noise and fanaticism had died away, reassured me about which way the arc of history bent.

Tomek drove us to the nearby summer palace, a mansion on the banks of the Prosna River, which lay in the valley below a medieval fortress. As the water trickled gently past the overgrown garden, it struck me that there had been some truth in Oma's words. "These were the beautiful days," she had said about the years in this place.

Tomek and I walked along the length of the road leading to the gate of the mansion while Robert took a phone call. "One of the women in the village, an aunt of mine, was raped by the Russians when they came here," he said. "She never spoke about it and never had any children. Those were terrible times."

For some reason, this provoked me to share the story of Aunt Gise. Tomek stopped, and the rawness of this information filled his sky blue eyes with horror and sadness. His mouth flinched, and he put his arm around my shoulder as we continued on our path.

As we neared the jeep, Tomek added more detail. "There was a mother home just three kilometers away from here," he said. "Local people say there were Jewish girls held there and the names of children born to them were struck from the birth register." At first I struggled to follow the thought because it was so gruesome. Then there was a moment of denial, because these homes had been supported by the local NSV, women like Oma who were "welfare workers" for the Reich. The rape of Jewish girls had become a standard weapon of the SS's dirty war in the East. At the same time, fraternizing with Jewish women was illegal. Had the mother home been used to cover up an awkward problem or to run racial experiments? It was impossible to digest the monstrosity of what Tomek had said, and so I left it for the moment, knowing that it would inhabit my dreams.

As we pulled into the driveway of the baroque palace, the director of the forestry institute ran down the steps anxiously with a small slip in hand. "You must drive to visit this man. He has written about your grandfather," said the director, nodding excitedly as he handed over the slip.

Tomek turned to me, his face bright with emotion. "You are an uncommon person," he said. There was nothing left to do but to grip his hands and then to hug him. In that embrace was the healing the generations could offer if only we bothered to take the time.

"I will write," I shouted and waved as Robert and I drove down the driveway, away from Opa's last conquest in occupied Poland.

It was dark outside and clearly it was going to be a late night. "My wife made us dinner, but I understand this is important," said Robert sheepishly. Robert's wife, Olga, had been endlessly patient with my hijacking of her husband.

———

As we entered their apartment, Matysiak and his wife stared at me in wonderment, as though history itself had just climbed out of the books. Matysiak was an octogenarian who had survived Opa's fiefdom as a boy and written about it. His wife, a tall fair-complexioned woman, had been sent to the old Reich for "Germanization" as a child, returning to Poland after the war.

"Guten Abend," he said in perfect German.

We sat down at a table laden with fine porcelain, tea, and biscuits. Next to Matysiak's tea setting was his book, which he immediately picked up and began to leaf through. Then he closed the book and looked straight ahead, recounting from pure memory.

"He was an unhappy man," he said. It struck me as remarkable that this is what so many remembered about Opa, who was just another of the many oppressors in a gray or black uniform who had passed through.

"I have heard that before," I said. "What do you mean?"

"He had a temper like spitfire that he was barely able to control," Matysiak explained. "His wife and children just cowered around him. Their nerves were scratched raw by his daily terror. It was awful for all of us to see. My father, in particular, became very depressed watching it every day. I remember this like it was yesterday."

"He wasn't the first to occupy this place during the war, was he?" I asked.

"No, we had a fairly reasonable type here beforehand, but he wasn't radical enough so they sent your grandfather." Suddenly, the pace of the day lagged, and everyone around me was on mute, moving in slow motion as one realization dominated my thoughts: What a hell M had been born into.

Noticing how pale I had suddenly become, Matysiak's hitherto-silent wife served tea. "You speak very good German," said Robert to Matysiak.

"I learned it from my father," Matysiak clarified, then turned back to me.

"He was your grandfather's interpreter. My father was good at adapting to the enemy at the same time as managing to preserve some of our pride. It was most skillful. When my youngest sister was born, my parents were ordered to call her Kazimiera, just as all Polish girls were, as punishment to the Polish nation for allowing Jews to settle in their land under the reign of King Kazimierz. At home we called her only by her second name, and our father told us never to forget our Polish street names, which the Germans changed soon after they had taken over. There was only one in that family who knew these things about us and never told, and that was Harty."

"Uncle Harty?" I was surprised at Matysiak's memory of the name.

"Yes, we were friends, although we were not supposed to be. In fact, Harty despised his father for his cruelty and told all the Polish boys as much," said Matysiak, and then chuckled at an afterthought that I wished I could capture. "Harty waged his own private war on his father by speaking Polish with us local children. We were forbidden to mix, you understand."

"My Uncle Harty disappeared in Brazil," I said.

"Brazil?" Matysiak looked over at his wife in wonderment and shook his head. "Maybe I shouldn't be so surprised. Harty was the oldest of the children and smart enough to see what his father had become. What happened to his sisters?"

"They are all scattered in different countries now," I said, not wanting to get in the way of Matysiak's storytelling.

Robert kept uncharacteristically silent, feeling guilty about missing the dinner his wife had prepared for us. He looked at me skeptically as Matysiak's wife served us another round of tea while her husband leafed through his book again.

"As time passed we noticed him becoming increasingly paranoid," Matysiak continued. "He was constantly accompanied by that one-eyed henchman, Meische, a veteran of the front tasked with protecting him. He had become one of those 'creatures,' the cruelest and most corrupt of the Party establishment."

"In his denazification papers, which I found in a German archive, his lawyer states that he was politically and ideologically disinterested—only wanting economic progress."

"I am sorry," Matysiak said, shaking his head in pity. "That was most certainly not the case. He created a farmers' inn in these parts for political and propaganda meetings. Everyone knew about that place and stayed well away from it."

Tomek had shown me the distillery and the brewery, which were just a stone's throw away from the baroque palace. Paranoia, alcohol, and violence: the picture Matysiak painted explained Oma's spine-chilling experiences at home.

"He changed his tone a little toward the end," Matysiak added. "Stopped shouting as much. The sound of enemy aircraft and artillery from the East turned his attentions to escaping. Special food deliveries were ordered, as were new carriages and other supplies. All of us remember the meticulous way he organized their departure. It was the 18th of January 1945, and it was unforgettable. There were many convoys passing through our town on the same route back into the Old Reich, but your grandfather led his string of hay-laden carriages out into a freezing midwinter's night on a completely different route to avoid the partisans. They were after his head, you see."

M's frightened eyes peeped out of the hay next to her older siblings. What had this three-year-old been told by her mother, now pregnant with a brother or sister who might never make it into this world? The adults kept to their unremarkable legends, even in situations like this.

"We saw so many of those convoys pass through our town during the following days," Matysiak continued. "I will never forget the mothers holding their infants, who had already frozen to death. Whatever their parents had done, we felt sorry for all the children who passed by us in those convoys."

—◦—

As we drove home in the dark, Robert stepped hard on the accelerator. It was close to midnight and we had missed Olga's carefully prepared dinner.

Matysiak's final comments for the evening wouldn't blend into the mass of impressions for the day. "We remember his wife well," he had said, referring to Oma. "She wore the NSV pin daily and was proud of it."

Images of Oma passed before me like pieces of a torn canvas. To the young Januszewski she had been the angel who had called the apothecary and adored her garden. There was the image of the stalwart NSV leader, working for "maternal health" in her area. There was the pregnant woman surrounded by her children, frightened on a freezing night in a hay-laden carriage uncertain of survival. There was the desperate wife who wrote letters to restore her husband's reputation and the chance to make a living for their family of seven. And there were the delicate hands with the antique ring that stroked mine with the gentleness of a good grandmother. As I looked through the windshield I saw the rawness in Tomek's eyes as we had walked along the Prosna. The rain fell past the headlights, like the many lost children.

———

As I returned home, I found that more photocopied documents had arrived in the mail, this time from the Central Office. Without the fast-ticking clock of the Ludwigsburg reading room threatening, I examined details of the many testimonies about events that had taken place in the forest and at the monastery. There, in an account by a comparatively well-educated man, who, unlike some of the others, had been a mature adult of over forty years at the time of the events and an interpreter for the Gestapo, was Opa. According to this account, he had collaborated with the so-called overlord over life and death, that member of the Blood Order. The forest in which Robert and I had stood had been the site of their "eradications" of unarmed locals.

I began to feel disgusted with myself. How much more horror did I need to dig out in order to comprehend? I had already read several accounts of whippings and beatings to unconsciousness meted out to unsuspecting civilians who had fallen into sadistic traps, which Opa had taken pleasure in rigging. I was convinced that behind the gentle, forgiving eyes of Januszewski and Matysiak were unspeakable memories that they had withheld to spare me the burden.

With a heavy heart, I called Oma. I had phoned twice since our last meeting to check that she was all right, but now my reason for calling was my own heartbreak.

"I must say, you went very hard at me," she said angrily, leaving no time for offloading sadness. "I haven't been able to sleep at night." Her complaint was like sandpaper that scratched open my guilt wound, so I listened. "No one talks about the good things from that time! People were well paid and the milkman who was wounded during the first war only had to work part-time. Your grandfather got on well with him."

I had already heard the unremarkable story of the milkman, a Reich German with a limp who worked at one of their estates before the out-break of the second war. It was usually presented as a counterweight to Opa's otherwise poor treatment of employees and indentured labor, and reminded me of the many Persilscheine in Opa's denazification docu-ments. The milkman was the author of one of them.

"You are a direct descendant of your grandfather. Yes, you are!" Oma insisted, as though I had attempted to deny it by my discoveries. It sounded like the same accusation she had hurled at M throughout the years and I could feel how it hurt. "And now you should let him and this history rest in peace. I don't know why you look into it! You know noth-ing about that time. It doesn't *belong* to you!"

In the barrage of disconnected statements, these last words stayed with me like a bullet in the flesh that could not be removed. Did any chapter of history belong to certain persons and not to others? I pictured Oma sitting next to her thick tome, *War and Peace*, which occupied a proud place on her book shelf, and I was certain she never wondered whether she had the right to read it. All the same, I could never escape the inborn naiveté of my generation—we had not lived in our grand-parents' times.

The ensuing conversation turned ugly as fragments of the old NSV volunteer's memory were tossed out into open view. "You've brought real concerns into our family, you know." I assumed this was a reference to my insistence upon digging into the past, but now her argument took a turn I could never have guessed at. "Your marriage has brought genetic uncertainties into our family. Really you ought to spend your time more usefully looking into those instead. Just think, I am sure your daughter is already ripe for marriage." My husband had three disabled siblings who had died young of their condition. No one had ever been able to diagnose their illness. My daughter was only fourteen years old. Whatever did she mean? I couldn't find an apt reply.

"Well, yes, I didn't think you had thought about it. All it takes is one kiss and there will be children. So, busy yourself about other things. You have far greater concerns on your hands."

Perhaps I lived with the blinders of another time, yet in that moment it seemed to me that the vulgarity at the core of history's unprecedented racial experiment was laid bare. Oma had gone to a wilderness with a man she feared because she too had participated in that experiment and felt the need to hide. No further evidence was needed.

"I have to go now, Oma," I said, trying not to fall apart.

She made sure to have the last word. "Remember that quiet is the best. That's from one of my favorite poems by Uhland, and it is so true. Quiet really is best."

CHAPTER 12

Auschwitz, 2013

I HAD RISEN WITHOUT SLEEPING. MY HEAD ACHED AND THE SKIN ON MY face felt dry and lifeless. I would go down to the kitchen, make myself a cup of tea, and everything would be all right. Or would it? My husband lay curled on his side, rejecting me with his back on this dim morning when only the falling leaves offered solace. I hoped that my imaginings were the short-lived gnomes that trampled on my spirit after a sleepless night, but there was no way of denying that I wondered whether he was growing weary of my obsession with the past. Had I become the dark creature of my childhood diary?

Today I would travel from my home to Auschwitz, the place I had been told was an exaggeration, a lie. According to these same voices, it was the place that had damned us eternally to the demand for an apology for things we knew nothing of; the place that had unjustly overshadowed our portrait of the hard-working men in the golden field; the prison in which we had been unfairly incarcerated so that the many tourists could pass by our works and misunderstand. Oma's voice had already made clear that it was accompanying me on the upcoming trip, and there was nothing I could do about it. Her voice dominated my mind and was impossible to switch off.

I had no evidence that Opa had ever set foot in Auschwitz. However, just over an hour from the estates he had occupied during the early years of the war was Chełmno, or Kulmhof, as the Germans called it, the "pioneer" extermination camp where hundreds of thousands had met their deaths in intense periods of mass slaughter up to 1943. Robert and

I had stood at the gaping trenches in this small isolated village next to a forest near the railway lines. "Death trucks" had been packed full of naked men, women, and children from the castle where they were kept, and gassed during the fifteen minutes' drive to the trenches in a forest clearing where their bodies were dumped. The entire operation was supervised by the SS, but conducted by victims who were aware that they too would shortly meet the same fate. The "death trucks" were no secret, rather a subject of hushed conversation in the surrounding towns. As Oma continued to comment incessantly during my flight to Auschwitz, I was sure that she knew.

Early the following morning, before the tourists and school groups had gathered, Robert and I walked under the wrought iron sign, "Arbeit macht frei," originally designed to delude hundreds of thousands of men, women, and children into believing that they were going to work. In 2009 the sign had been recovered from a Swedish neo-Nazi who had stolen it together with five Poles during the same year. A similar sign was stolen from the Dachau concentration camp memorial in 2014 and was found in a parking lot in Norway in 2016. Europe seemed unable to shake its endemic fascist disease.

"This never happened," said the voice in my head. How well I had come to know that conniving creature, deception.

Ahead of me, Robert dodged the cold muddy puddles between the prison blocks, which had been transformed into museums by the many nations that had lost their citizens to the crematoria. Traces of what had happened collected in the grooves of my rubber soles. The air seemed dense, as though the human dust that had once filled the air hadn't quite settled. My body was a vulnerable thing with a skull that could easily be smashed, lungs that could easily be asphyxiated, and intestines whose membranes could easily be dried to paper by poisonous gas. To the left was the execution courtyard with its stone wall against which countless men and women had stood unclothed and freezing, and had fallen lifeless at the whim of a firing squad. There were different ways to meet death in this place, but the aftermath was always the same: to be dragged by fellow inmates who would themselves soon join the mounds of limbs and stunned faces that turned to ash in the furnaces. To the SS they had never existed, and history would be rewritten.

"This never happened," repeated the voice in my head, and I thought I would go insane until Robert called me to join him inside one of the blocks.

Both of us looked glumly at the contents of one of the display cases, which exhibited a standard registration form for prisoners entering Auschwitz. Nose, eyes, teeth, posture, face, and ears were among the many features to be described for each inmate in terms that fit the SS's parody of science. The skeletons of those with so-called deformities would be put on display in the museums of the Reich after their deaths to serve as a reminder of the danger to the Aryan race that had heroically been overcome.

"Only quality! Only the best!" the voice shouted until I felt ill.

In another display was a tangle that looked like modern art from a distance. Closer examination revealed the thin round spectacles of prisoners who had gone into the gas chambers in a blur. As I looked into the heap of bent metal, I saw Oma's batting eyelids and consciously kept my eyes wide open.

Behind the glass were seas of brushes, combs, and other grooming items, which had been taken from the prisoners upon entry. In their new environment these would not be required, because they would live on lice-infested hay with overflowing latrines and insufficient space, time, or energy to wash. In a room around the corner, I discovered the customary bunks that inmates had been forced to share. Those who were still alive in the morning used up whatever scarce energy reserves they had summoned during the night to remove the dead bodies and remake the beds to military standard.

"They were dirty and disorganized. We brought order!" I wanted to scream at this voice that tampered with my sanity, but this seemed cowardly and disrespectful in a place of such suffering.

Auschwitz had been a mandatory part of Robert's school education, so he remembered where the gas chambers were. "Come, this way," he said.

As we stood in the dull gray cement building his head brushed up against one of the openings in the low ceiling. Through it members of the "SS auxiliary health service" had poured in deadly Zyklon B crystals from the roof. Afterward, they drove off in their truck, marked with the sign of the International Red Cross. This charade continued despite the fact that the odor of acrolein, a pungent smell produced by burning fat, filled the air of the camp. In the room next door were the sliding berths where the gassed bodies were placed to be pushed into the furnaces. The inmates put to this gruesome task knew all too well that their bodies would be on those berths within four months of starting their assignment, before a new team of doomed men took over. It was all a part of the monstrous pretending, so that no one outside would ever know. As these men washed away the excreta that the gassed bodies could not retain, the thought of lying lifeless in their own waste must have been near.

My inner pendulum swung fitfully to the left and to the right, unable to find rhythm, unable to divine. I could not explain this place, only behold it in the furnace ahead where I saw my own scatological existence. How could I have listened? Why hadn't I spoken up earlier? Why had it taken me all this time?

CHAPTER 13

Bosnia Herzegovina, 2014

TWO TINY PUPS SCAVENGED AROUND THE STEPS OF THE COMMUNITY center in the tiny rural village in northern Bosnia where we had been working. One of them sniffed energetically, intent on surviving by finding scraps of pastry that had fallen to the ground during our coffee break. The other walked aimlessly across the grass, weary of life even as it had just begun, and lay down in the shade, indifferent to the warmth of the sun on this early autumn day. I petted the more active of the two, which responded enthusiastically to my affections. What choices were there in a world in ruins? Exactly one year after Auschwitz I found myself in an environment that raised difficult questions about how to live in the aftermath of apocalypse.

On the other side of the potholed dirt road was the ruin of a house destroyed during the war of the early nineties. The bright blue graffiti, a gift from the annual youth arts festival to the community, contrasted starkly with the pastoral scene and the smattering of houses and ruins scattered across the overgrown meadows that made up the village. Next door to the ruin, elderly men stood outside the local shop smoking and eyeing me skeptically. My colleagues and I had spent the past days inside the building across the street from them working with their youth on peace-building. Didn't I know that just a few years ago with their own bare hands they had exhumed hundreds of bodies from the nearby mass grave and placed them on the white-tiled floor of the youth center for identification? What could I possibly understand of the ordeals they had endured?

A herd of unshorn sheep wound its way around the potholes, followed from behind by a white draft horse that sauntered, unbridled, next to its master. The animals brought peace over what seemed to me a troublesome scene of ruins, death, and skepticism. Unhurried by their human master, they poured into the field surrounding the center and grazed in the same spot where men of the community, identified as Muslims, once had been gathered for sending to the mine that had been converted to a concentration camp farther down the road. Neighbors had turned on one another overnight. Suddenly, some were inferior, receptacles for the myths and furies that had been passed down through generations. Someone, some group, would always have to play that role for as long as a lid was put on openly discussing the substance of the rage.

As visiting workers, we had been told explicitly not to discuss ethnic conflict or the war. None of the surrounding villages would collaborate with us if we did. We must help to build peace without discussing the reasons. To the youth in our group, the war was history, but to their teachers it was memory, and for them to participate we had to find another vocabulary that didn't include words that recalled what had happened here. A veteran of destructive taboos, my instinct was to speak with them about what had happened to their families during the war, and how personally they had been affected; but it was forbidden and so I refrained.

What stopped us from talking about these things? Would the pain and the misery of it turn us insane? Or was it that if we examined it closely enough, we would have to let go of the myths and face the facts that people had murdered people and that all of us were people. The closer one came to the truth, the more difficult it was to moralize.

⁓

Shortly after my return from Bosnia, the news came that Oma was dying. She was two months shy of her one hundred and third birthday. During the year since we had last spoken something had shifted inside me. I had talked publicly of my discoveries to people I had never met before, who repeatedly and patiently provided a safe space for the untangling of my emotions. By doing exactly what I shouldn't—breaking an old family taboo—a healing had begun so that wherever I looked in our broken world, light shone through the cracks. My ears had ceased to hear the echo of Oma's hard words that had scolded me as I walked between the barracks at Auschwitz. Now all I knew was that a life that had survived a terrible century and was closely tied to mine would soon end.

I rose earlier than usual to walk the dog. The night had been troubled after a luxurious run of nights when sleep had returned. During all the years I had lived in a time warp, sleep had been fleeting and sometimes undesirable because of what awaited me there. The night had been a stormy one, out in the sea of memories of the times that Oma and I had spent together. Before going to bed I had spoken with Auntie Best, the loyal nurse at her bedside. "We've missed you, dearest, where have you been?" asked my loving aunt, who made everything seem so uncomplicated.

Now as I walked between the trees, the frost-encrusted leaves brittle as life under my feet, I searched my memory. Oma stood at her kitchen counter with a small, round child fascinated by her careful measuring of each ingredient. I gazed into her sad-looking eyes, which had twitched only slightly then, and were the same as M's and mine. They looked determinedly into the pot where her lithe fingers with the antique ring handled an apple with an elegance no one I knew could match. Oma spoke to me throughout, passing on whatever she had learned about survival in her turbulent century. As I had boarded the train to return to the university, I looked into her eyes that expressed such concern. "Do you have those sandwiches handy? It's important you eat up every last one, you hear?" Oma was always worried that I might not have enough to eat, and had prepared two high towers of sandwiches, which I had obediently placed on top of the belongings in my handbag. They were very good sandwiches.

It was these images, not our last conversations or all of the other things I had learned about who she had been, that came to the fore. Her crystal-clear High German soared above the low voice of bitter frustration. I could reject my grandmother's ideology and reject things she had done, but there was something beyond this, a person, I could not simply cast out. That person had formed me in ways that neither she nor I could ever guess the extent of, and whatever she had done or said, the prospect of her loss and the knowledge of her tragedy left a gaping hole in my heart. People were people and it behooved us to know them.

As the dog circled a tree trying to figure out how it was going to pursue the tiny shivering squirrel that looked down upon it from a high branch, I thought of M. As a child I had felt her suffering, not been able to carry the burden, and turned it away. Today I forgave that child because I knew that her mother had borne a weight so heavy that it could have left both of them crushed. With this one small forgiveness, the possibility of many more opened up.

There was a kernel of deeper truth in Oma's words uttered in anger and frustration. I was the direct descendant of Opa, and he would always be my grandfather. Yet I was no longer the blond toddler who looked up at him in wonderment, but rather an adult who saw his brokenness and remembered that he had once been the youth with a thirst for life who had hugged the foal.

The telephone in my pocket vibrated and, noticing that it was my sister, I struggled to pull off my right glove to answer. "What are you doing?" she asked, sounding remarkably awake at such a late hour on the other side of the Atlantic.

"Walking off my worries," I replied, happy to hear her voice. "Busy gestating?" I asked jokingly, referring to the fact that she was due to give birth any day. "One life goes out just as another enters. Feels a little strange," I said, trying to resist all references to superstition, but failing.

"Yeah," she said, her sentiment with impending motherhood not entirely aligned with mine.

"I think a lot about what I have done during these years," I said.

"I get that," she replied. "I only wish I could have been there with you. I kept up with everything you sent to me." During the five-year journey, I had shared every piece with my sister. I didn't know whether this was good or bad—it might increase her desire to rebel and become more self-destructive—but I believed that this history belonged as much to her as it did to me.

There was a momentary silence when both of us could feel the misery and the pain of the past, but also the intense joy in one another that would never cease. "You have to know, that what you have done has freed me." She sighed, her voice shaking at the power of love between us. "Never think that what you have done is wrong. Whatever anyone said, you stuck with it. Thank you."

"I'm so glad," was all I could say. I would never be able to determine whether what I had done was right or wrong. Those judgments were beyond me, but I was happy that my sister felt better. Living within the confines of a taboo had distorted life for both of us.

Still, there was no danger that this work would leave me in the smugness of satisfaction. It would never be "done" and, in this sense, perhaps closure would never come. I had begun to suspect that the very idea of closure was perilous. To me it still suggested forgetting, or the fallacy that everything that needed to be known had been discovered. Robert had continued to investigate independently in the town of Pzydry, Peisern during the occupation, where records showed that Opa had also brought his wartime reign of terror. Nothing about him could be found there. In fact, any records of that town's wartime experience appeared to be absent or unavailable, raising the prospect of buried guilt. A few interviews with eyewitnesses revealed that the townspeople—ethnic Germans, Poles, and Jews—had turned against one another after the German invasion. Jews ran most of the shops, but soon there were none left, just as in so many other Polish towns.

The winter sun teased the horizon as I approached the entrance to my home. The dog sat before me with ears pricked, eager for the door to be opened. I waited to observe the daily battle of light and darkness, knowing that the morning news on the radio in the kitchen would remind me that we were not free of my grandparents' ideology. Its echo, so many decades later, bellowed through the hallway past the photograph of the sad-eyed toddler in the dirndl into a world torn and dismayed with the picture of itself. The same eyes as those in the photograph, now with the crow's feet of age, looked out into the world and wondered when it would awaken.

The front door creaked as I opened it and the dog raced past, hungry for breakfast. As I walked past the photograph of the boys playing on the raft and finally of Jülchen in the dirndl, I asked myself how we would do it: How would the generations rise out of the wasteland?

PART II
THE RED DUST

CHAPTER 14

Sweden, June 2015

UNCLE HARTY HAD DIED COUNTLESS GRIM DEATHS IN THE STORIES told in Oma's apartment, but now after forty years of eternity he was back, or at least so it seemed. I had tried to give Oma some calm by investigating the Hartmut who had died in Florida, and who, according to an obituary, had been loved by his family, but the slight discrepancy in birth dates warned of a mismatch and so I continued to keep an eye out.

I'd first seen credible evidence of Uncle Harty's existence on the mobile phone of my Brazilian friend Igor, an IT expert who had accompanied his wife, Patricia, to Sweden to study at Stockholm University for a year. Patricia had become a friend and suggested that she and her husband could provide some insights into how to begin planning the trip into the interior of Brazil to find my grandparents' hiding place, scheduled for the following late February. My alma mater, Wellesley College, had miraculously stepped in with a traveling fellowship, just as I was being forced to the conclusion that I'd have to concede to the need to make a living. There was work still to be done, and I knew that if I didn't finish it, it would always haunt me through the empty space like an amputated limb.

"Could this be him?" Igor asked, holding up his iPhone just as we had finished eating the main course of our meal in our dining room at home. By scouring the Internet, Igor had gathered a first tranche of documents that could help me with my research in Brazil. Among them were property documents suggesting that the ownership of a portion of my grandparents' old property, which had been divided, was disputed, and various traffic fines and other police reports attesting to Uncle Harty's wild nature as a young man. So far, almost anything was available to anyone on the Internet, but language still divided us in this vast new frontier of human activity, and therefore I was extremely grateful to my savvy new Brazilian Sherlock.

On the screen of Igor's iPhone was an older man of European origin who stood with one hand folded over the other against a dark suit at an altar next to the bride, an attractive woman of middle height, slim, with features that intimated a native Paraguayan parent. The caption revealed the names, one of them Uncle Harty's, and the bride shared his last name. His hair wasn't white or even visibly gray, and the hands didn't seem to be those of an eighty-year-old.

"No, that can't be him—it has to be someone else with the same name," I said.

Igor zoomed in on the hands. "What about now?" he asked. The hands showed signs of protruding veins and liver spots, and of course his hair could have been tinted. Doubts showered over me like wedding confetti over an uncertain bride. What if this really was Uncle Harty, and what if my uncle had only been dead in our family myth?

"But is he getting married to that young woman?" I asked Igor.

"No, that's his daughter," Igor replied, examining the screen more closely. "She married two months ago." His daughter—my cousin? It all seemed beyond belief, but of course it was the reverse. The reality *was* my Paraguayan cousin, laughing under her fine-lace veil; a symbol of resistance to the mythology that I had lived in.

On the same evening, via social media, Igor tracked down not just one cousin, but two—the brothers of the bride who was slightly younger. The next day I sent them a message, attaching a photograph of Oma serenely holding a bouquet of flowers on her hundredth birthday, informing her Paraguayan grandchildren and son that their grandmother and mother had passed away during the previous winter. The reply was immediate and confirmed Uncle Harty's recognition of his mother. "What a lovely grandmother! He thanks you," it read.

I wasn't certain that Igor understood the enormity of what had just transpired, although he and Patricia smiled brightly. "We are happy for you," Patricia said.

I didn't know how to feel. The sight of the mature Uncle Harty juxtaposed with my memory of the young man in the black-and-white photograph that Oma had held her pendulum over was like staring at a tree with the largest part of the trunk absent. I was unnerved. The days began to bend as though reflected in a distorting mirror. Food didn't taste the same, the flavors overpowered by the metallic taste of tension.

After a week of feeling this way, I understood that there was nothing left to do but to request a revision of travel plans from the fellowship committee at Wellesley. Uncle Harty might be able to put pieces of the puzzle into place that no one else could. "We see no reason why not," was the reply, and it was thus that the first stop on my Latin America trip became Asunçion.

During the months of preparation that followed, I returned to Germany to pull together the loose ends of my research there, and to meet people who could potentially help me to organize my Latin American adventure. My feelings of apprehension were only compounded by stark warnings of what lay ahead.

—◆—

"Take care of your family," Danny and Paula had urged over dinner when we met in Bremen to discuss how they could help with my Brazilian journey. Paula had grown up in a Jewish community in São Paulo, an experience she had written about, and now lived in Germany with her husband, Danny, working in film. Both understood the draw of a good story, the existential need to work through strong personal experiences, and the importance of remembering. Danny spoke to school students about his family, who had survived or perished in the Holocaust. They understood me perfectly and yet both cast a look of concern over the dinner table that said: "Don't get lost in the past." A friend of Danny's had done just that and never reemerged as himself again.

Their concerns echoed the sentiments of others around me, but I pushed back at them with all of the inner resources I could summon. The fact was that in order to manage the trip, which I was absolutely committed to—not least because of my traveling fellowship—I needed a travel companion. It had to be someone who not only could speak Portuguese but who could also negotiate with the fearsome ranchers in the interior of Brazil. I would manage the Paraguayan leg myself.

"You need a strong man with a big gun," Paula warned, lifting her delicate shoulders and cupping her arms around her petite body to suggest the need for a person of a completely different size and build. "Even if I came with you, it wouldn't be enough. Out there, locals handle unwelcome intruders in the only way they know how: with force. Two women turning up with troublesome questions in a macho environment like that. . . " She shook her head. "Well, it just won't do." Danny looked at his wife lovingly but skeptically. They had their own family to think of. He didn't want to lose her to my past and I couldn't blame him for it.

As we parted after dinner in a dark parking lot in Bremen, I felt like Indiana Jones after a stark reality check. It wasn't the first time I had heard such stories, but I had preferred to dismiss them as an exaggeration. Now they had been confirmed by people who seemed to know what they were talking about. Were there really such wild places left in the twenty-first century?

No sooner had the pendulum of my thoughts swung toward doubt than someone appeared to make it swing the other way. After the meeting with Paula and Danny in Bremen I returned to the countryside west of Hamburg to meet Gerhard Hoch, a historian in his nineties, who had done everything he could to face the past of his northern German origins with integrity—something that Oma and Opa had avoided because of the existential risks. He wasn't certain how he could help but had agreed to meet me, and, as I parked my car, stood on the pavement in front of his modest home in an oversized khaki gardener's sweater and baggy corduroys. Townspeople had avoided his side of the street for years, walking on the other side of the street in order to avoid his penchant for truth.

Gerhard's story was an offense to all efforts to leave history behind. At the age of eighteen he had been drafted into the Waffen-SS, with an enthusiasm for the cause imbued by the Hitler Youth. The horrors of what he had seen during the war in northern Russia, and years of postwar military imprisonment, drove him to seek refuge from the world in a brotherhood of Benedictine monks. Eventually, love drew him out of the order as he married and became a university librarian. In time he also became a vocal member of the leftist Green Party and, not least, a historian responsible for initiating the difficult task of facing the reality of what had happened in his native Schleswig-Holstein under Nazism. I wasn't certain how much he cared for the honors and medals that had been bestowed upon him in recent years, once neighbors had stopped deliberately choosing the pavement he wasn't on. The pain of living with the truth was drawn in the lines of his face as we shook hands.

To sit at Gerhard's table was to renounce all delusions about ourselves as human beings and to live daily with the discomfort of knowing what we are capable of. As I looked more closely into his face it began to transform into that familiar painting of human suffering by Edvard Munch, *The Scream*. I had always believed in our capacity for progress, but at Gerhard's table I knew that this picture was dangerously incomplete. We must also accept the discomfort of knowing the suffering that we as a species had wrought and that, as a consequence, we would ourselves endure. In the juncture, where truth lay, we would find love for our fellow human beings. He never asked me to give up on my treasured idea of progress. The weight of his presence simply forced me to stand nakedly before the question of what I believed in.

Gerhard had information I still thirsted for: detailed knowledge of the SS in Schleswig-Holstein, where Opa had become radicalized, and its marked influence on politics and society in this SS-friendly area even after the war.

"A Sonderführer. Ah yes," he said in his precise librarian's style. "He will have been given special indoctrination in one of Himmler's fortresses, so that when he came to manage his domain in the East he would be especially fanatical and run things according to the accepted race ideology. Early in the war, Himmler passed a law giving the right to those people to make their own law in their Eastern domains. He knew that most of them would act in line with his thinking. He had trained them well. That was how it worked." It was a rounding out of the facts I already knew from reading the remaining documents about the Reichsgesellschaft in the Bundesarchiv.

I revealed to Gerhard how splintered I felt about my chosen path. "Frau Lindahl," he replied, "it is where we do not seek truth that ungoverned guilt does its unholy mischief."

A month after our meeting, Gerhard wrote me a long missive on All Saints' Day to remind me of the importance of what I was doing. Only three weeks later his wife informed me that he had passed away. I felt lost. Without the eyewitnesses to consult, how would we know what had happened? Where could we continually find the courage to remember? Whenever mine failed, I read the letter from Gerhard and understood why he had written to me. He had become one of the many angels who saw to it that I didn't stray from my path.

I hadn't anticipated how hair-raising it can be to bring someone back from the dead. In the eight months since I had first seen the evidence suggesting that my lost uncle was alive and had his own family, I had kept it to myself, informing only my sister, in the belief that this journey was also hers. The finding had to be confirmed before anyone else was informed.

As the new year dawned and the date of departure neared, I struggled not to crack, but the pressure couldn't be borne and eventually found an outlet in facial paralysis with a diagnosis of suspected stroke. It was as though Oma's harsh god, Nature, had determined that the past was best left alone. Surprisingly, I found temporary peace in capitulation. After eight obsessive months of living in a proverbial closet with my travel and research plans, I found myself once again able to notice the fine details around me.

In mid-January I watched from my hospital bed as a woman with a white cloth wrapped Bedouin-like around her head sank a mop into a bucket of soapy water. The color of her headdress contrasted starkly with her even copper skin, and her fine features were unmistakably Somali. She ran the mop over the linoleum floor once or twice and then, unable to resist the rays cast by the late January sunlight, paused to look out the long window of this spacious room with six hospital beds. Only mine was occupied, but the others would soon fill up with other stroke patients as the clock ticked on and time touched other lives.

Perhaps the Somali housekeeper thought this Nordic winter sunlight puny; or, on the contrary, lived in wonderment as each New Year it showed signs of gradually emerging from months of shyness. The rays transformed her profile into those of a classical statue, which caught me by surprise when she spoke.

"Just like in Somalia," she said, turning to face me as a broad smile broke over her face. How was it possible that there were people in this world who hated this smile and the profound contribution it made in hospital wards and elderly homes? At best, it was grudgingly accepted, because there were few who would mop the hospital floor if people from Somalia didn't. How close we remained to Hitler's view that not all smiles belonged to humanity.

I tried to respond, but the best that my damaged facial muscles could muster was an awkward jerk. The elegant woman was unfazed by the erratic movement of my face, a common affliction of patients on this ward, and continued her silent mopping.

The ceiling above me was divided into white squares with metallic borders. It interrupted the moment of peace like a scolding schoolmarm: What was the point of carrying on with such nonsensical behavior? Now see where I had landed myself—in a hospital bed with a suspected stroke from the stress of work. At best this was a warning against the naiveté of continuing my search into what would no doubt be its wildest phase. In hopes of finding a kinder ceiling, I rose from my bed and wandered into the common room next door.

"Zika declared a global health emergency," read the crimson banner that ran across the bottom of the television screen. Like a child obstinately blocking its ears, I turned my back on it and made my way toward the modest breakfast buffet for patients who could feed themselves. Eventually, I couldn't avoid the reality blaring out of the television, and succumbed on the sofa with a cup of tea, joining two other patients, who were oblivious to all but the screen. Images of children with tiny heads, and adults paralyzed from head to toe, unable to control their eye muscles so that only the whites of their eyes showed, flashed across the screen. Interviews with hapless doctors in disorganized, underequipped clinics were followed by a map of Brazil highlighting the worst-affected areas. I stole a look at the two patients next to me. Each of them sipped their tea intently. What else could we do when Nature decided to inflict misery upon us?

The warm tea dribbled out of the side of my mouth that I couldn't control. I wiped it away and left the sofa, irritated by the entire situation; in particular, the emergence of a strong counterforce to my plans, which fed my own doubts and fears, cultivated in the many discussions I'd had with acquaintances during the previous autumn.

Tired of the Zika reports, I lay back in my hospital bed in what seemed an eternal waiting for the results of the many tests. It was only the kindness and steadfastness of the hospital staff that kept those unthinkable reflections on mortality away. A Syrian doctor who no doubt had seen many die in more stressful circumstances told me that I was strong when I whimpered as he tapped my spinal fluid. A Spanish doctor with warm olive eyes cupped my hand in hers when I was afraid and told me that everything was going to be all right. Yet they knew the truth, which was that all of us would end, and that some of us on this ward would end sooner than others. Still, they didn't talk about it and instead focused on keeping our spirits up. I began to wonder whether the truth was really so important. I had pursued it doggedly, but to what end?

As on so many other subsequent occasions when I questioned my priorities, Gerhard's shadowy eyes looked right at me, and like the deep lines on his face, cut through the chaos and the nonsense with those unforgettable words: *It is where we do not seek truth that ungoverned guilt does its unholy mischief.*

Now a nurse pulled back the curtain I had drawn around my hospital bed to fend off doubt and the news of Zika. "Enough with the hiding! They're sending you to an ear, nose, and throat specialist," she said, grinning with the knowledge of my test results. "No stroke." She smiled. "Probably just a little temporary paralysis, but you'll have to take it easy for a while." She patted my hand reassuringly.

CHAPTER 15

Latin America, February 2016

OUTSIDE MY CABIN WINDOW, THIRTY THOUSAND FEET BELOW, THE great river pulsed like an artery that gave the wild land its vitality. It wasn't blue, as one expected a river to be. Rather, it was a rich, rust red, just like the dust Oma said had covered her shoes. It was impossible to look at it and not be infused with its extraordinary power. The thick, primal core pushed through the earth leaving shapely offshoots like colonies left in the trail of an empire, or pretty concubines that clung to their master for fear of what he might otherwise do. This was the land where the strong had the right, and where my grandparents who believed in this creed had once found refuge. The photograph of their jeeps on a raft-like ferry crossing the river below came to mind. On the other side was the promise that the Third Reich had never delivered: Lebensraum, more beautiful and more brutal than they could ever have imagined.

Next to me, my friend Lilien, a colleague in the Stockholm-based nonprofit organization I had founded, bristled with excitement. To celebrate her sixtieth birthday, she too had decided to return to the land of her birth and formative years, after decades in different parts of the world. Those of us who lived between cultures seemed forever in search of belonging.

"This is going to be so great!" she exclaimed, jumping up and down in her seat like a young girl, as our aircraft crossed that rust red divide that seemed like a point of no return. For Lilien, this too was a journey into family, remembrance, and meaning. She was the daughter of revered Swedish missionaries who had once worked in Paraguay. Now that her father had passed away she was a living descendant and could expect a hero's welcome by the congregation. Whatever the difference in our situations, I had to admire Lilien for her enthusiasm. She had faith that everything was for the best, while all I had at this point was the uncomfortable spur of doubt.

Only a few hours ago, as Lilien and I flew over the Atlantic, I received contact details from my Paraguayan family via social media. We had communicated in this way for months. Repeatedly, I had requested further details of their whereabouts, but received no addresses or telephone numbers in return. Without these I wasn't sure how I would find them, and had begun to wonder whether Uncle Harty really wanted to be found.

"We will be there to pick you up!" reassured cousin Bibbi. A parade of affectionate emoticons followed her message.

"See! Everything is going to be fine. You're doing the right thing," said Lilien, in whom I had confided all my worries during the long flight. She turned over to rest in her seat crammed with bags full of gifts for the adoring congregation.

As I walked through Paraguayan customs, Bibbi's was the first face I saw in the lineup of the four relatives who had come to greet me at the airport. Although we'd seen one another's images online, she held a sign with my first name written prominently on it. Soon she lowered the sign and smiled with the satisfaction that finally we had found one another. Behind the mild face was a searching mind. In several of our exchanges, both Bibbi and her brother, Mikael, revealed that they had independently been trying to find their father's family for years without success. "Pappa doesn't talk about his family," they'd said.

A tall, strong man in jeans and a checked shirt, who looked like a blend between Auntie Best and M, rushed forward and raised his arms in a gesture of enthusiastic welcome. The last time we'd met, he'd held me in one arm. A half century had passed and I thought he was dead, but none of it was true, just like so many other things left in the dark, unquestioned and undiscovered. Bibbi and Mikael had portrayed a man who worked hard and didn't talk much so that I wondered whether the excited and jovial person who now stood before me was one and the same.

With his eyebrows raised in disbelief, his face adorned with an irrepressible smile, and his chest filled with pride, Uncle Harty clasped my hands in his. They were the same hands as in the photograph on the Internet. All my plans for what I would say collapsed under the enormity of this meeting. How did one greet a person who had been "dead" for fifty years? "Good day, Uncle Harty," I said.

"*Bueno*, Julie! Welcome to Paraguay. We have been looking forward to your visit." He spoke German laced with Portuguese instead of the local Spanish, a legacy of the many years spent in a Brazilian wilderness managing his father's estate. The voice was strong and straight, broken only by a mischievous laugh. In the familiar green-brown eyes, Oma's eyes, I could see that he was sincerely glad to see me, even if he hadn't been sure up to now.

Behind Uncle Harty, to the right, a pair of dark brown eyes framed by stark brows stared intently from behind a delicate bouquet of flowers. These were held in strong hands at the end of muscular arms. As Mikael's lips broadened into a warm smile, I realized I had just met my most handsome cousin. The lucky woman standing next to him, his girlfriend, Lara, looked alert, as though analyzing every move with sharp intelligence. Her classic Hispanic looks evoked the image of a proud matriarch on a hacienda, her hair strictly parted down the middle in an elaborate updo with a mantilla.

Bibbi broke the nervous lineup, stepped forward, and hugged me. "Hola, Julie," she said warmly, without pretense. The fact that we would somehow have to cobble together our conversations in English, German, Portuguese, and Spanish didn't seem to matter. We had a common, as yet unspoken, purpose and, for this reason, all of us wanted to be here.

Contrary to what I had expected, Lilien's welcome party was late and mine was robust so she piled into one of the two cars with us, informing her contacts that she was already on her way. This was a fortunate coincidence, as she was fluent in Spanish, and could help us to begin our communication more easily.

Uncle Harty wasted no time asking questions. "How are my sisters?" he asked. "Where do they live? Tell me of my mother." I glanced at Bibbi, who was deftly navigating her way through the chaotic Asunción traffic. Mikael and Lara were already far ahead of us in the sea of honking taxis and air-conditioned SUVs with darkened windows. I imagined these questions were as much of a surprise to her as they were to me. Her father hadn't spoken of his family in her lifetime.

After almost thirty hours of travel I answered his questions as best I could. Uncle Harty listened attentively, and all the time I wondered why he had lost contact with the rest of the family for over four decades. He changed the subject, sensing we might be approaching a question laced with complications. "Your Opa had a great deal of land just across the border in Brazil, you know."

"Yes, I know," I said.

"Si, he was SS during the war and then he came here. What ideas he came up with!" He whooped, and then continued: "The machinery and the land we had. I tell you . . ." I was startled by this unencumbered admission of Opa's engagement in the SS. It was as though it was a side issue—a less-important precursor to the ambitions he had tried to realize in Brazil.

Uncle was about to continue with the story of his father's land con- quests when I stopped him in his tracks. "Did you know that he was SS?" I asked, surprised at the ease with which Uncle Harty shared this infor- mation that I'd gone to great pains to dig out of an archive in Berlin and wept over in the Holocaust memorial of stone blocks years ago. "Siii!" he said, in a long, deep yes, wondering where on earth I had got the impres- sion that my grandfather had been anything else.

This was without doubt one of the strangest moments that I could remember. Without hesitation my uncle had opened the door to talking about things that others in the family had shunned. I thought it would take days before we could discuss the past, but we were into it within twenty minutes of meeting. I felt as though I had struggled with a locked door for years only to find that I had been turning the key the wrong way. Could it really be as simple as just asking?

"Deutschland, Deutschland über alles!" he joked, reciting the now forbidden opening lines of the old German national anthem that matched the overlord mentality of the SS. The touch of nostalgia in the joke grated on me and was the first moment of dissonance between us. In Europe, the first stanza of this anthem represented an abhorrent racist supremacy that had brought civilization to its knees and was banned in Germany. Yet, I had been forewarned. A friend of mine back home in Stockholm, who had frequented the German Club in São Paulo during the sixties and seventies, described outbursts of defiant national pride, unacceptable in postwar Europe. These, he noted, found a vent in Latin America, where judgment about the war was clouded by distance, far-right nationalist and military governments that didn't hesitate to employ torture as an instrument of governance, and local sympathies for strong men. Conscious that exhaustion was amplifying all the sounds in my head and possibly resulting in oversensitivity, I didn't respond.

Lilien had stopped translating our conversation into Spanish, aware that this might be the first time that Bibbi had heard the story, and that it might be too much all at once. Yet Bibbi's German comprehension skills were good enough for her to understand what had been said, and she cast a brief glance at her father, shaking her head before returning to concentrate on the traffic. Her mild face, eyes hidden behind large sunglasses, made it difficult to determine whether she was shocked or merely disapproved of his mischievous schoolboy behavior. Even more confusing was Uncle Harty's enthusiasm to share this story. I tried to listen for evidence of anger toward Opa, which his Polish childhood friend had described so vividly to me, but couldn't find any. Life didn't progress in straight lines, but what had changed? How had Uncle Harty changed? The years had a habit of grinding down the hardest of emotions.

I wondered about Bibbi's feelings. Was it right for me to barge into this family and shackle it with a subject that it had seemingly escaped for so many years? Did she really welcome this new openness about the past I had unleashed in her father?

We said our farewells to Lilien, whom I would meet again for the journey home three weeks later. Now I was on my own.

—◦—

That evening we settled into the spacious, terra-cotta veranda of Uncle Harty's bungalow-style property on the outskirts of Asunción. The soft, warm air felt eerie on my skin, and the terrace lights were shockingly bright after the sudden change from the Scandinavian winter. Uncle Harty continued with his enthusiastic storytelling, now mainly about his farming machines that he rented out to make a small income. Mikael sat to my right, silent and polite, although his tight muscles flinched, making me wonder whether he was in pain. Lara draped her girlish body over the arm of his chair and looked considerably more confident, perhaps because she and I could communicate easily in English.

Eventually, a small Paraguayan woman with jet black hair and a glowing, slightly pockmarked face appeared and gave me a kind, measured embrace. This was Uncle Harty's wife, Luna. She sat down slowly, spoke softly in Spanish, and moved her hands deliberately as she untied the ribbons around the presents I had brought. She had been married to her husband for well over three decades and had never met any of his family. I wondered what their discussions had been like in advance of my arrival. Had I stoked conflict and questioning? Whatever I did, I was certain that I had smashed an old urn that had sat perched with everyone's deep awareness on the proverbial family mantelpiece for years.

"We are very happy to see you. It means so much to us. We don't know any of Hartmut's family," Luna said, as her son's girlfriend translated. Uncle Harty showed no signs of wanting to defend himself. It seemed that Luna, over twenty years his junior, half his size, and a woman with Guarani heritage in a place where European men were still gods, had assumed the translucent power of the moon after which she was named.

She rose so regally, without excusing herself, that I wondered whether she came from tribal royalty. Mikael followed her into the kitchen to help Bibbi finish the dinner preparations, and Lara slipped into the empty armchair and continued to watch from under her strong, discerning eyebrows, analyzing our body language with her trained lawyer's mind. It didn't matter to her that the conversation now turned to German, which she could not understand.

"All the European wives just pined to go home after a while," said Uncle Harty. "So I chose a Paraguayan. Si, much better. I wanted to stay here, and Luna and I understand one another." He nodded, affirming his choice to himself. I sensed the anguish of his parents' separation still with him, all these years later, and at the same time tasted the bitterness of racism that slinked, unconfronted, through families. How many times had I listened to family stories of that "little mulata" of my grandfather's, as though she had been a sort of leech on our collective purity? I was certain Uncle Harty saw me as an emissary of that family, a bearer of the idea that not all humans belonged to humanity, and that therefore I would judge his marriage to Luna.

"I'm here on my own, Uncle Harty. Your wife is lovely," I said, hoping he would understand.

"Si, bueno," he said, although I wasn't sure whether he acknowledged my intention. "But what does your husband think of you being so far away from home?" he asked with genuine curiosity.

"He is very supportive," I said. "But he misses me, I hope."

"Si," he acknowledged, and then left that topic behind.

I could tell that he was old school, and that he must have seen me as one of those European women with an amusing but troublesome will. He had been raised in a National Socialist household in which women were seen as incubators of the master race. As a young man he'd moved into a hyperpatriarchal environment, where a woman was a piece of a man's puzzle rather than a full being with choices and desires in her own right. Yet, despite all this, one of the qualities that I was beginning to appreciate about my uncle was that he didn't dwell on disagreements or differences, and didn't cast judgment. His careful interaction with his wife, which contrasted starkly with his otherwise ebullient style, suggested that he had learned a few things in his life with her.

I glanced at Lara, who smiled knowingly at me. She was an intelligent woman, who must have regarded Uncle Harty as a lovable chauvinist beyond reform. How many of those knowing smiles had intelligent women shared with one another through the ages in the face of the idea that women were there for a man's choosing?

Lara left to help with setting the table, and I felt the urgency of touching upon history before dinner started. "Do you remember anything from Poland?" I asked.

"Siii!" replied Uncle Harty in that of-course-what-do-you-think style of his. "Those Russian prisoners on our estate kept asking after potatoes. 'Kartofel! Kartofel!' they begged, and when they got a hold of them they ate them raw. *Shww!*" I wasn't certain what the strange sound at the end meant, but it was achieved by sighing through puckered lips, and accompanied by a slight raising of the shoulders, and the exposure of palms to the ceiling. I suspected he meant that he had no idea why they did that.

"Everyone was treated well," he continued. I wondered what had influenced Uncle's memory. It hardly took much to work out that Russian prisoners wouldn't consume raw potatoes unless they were starving. More difficult to understand was what had happened to this child's resentment of watching his father's hatred in action.

"This was in Schemmingen, Silesia?" I asked, realizing that Uncle would have been too young to remember more than the last estate Opa had occupied in Poland during the war.

"Si! How did you know that? Have you been there?" he asked, in disbelief at the prospect that I knew this place that must long have dwelled in the recesses of his memory without anyone to share it with. I nodded, and an avalanche of stories followed about the caliber of guests Opa and Oma had entertained at their last grand estate in the occupied territories.

"Si! Panzermeyer was a great friend," he said, somewhere between pride and enduring amusement at the nature of his parents' guests. I still wasn't certain whether he in fact considered them infamous or just famous. Listening to Uncle Harty was like walking a tightrope of interpretation. "He and several other bigwigs in the wartime armaments industry and from the SS on the eastern front visited Vati's hunting estate in Schleswig-Holstein after the war. We had Waffen-SS weekends with some of the most influential people!"

Now it began to dawn on me that there was something odd—something missing—about Uncle's perspective on the consequences of the

Third Reich. Panzermeyer, whose real name was Kurt Meyer, had been tried and imprisoned for crimes against humanity after the war, but was pardoned in 1954 due to the diversion of the Allies' attention by the chilling of the Cold War. He became one of the most vocal revisionists of the history of the Waffen-SS, claiming falsely that it was a regular military organization with no political interests and no involvement in war crimes. To represent this view, he had formed an organization, the Mutual Aid Association of Former Waffen-SS Members (HIAG), which echoed the thin arguments I had read in my grandfather's denazification papers about lack of political motivation and a keen interest in riding.

"Kiev, Ukraine! Si! There was so much land to be had—it was all the talk among Vati and the other men." He whooped at the thought of the vastness. I wanted to scream, object, and tell him that it was all wrong, but we barely knew one another. We needed time, and Uncle Harty showed no signs of being a racist—he just had a strangely abbreviated sense of consequences; it was as though a part of history had been amputated away. I sensed that I was playing with danger. Wasn't it exactly these types of conversations, in which ethical considerations were set aside for the sake of pleasantry, that smoothed the way for the slippery slope? Two well-meaning people conversed about the unthinkable without decisively rejecting it, and then the unthinkable happened.

"Why did you come to South America?" I asked, determined to understand the decisions that had formed my uncle.

"I was young and keen for the land," he said, remembering with a hint of rare regret in his eyes, which he quickly blinked away. It was that familiar mourning for an irretrievable moment in time when there were still other choices to be made.

"Vati paid for my three-week journey on a French liner. After that I traveled for months in the interior—all by bus—first north and then made my way south. Even got to know Baron von Thurn und Taxis along the way. Those were the days!" He whooped again, evoking memories of the wild, sexually adventurous parties that the baron, a multimillionaire landowner in the interior of Brazil, was famous for. Yet, this time the whooping felt like a cover-up for divided sentiments, and so I turned my attentions to a subject that might help us to explore them.

"Who was Baron von der Kleist?" I asked, convinced that the young Uncle Harty hadn't been entirely responsible for his own choices, and hoping to discover von der Kleist's real identity.

"Si," replied Uncle Harty, without asking about the source of my knowledge about the mysterious baron. "He was the first point of contact—visited at the hunting lodge in Schleswig-Holstein and made a business out of parceling out land in Brazil to Germans worldwide. Vati originally wanted to go to Ecuador, but von der Kleist convinced him that Brazil was the place for us, although Vati didn't in the end follow his suggestions about where in Brazil to buy. He followed mine instead."

Uncle Harty didn't for a moment seem to doubt von der Kleist's identity or that his business was entirely legitimate. This strengthened my theory that Opa had used his young son as a pawn in the delicate game of finding a haven from the hostile world of justice that he feared might ensnare him. Among old comrades true and false identities were usually known, and a service like von der Kleist's was an important dimension of the sprawling ecosystem that had been built up to assist former Nazis out of uncomfortable situations. Von der Kleist himself appeared to have benefited from it.

During the previous autumn, Gerald Steinacher, a scholar who had devoted years to tracing the "rat lines," including the passages that cut through his native Austrian Alps, strengthened the conclusion that the name von der Kleist was an alias. Gerald, who had cast his trained eye over countless hastily issued travel documents, noted that von der Kleist's temporary passport had been issued to him on the ninth of November, the date of Hitler's Beer Hall Putsch, and a red-letter day for all die-hard Nazis. It could have been a coincidence, of course, he noted, but then added another observation to the already damning pile of evidence against "von der Kleist." The passport had been issued by the German Interest Section of the Swiss Police Department, which in 1948 was run by Dr. Hans Fröhlicher, the former Swiss ambassador to the Third Reich, who became Switzerland's most controversial diplomat for his German-friendliness.

Several other pieces of the puzzle were falling into place as Uncle Harty spoke. As the fifties wore on, Opa's revisionist circles—the Panzermeyers who sought to rewrite history in order to save their own skin—began gradually to lose their arguments, despite the Federal Republic's policies of amnesty for war criminals and the return of many former Nazis and their sympathizers to respectable professions. As the first documentary films and books about the Holocaust emerged during the midfifties, von der Kleist likely saw an opportunity. Opa's hotel, which had chosen hunting, a favorite motif of the SS, as its image, was a place where he knew he could find a receptive clientele, particularly on those Waffen-SS weekends. Even a well-known Nazi like Josef Mengele was able to return to the Federal Republic to get divorced in 1954 and to take a Swiss holiday using a German passport issued in his own name in 1956, so the risks for von der Kleist to return for occasional visits with his changed identity, at least until the late 1950s when trials restarted, were low.

Despite the fact that the baron did not become the final broker of Opa's land purchase, his intervention had determined the fate of the family. By 1960 Ecuador was equally as popular as the interior of Brazil among former Nazis, if not more so. Both were perceived among former SS as places where the Nazi hunters did not so easily venture. There was something even more personal that haunted me about the intervention that had determined my own fate, and that was von der Kleist's wife's first name, uncommon for a German, that was the same as mine. It could have been unrelated, just like all the other uncanny coincidences I kept stumbling upon, but at this moment Julie von der Kleist, in the high-necked lace collar and neat chignon she wore in the photograph on her immigration pass into Brazil, stared at me with disturbing familiarity.

As these thoughts turned like a tidal wave in my head, Uncle Harty continued his revolution of openness that my appearance seemed to have unleashed, now returning briefly to the memory of his father. "His legs were very swollen in the end. Too much drink and he had diabetes. *Não!*" exclaimed Uncle Harty, suggesting his own rejection of such an imprudent path in old age. "I stick to my maté on this cool terrace in the early mornings and write in my diary," he said.

"Do you know what maté is?" he asked, as an aside. "Paraguayan tea—here, try some." He offered me a sip from an engraved silver mug with a matching straw that jutted out of the middle of the closed top. This could be a bonding gesture that I shouldn't turn down, so I sucked up some of the lukewarm, milky, medicinal-tasting liquid. "Good?" he asked, eyebrows raised. I tried to smile politely, still uncertain what I thought of maté. His vast torso shook with laughter.

More interesting to me was the fact that Uncle Harty kept a diary. He seemed all too practical a person to be spending time brooding over the events of the day in writing, just as his big farming hands contradicted the delicate affection he now lavished on a small white poodle that jumped up and nestled in his lap. "Si! My friend and I sit here quietly then. Why don't you come and join us in the early morning and we will talk more?"

I looked to my right and saw that I had been so absorbed in the conversation with Uncle Harty that I hadn't noticed Mikael and Lara's return. They sat in the same armchair, in their previous positions, watching attentively as though they had never moved.

Luna returned from the kitchen with Bibbi and placed a pile of thick, beautifully wrapped gifts before me on the table, which put the small, touristy offerings I had brought with me from Sweden to shame. I looked at each of the family members beaming in anticipation of how I would react to the gifts, and awoke to the miracle that I had found them in this faraway place I had never expected to discover.

Each of the gifts—soft cotton towels and a kitchen apron—had my first name embroidered onto it. "Luna's mom sewed your name onto those," Lara explained.

"It's beautiful," I replied. "But where is she? I want to thank her."

"You will meet her soon—another day," said Bibbi. My name had been embroidered by hand in a swirling script into these fabrics, as though by its repetition the reality of my existence would sink in.

CHAPTER 16

Asunción, February 2016

As the sun hit the windshield on a humid new day, Bibbi deftly navigated the morning traffic. I sat in the passenger seat and felt strangely at home in Asunción, as though transported back to places in the developing world I had grown up in as a child. Crucifixes and portraits of Christ and the Madonna swung from the rearview mirrors of the taxis, as though it made no difference whether the drivers could see what was happening behind them or not. Divine Providence decided; no need for seat belts or traffic rules. The drivers sipped their morning maté through engraved silver straws, a reflex that passed the time in the inevitable morning chaos.

"Nice day," I commented. The eeriness of being able to expose my skin to the air in February had passed into a light, airy feeling that temporarily buoyed me over the weight of jet lag.

Bibbi looked deadpan behind her oversized taupe sunglasses. I wondered whether I had done something wrong—upset her father with all my questioning. She must want to know what I was doing here, thousands of miles away from home without my family. During the relaxed dinner at Uncle Harty's on the previous evening, her family appeared to be close, the members a part of one another's lives in work and personal matters. The family businesses were in or near mother's and father's home, the gravitational center of life. Who was this lone woman from Europe, and why was she here?

"I want to know about Pappa and his family," she blurted out. "Who were they and why has life been the way it has?" Her face was drained of energy, turning it taupe as her sunglasses. How strange it was that people we had known all our lives and from whom we came could seem such mysteries. Shouldn't we know them instinctively by the shapes of our eyes and the beating of our hearts that were so close to theirs? Yet all I had learned through these years was how difficult it was to know those who were closest to us.

I fell from my perch of lightness in the soft Paraguayan air back into the reality of my own experience. I hadn't wanted to admit it, even to myself, but the trigger for the work during all these years had been precisely Bibbi's questions: Why was life the way it was, and why were our parents the way they were?

As Bibbi looked into the unrelenting traffic it was as though she stared into our common existential wound that was seeping and swollen, having been ripped open too many times. How did I know that she had tried to turn her sights from it; turn her heart inside out and try to make it bigger so that it could absorb all of the beloved parent's acute pain? Whatever the parent came to the child with and however that pain expressed itself—even if it meant allowing her soul to be trampled with regularity—the child would make the space, try to be bigger, manage. Somehow.

"You don't know how hard it has been," Bibbi added.

"I think I do," I replied. Bibbi removed her glasses and her chin trembled with tearful emotion. I put my hand over hers that was on the gear stick, and the alchemy of acknowledgment began to work its magic healing.

A shiny black SUV honked and pushed its way in front of us, like a dark force intent upon blocking the sharing of essential information that might deprive it of its power. Bibbi was forced to turn her attention to the intrusion. The anger at the older generations welled up in me, and I felt rage as never before. How dare they be so arrogant as to keep Bibbi, Mikael, and me separated, taunt us with their unresolved traumas, and use us as unknowing scapegoats for the sins of the past? Did they really think that we did not have the right to discover it and one another? This selfish arrogance was no better than that which I saw all around me: bred by the inequality that was plain to see on these streets lined with shacks ready to be carried away by the next floods.

No sooner had the anger washed over me than I sensed the guilt of feeling it. Compared to the tribulations of those who came before us, it seemed illegitimate. Moreover, we, the descendants of the perpetrators, did not feel that we could speak of it, let alone that we were allowed to call it as such, but it was suffering all the same.

A dear friend of mine—a respected Swedish journalist and historian who had moved to Hamburg for love in the mid-1950s and become immersed in the question of war guilt—had begged me to dare and to give my experience that name. "You can and should say that you were hurt—it's important," she implored. Yet it had taken a few more years and traveling across the world to look into the mirror provided by my cousin, whose existence I hadn't known of for almost half a century, in order to be able to call that feeling its true name.

"Our grandfather was a fanatic in the SS," I said to Bibbi, uncertain whether she had been able to take in the significance of this when Uncle Harty had mentioned it in the car on the way from the airport the day before. "This had a strong impact on our parents' lives and we have felt the aftershocks. Violence of that kind doesn't wash out easily."

Emboldened by the feeling of solidarity between us, Bibbi shared her experiences. It surprised me but didn't. There was no longer any question that we had lived in deeply dysfunctional parallel universes, starving ourselves with undeserved shame and lack of self-esteem.

It had become overcast, and Bibbi lifted her glasses off her face onto her head. She looked at me with those eyes that I recognized. They were similar to mine, Oma's, and M's. "I am happy you are here," she said, clutching my hand as the tears wet her cheeks. She took a deep breath, as though to summon all the strength in the world. "Pappa has a sick heart. Maybe he won't live long. He doesn't go to the doctor or get medicine."

"But why?" I asked, and then reflected that it might be a foolish question. Uncle Harty had long ago submitted himself to the wilderness, and there he would die without help or hindrance. Bibbi shrugged her shoulders hopelessly, at the same time as it was clear to me that, despite all, she cared deeply for her father. This visit had occurred just in time. By necessity, our parallel universes had been merged into one.

As we pulled into the driveway Uncle Harty laid his diary and pen down on the table, and rose from his usual spot on the terrace. I stepped out of the car, and Mikael walked casually past, pecking me on the cheek, as though I had lived here for years.

"Ola, Julie. Coffee?" he asked in his husky voice, as he strolled in the direction of the kitchen.

"That would be great," I replied. Mikael and I had established that we were the only ones in the house who preferred coffee over maté.

Bibbi kissed her father on the cheek and went inside to help her mother with the morning chores. "I have a strong-minded daughter," Uncle Harty acknowledged. "Si, she will be all right."

"How are you today, Uncle Harty?" I asked. Today I saw a different man—one without much time left to make amends.

"Me?!" He laughed. "I am absolutely primo," he said. "Couldn't be better." He patted his heart defiantly as though to suggest that *that* old problem wasn't going to get the best of him.

Mikael served the coffee and then left for work in a place nearby, where trusted customers could enter in order to shop away from the danger of rampant crime. As I poured some milk into my cup from a porcelain pitcher, Uncle Harty watched carefully with raised eyebrows. "Just like my mother held the milk pitcher. Very delicate and proper." He whooped a little and shook his head in an expression of pleasurable disbelief. "You remind me of her," he said, delighting in his own observation of something from the Old World—once his. Whatever had passed between Oma and me, it felt fine that I reminded him of his mother. I could see that the wheels of memory were turning behind each of his observations, and wondered why he had lost contact with her so many decades ago. Oma's pendulum swung back and forth in my thoughts; this time not with the question of whether, but of why.

"Have you been writing in your diary again this morning?" I asked.

"Si," he said. "Every day—let me show you." He jumped out of his low armchair with an energy one could hardly expect from an eighty-year-old with a heart condition. What was it that sustained him? I abandoned my cup of coffee and followed him into the house.

The rooms were invariably dark, designed to keep the interior cool during hot, sun-scorched days. We entered a moderately disorderly room with yellowing photocopied pictures thumbtacked to the wall next to a heavy wooden desk. They were of a slender Uncle Harty in middle age standing proudly in front of a light aircraft. Teetering piles of old notebooks with pages rippled by humidity rose from the desk surface.

"I used to fly a lot," he said. "Own planes—best way to travel between Campo Grande and Maracaju in the old days, when the roads were bad and the floods came." I didn't mention that during the following week I would travel to these places in Brazil, as I didn't want Uncle Harty or Mikael to feel obliged to accompany me. I knew that they would if I told them, because it wasn't safe country for a single woman, and they both knew it.

"And there are my diaries!" he said proudly. "I have been keeping them since I arrived here in Brazil over half a century ago. Every day I wrote in them." I looked at his hands. They were thick from decades of farm work. One of the forefingers was amputated at the second joint as a result of a childhood accident after the war. It was a detail that hadn't been visible in the wedding picture but that Auntie Best, his sister, had told me about, in shared memories of her brother, believing him to be dead. The fact that one of these hands had gripped a pen and patiently recorded the reflections of its master once a day since 1960 continued to surprise me. Uncle Harty clearly had an insatiable need for processing life. What stories there must be in those records, and how I longed to be left alone with them and read every one. Yet a diary was an intensely private thing, so I dared not ask. Soon he revealed that they were mainly written in Portuguese, which my uncle had quickly adopted as his principal language after arriving in Brazil in the spring of 1960. Maybe it was a sign of how eager he had been to leave behind the sullied Old World and his German beginnings, or perhaps it was just a survival strategy.

Opa had chosen a place that was far from everywhere and had resisted learning the local language.

Luna appeared at the doorway to Uncle Harty's study, like a silent angel whose presence could not be ignored. After what Bibbi had told me about the family's past, I was afraid that Uncle Harty might be provoked, show an authoritarian streak and override her, but there was no sign of it. As before, he submitted to this delicate woman who was half his size, and instead stood there next to his piles of recorded memories, looking like a deserted lapdog as she took my hand and led me away. I didn't know where we were going, but she had an extraordinary power about her that meant that one followed without asking questions. We stopped at the doorway and she said something in Spanish that sounded like we were going for a drive and would be back for dinner. "Bueno," said Uncle Harty, resigned. "We will continue later."

That afternoon Bibbi and Luna drove me to a nearby village by a lake, where the rising upper middle class had summer homes they retreated to on the weekends. In this landlocked country, a waterfront view was gold. With few customers shopping midweek, vendors fanned themselves sleepily in the shade amid paintings, ceramics, and other handicrafts. An art gallery in an elegant mansion-turned-museum across the street was one of the signs of this country's gradual emergence from obscurity into greater economic dynamism. Bibbi and Mikael, with their thriving modern textile businesses and ever-present smartphones, were a part of it.

We strolled past the many adjacent stalls of pottery, hand-painted in colorful rustic patterns, and attempted to avoid direct eye contact with vendors desperate to sell their wares. Eventually, the bad conscience of evading their hopeful looks wore me down and I stopped at one of the stalls to admire some painted ceramic plates. Within seconds two of the shop attendants hovered behind these objects of my interest, all smiles, ready to package my choices in thin plastic bags. "Do you like those?" asked Bibbi. "Yes, they are very beautiful," I said, and all of a sudden four of them were mine. I already knew where I would hang them, and that someday I would look at them on my wall at home and be reminded that all this hadn't been merely a dream.

We sat down in a lunch cafeteria where traditional foods were served in metal troughs. I picked my way through the buffet of deep-fried starchy yams and meat, leaving Bibbi and Luna disconcerted by my sparsely laden plate. Soon they had finished most of their food, while I continued to push around the small heaps on my plate. I'd been disconnected from any feelings of appetite for days now; all my senses turned from physical hunger to listening, watching, and asking questions.

"Thank you so much for the lovely presents," I said, referring to the wrapped plates in the plastic bags next to me. "I know exactly where I will hang them at home." Bibbi nodded her head lightly at her mother, encouraging her to speak what was on her mind. Luna took a deep breath and began to speak softly to me in Spanish while Bibbi translated in a blend of English and German. "We are so grateful that you are here. It is a gift from God. We have experienced very difficult times, and we didn't really know why." She paused and a smile that heroically bore the burden of pain came over her face. I couldn't know what was to follow, but somehow I did.

I looked at Bibbi, her eyes reddening and her lips trembling as her mother continued to speak. Luna's story was a confirmation of the exchange between Bibbi and me the day before. Both these women seemed used to sharing their grief with one another, perhaps here at this very table in this cafeteria.

"But you are so good and kind to one another. All of you. How have you managed?" I asked. Luna looked once again at her daughter for courage and consent, and then back at me.

"Forgiveness is the highest privilege God grants us," she said. "Today our family lives peacefully."

There was something about this delicate woman that could move mountains, and it was that very thing that Oma, a much bigger woman than she, believed had eluded her. What would Oma have thought of her native Paraguayan daughter-in-law who lived in a state of peace with God? Younger generations had a habit of tossing the old prejudices and insecurities of the previous generations back at them, often inadvertently, and in marrying Luna that was exactly what Uncle Harty had done.

Although I didn't know whether my own spirituality could ever be framed by the idea of God, I recognized that Luna had stood up to the rage of an unknown past armed only with the power of faith. Her gentle crusade of forgiveness made my sometimes severe crusade of truth feel self-righteous. Was the search for truth as important as finding the grace to forgive? One could lead to the other, but truth must by its nature always be incomplete and therefore unsatisfactory. Forgiveness wasn't itself unless it was total.

At the same time, I knew that without my terrier-like desire to know, we would never have met one another, and our meeting seemed to be important to all of us. The question of "why" had remained a gaping sore. Perhaps now, in the last phase of Uncle Harty's life, his family could be allowed to heal, but what of my own?

CHAPTER 17

Asunción, February 2016

"BOM DIA!" ROARED UNCLE HARTY, AS MIKAEL AND I PULLED INTO THE driveway in his pickup truck. "We missed you last night. Walter's pizza was good. Come here and sit down with me," he said, eager to talk.

Compounded by jet lag, the afternoon outing with Bibbi and Luna on the previous day had left me emotionally drained so that there was nothing else to do but to excuse myself from the evening's planned dinner, which had been prepared by Bibbi's husband, Walter. Instead, I had returned to my apartment, and fallen asleep on my travel notes.

Now strewn across the table near Uncle Harty's diary and his maté were photocopied images of farming machines, rolling like panzers through the muddy soil. "These are mine," he said warmly, as though referring to his other children. "There are floods now and we just have to keep cool until they pass, so that we can get into business again and continue to rent them out. It's a good business, you know."

He looked into the skies that tested him. It was the first time I saw anything resembling uncertainty in Uncle Harty's face. "Si, when the water recedes all will be fine and we will be in business again. Just look at these pictures—aren't they prima?" I understood that those machines were my uncle's bread and butter—his attempt, after years of living in turmoil, to make a steady living. The precariousness of Uncle Harty's life brought on a feeling of urgency, both for him, in creating security for his family, and for me, in learning all that I could about the family's past.

"Have you always been interested in farming, like your father?" I asked.

"Si!" he replied. "Now I have my own *chaco* near the border with Brazil, but it's not possible to go there now—too much water. It's not so far from Maracaju where Vati and I started—farmed it mostly ourselves." Uncle hooted and shook his head. "He kept having such crazy ideas—insisted I build pigsties for him, which I did, and then he started breeding those animals so that their legs got too long. They couldn't walk properly. What a crazy project!"

The thought of my race-obsessed grandfather exercising his genetic fantasies on pigs passed quickly from the humorous to the macabre. I kept looking for traces of resentment in my uncle's voice when he spoke of his father, but found none. Oma had lamented that they'd fought tooth and nail, but so far Uncle Harty had not mentioned it once. What had led to this pardoning? Was it the forgiving influence of Luna or was it something else?

If there was one thing my uncle craved it was adventure, and I felt as though a passenger in one of his small propeller planes, as we soared across the memories of his father in the vast Brazilian wilderness together. "Then he took off and crossed the Rio das Mortes, the river of the dead, a dangerous place where there were disputes with the Indians in that rain forest." He swiped his hand swiftly across his neck, in a cutting motion that described the danger.

"But why did he do that when he had a running business?" I asked, puzzled.

"He always wanted more—got ahold of tens of thousands of hectares of grazing land farther north in Bara do Garça and stayed there most of the time."

Uncle jumped out of his seat like a twenty-year-old. "Stay here—I want to show you something," he said. The towering figure stormed into the house, his jeans sagging like an irreverent youth's.

Soon he reemerged holding a thick book bound in green fabric with the words "Unternehmen Barbarossa" engraved in gold in the lower right-hand corner. He placed it on the table before me and said: "This is the only thing Vati left to me." I opened the book to find Opa's signature on the inside cover, and recognized it from the many SS documents given to me in Berlin five years ago. The table of contents was a list of the tactical and strategic military turning points in Germany's fateful invasion of Russia, Operation Barbarossa, which had turned the war in favor of the Allies. I leafed through the pages, and noticed that some of the paragraphs were marked in red in the left-hand column.

"He must have read it fourteen, fifteen times to try to figure out why we lost it all. The pen marks are his." I ran my finger over one of the marks that were like ominous small paths into my grandfather's mind. "I read it a few times too," Uncle Harty added. "Imagine, if only we hadn't made those dumb mistakes—what we would have inherited!"

Uncle Harty wasn't a callous man, which made my unease about his words all the greater. Suddenly, he seemed to have become a mouthpiece for a voice from the dead, unmoored from the hellish effects of man's hunger for land and resources. Operation Barbarossa hadn't been lost because of tactical mistakes, it had been flawed from the very beginning, grounded in the misplaced racist delusion that thirty million Slavs could easily be murdered, starved, or driven out of their homeland because they were inferior.

The author of the book, Paul Carell, as he was known in the post-war years, had made a successful career as an author writing revisionist accounts that whitewashed the Wehrmacht's participation in the Holocaust. Earlier, as Paul Karl Schmidt, he'd been the chief press spokesman in the Reich's Foreign Ministry and authored propaganda for the foreign press, specializing in "the Jewish Question." Like Opa, he'd served in the General SS.

With all this in mind, the time had arrived for me to ask the unthinking voice that question. "But what of the Holocaust?" I asked, attempting to keep my calm to encourage an answer.

He looked down at his hands and pursed his lips. "Si, that was a bad business," he said, speaking in a low, barely discernible tone. The voice I heard now seemed to have been temporarily released from the spell of the green book. I felt some relief, but then he tapped the cover and added: "But just imagine if we hadn't made those mistakes, eh?"

As the curtain fell on my efforts to evoke a satisfactory appreciation of consequences by my uncle, I could see the image of a young boy running as fast he could away from me; away from this awkward theater of reckoning with the past. The child was blond, and had skinny legs, like a young colt's, that jutted out from the lederhosen that were customary for patriotic young boys in Uncle Harty's childhood. It was the same boy as the one in the family albums that I had uploaded onto my computer before leaving home.

"Do you want to see some of the old photographs from your mother's albums?" I asked, sensing that I shouldn't give up just yet, and follow that boy to see where he went. Uncle Harty looked at me curiously. Beyond possessing a mobile telephone, he didn't have a digital life. "Si, my children play around on those computers, but not me. *Não!*" he exclaimed, shooing away the thought.

"That's okay," I reassured him. "You don't have to do anything. I'll fix it."

We moved to the dining table in the shade of the house so that the pictures would be visible on the computer screen. I opened the file of scanned black-and-white photographs from the albums Oma had given to me. She'd said that otherwise they would be destroyed after her death and had welcomed me to remove them from her cabinet in the corner of her small apartment. She would never know just how important her willingness to pass them on to me would become.

I chose the oldest photographs first: those of Uncle Harty as a one-year-old toddling on the lawn, as his father sat in a reclining lounge chair reading of the Reich's latest triumphs in the newspaper.

At first Uncle looked at the photographs deadpan, as though he didn't recognize anyone. "That's you," I said, pointing at the chubby toddler.

He moved closer to the screen and examined the photograph in detail. "Ah." He sighed and smiled gently, surrendering to the image. "Si, that is Vati and there I am." His mouth was half open in wonderment.

I switched to another photograph, of Oma standing over the blond toddler. He gripped her long forefingers with his pudgy hands to avoid his wobbly legs from collapsing under him. "That is your mother," I explained. Uncle looked more closely at the photograph and swallowed hard.

I moved on to some of the other images that he might find more cheerful: photographs of him playing with his sisters in Poland, standing in a sweet train of blond heads, in which he was the tallest. He laughed with amusement, and his whole being seemed to light up.

"In that picture I was very happy because I had just been saved by old Meitsche, who looked after the horses of the SS cavalry and guarded Vati on the estate. He didn't tell Vati that I took off on one of the horses bareback, far off into one of the fields. It was dangerous, you know! The partisans were everywhere, and, what was worse, I fell off and couldn't find my way back. Meitsche rode out to find me and never said a word to Vati. He was a good pal. You see how sharp my memory is from that time?"

Maybe my mental image of a young boy running away was not so far from the truth.

He continued to recall details of a more three-dimensional world than history books could portray. Uncle's descriptions made it increasingly difficult to keep the figures of the past in narrowly defined categories. Meitsche, Opa's SA bodyguard whom I had learned about in Poland, was transformed from a one-dimensional brutish lackey to a man who also possessed compassion for a child.

Bibbi, Mikael, and Luna, hearing the chattering and laughing, gathered around us. "Que linda!" Luna exclaimed at one of the images of Harty with his younger sisters. Bibbi and Mikael stared in disbelief as their father continued to narrate his past through the images. I hoped they didn't feel I was stirring up things unnecessarily. Each of them had contributed to bringing calm to a turbulent family life, and none of us knew where this wrenching open of the past would lead. Bibbi held my hand to reassure me that it was all right, and Mikael folded his thick arms, watching with glistening eyes.

"Don't you have any images of them as they are now?" asked Harty about his sisters. I pulled up the most recent ones I had of Auntie Best, M, and the others. "Yes, that's them. They look very fine. And there is your father. A good man." Of course, Uncle Harty had known Father then, all those years ago when as a young businessman starting out on an ambitious career, he must have struggled to know what to do with his in-laws and their barbed past, which seemed not to have been a secret at all.

Now seemed the natural time to ask another difficult question. "Why did you lose contact with the others?" I asked. "What happened?"

I thought it would be an awkward moment, but Uncle didn't hesitate to answer. "Ah! I was tired of farming for Vati. His ideas were crazy and we weren't getting anywhere. One of my sisters wanted me to continue farming some of the land for all of us. I didn't want to have anything to do with the whole business. I was tired of it. The last time we met was at Vati's burial, and I remember it as a very cold, unfriendly parting. I never wanted to go back after that. To be sure, I did many foolish things— womanized, drank, didn't pay my debts, you know—but if there is one thing I didn't do it was to make off with whatever Vati left behind."

For the first time I noticed some anger in his voice, evoked by the pain of old wounds. The confession of past sins didn't surprise or bother the rest of the family standing around us. They had been through hard times and had emerged together on the other side.

I'd grown up with the suspicions about Uncle Harty that circled like preying hawks over family conversations. Everyone seemed to be in possession of their own truths without knowing. The pious Luna, who I was certain assumed she would be struck down if she told a lie, had attested to the state of near-poverty in which her husband had lived when first she had met him. Whom was I to believe, and did it really matter?

We returned to more cheerful memories and left the resentment that talk of Opa's estate evoked. Yet, hours later, as I lay outstretched on the bed in my apartment and mentally flew across the landscape of revelations I had just witnessed, I looked down and saw only the land and our perpetual wars over it, among nations and in families. Lebensraum was a delusional illness that humans must overcome in order to find any real space for living.

CHAPTER 18

Asunción, March 2016

IN THE COOL EARLY MORNING LIGHT THAT PRECEDES A LONG, HOT DAY, Mikael and Lara arrived at 6 am to pick me up for our trip to Iguazú Falls. Lara hopped out of the car on slender girlish legs to greet me, while Mikael waited in the driver's seat, his broad shoulders bent over the wheel with exhaustion.

"Ola, Julie," he said, in a deep, groggy voice, leaning his head affectionately backward toward me as I climbed into the seat behind him. "Late night's work with our business," Lara confirmed, stroking his neck. Both were so busy trying to make a life around their own business that it was a wonder they could find time for this trip.

To remain ahead of the curve, serving an emergent generation of young Paraguayans yearning for modernity in this traditional land, required an all-out effort. Their quickness, openness, attractiveness, and, not least, their attentiveness to the powerful network of communications they nursed throughout the day on their mobile phones, must have been considerable advantages. Two days of driving and sightseeing at Iguazú Falls with their older cousin was the last thing they could afford at this point. "Tranquilo," said Mikael, reassuring us that he would be fine, and turned the key in the ignition.

Once we had made our way out of the congested city and began to head south toward the convergence of Argentina, Brazil, and Paraguay, the location of the falls, I tried to take in the landscape. Still, my eyes always wandered back to Mikael's strained muscles straight ahead of me in the driver's seat. Often he leaned forward over the wheel or shuffled in his seat to relieve the discomfort. Lara attempted to soften the tight muscles by pressing them with her slim fingers with the well-groomed dark nails while she distracted his attention from the pain with amusing messages from friends, business associates, and clients that pinged constantly from the phone in her other hand.

At home Mikael had shown me the trophies for bodybuilding that he had been awarded as a youth, when he had traveled the world competing for his country. Maybe we had passed one another in an airport somewhere, the myth of my uncle's nonexistence always on the verge of being exposed.

When Mikael had tired of the strain and self-abuse required by that physically taxing sport, he'd gone onto motorcycle rallying and had an accident that had left him with a shoulder blade that protruded through the skin. Now only half the blade remained on one side. His was a body that had been battered and hardened, like a gladiator's, from an early age. One could try to put it down to that rite of passage, the ritual of high risk, that young men often subjected themselves to, but this was extreme. Eventually, when Lara tired of rubbing and pressing, I put my hands on the thick shoulders and took over that duty. They were hard as rock, and as self-denying as the starvation Bibbi and I had put ourselves through. All three of us were somehow gladiators who had served the hard master of past sins and were struggling to set ourselves free.

We spoke about the history I had uncovered, but Mikael interrupted, intent upon defending the male line of which he was the inheritor. After the previous day's run-through of Uncle Harty's sisters in the photographs, he had become aware that he was the last who bore the family name. Whether in hypermacho Latin America or elsewhere, a last name counted. It bore the story of forefathers, their places of origin, their occupations, and the soul of the times they had lived in. It was a signpost that explained and formed lives. In one moment he proclaimed respect for what he saw as the hard-working ethic and fearlessness of his father and grandfather, both men who had conquered the land; in the next his body twisted with unease.

I wanted to put a cool cloth on the fever of Mikael's heart that I recognized so well. His was the struggle among the descendants of the perpetrators shared by Bibbi, my sister, our parents, and me: who were our role models if they were not our elders? I recognized it in all of us: we walked the earth without direction, railing at the skies and beating the barren ground for someone to show us the way. The only remaining hope was to find stillness in one another.

By midafternoon we'd parked the car and were on the open tram that took us toward the falls. The white faces of the brown-coated capuchin monkeys watched us from the rainforest like partisans, and pounced on the platforms whenever the tram stopped, to scavenge from the food spillage of snacking passengers. Mikael and Lara hung dotingly over one another, so that at times I felt like an old aunt, and turned my sights back to the monk-like creatures in the surrounding forest. Lara broke the awkwardness by snapping photographs of us with her cell phone.

When we reached the end of the line, we followed the long wooden footbridges that led toward the Devil's Throat, the U-shaped three-hundred-foot (or eighty-two meter) drop, that was absurdly split between two nations. The falls spewed continuously on the hubris of the idea that we could divide such a powerful natural force. The wide river above hurled white water over the edges that dropped into a deep, bottomless chasm. We stood on the terrace closest to the falls with the many other tourists rushing into the cold spray in hopes of capturing some of its irresistible power.

We left the Devil's Throat and moved to a quieter terrace over one of the lower falls where the sun could bake us dry. As I stood looking over the rails, Lara removed something from her handbag that she clutched in the palm of her hand and gave it to Mikael. In turn, he placed the smooth, cool stones in my hand and closed my fingers over them.

"Throw them over," Lara said, recalling a story I had told in the car on the way to the falls. She held up her cell phone to film me.

I had told Mikael and Lara of a scene shot at Iguazú in one of my favorite films, *The Mission*. It had stayed with me since I had first watched it decades ago. In the film, one of the protagonists, a repentant sixteenth-century Spanish slave hunter, does penance for the suffering he has inflicted upon the Guarani by dragging his heavy armor and weaponry in a sack up the face of the falls. Toward the end of this tortuous journey, in which he has repeatedly forced himself to retrieve the heavy sack, which he drops accidentally back down in the river due to exhaustion, the Guarani themselves cut him free of his burden. The sack of armor plunges to its fate in the river, never to be retrieved again. His victims pardon him and he weeps inconsolably for the grace that has been granted him, but also for the extreme difficulty of parting with the guilt and shame that harm him. For something new to be born, and for him to be of any use to the world and his fellow humans, he must release these burdens. Subsequently he becomes a Franciscan monk and lays down his life to protect the Guarani. Each time I saw the scene of his freeing, it struck me that there were few moments in film that portrayed redemption so poignantly.

What I hadn't told Mikael and Lara was that I had sometimes felt like the former Spanish slave hunter, in search of redemption but in expectation of eternal self-punishment. The difference was that I didn't know what the crime was because it was buried in history, in another time. They hadn't seen the film, and I feared they might find it a peculiar, far-fetched analogy, but there was no doubt that the placing of those rocks in my hand was encouragement to overthrow that old inherited shame, maybe on behalf of more than just myself.

I looked into the falls and clutched the stones in my fist behind me. How hard it was to part with the familiar things that hurt us. Mikael and Lara remained silent, waiting patiently. Now was the time. As the stones flew in the air, they hurled toward a dim rainbow that emerged behind the spray. Mikael hung his strong arm over my shoulder and we watched together as the stones we could no longer see washed away in the river. "Tranquilo," he said.

There are moments after which life is quite simply different and this was one of them. It wasn't a forgetting, rather it was the undoing of our blindfolds, our understanding of the source of our pain, and our compassion for one another. In a flash, I saw the old man in Poland, the son of the gardener with the scar over his eye. It was as though he was standing behind us, urging us on.

We continued along the path of planks overlaid on the rain forest floor that eventually led us across the river farther downstream. I stopped and observed the water moving slowly through the wide channel between the river banks. The desperation was gone, and one wondered whether this was like life after death—the never-ending peace that comes when the great fall through the devil's throat is over.

Throughout these years of searching, the question of why it was necessary had loomed over me. I had tried to wring the answer out of friends and attempted unsatisfactorily, often with feelings of guilt for the betrayal of my family, to answer the question. It was like the Gordian knot that I had tugged at determinedly but that would not yield. In the flowing of the river I stopped struggling with this question. It didn't ask why; it simply flowed.

On the following morning I left the rental apartment of our Argentine motel early so that the lovebirds could awaken in privacy. After a swim, I sat on the terrace in the warm sunshine, sipped strong coffee, and began reading a short account of the life of Jochen Klepper. Klepper's 1935 novel, *Der Vater* (The Father), was one of the last books remaining in Oma's bookshelves when she could no longer read. It was a dense portrayal of Frederick the Great's father, adored by the Nazis as "the soldier king" and the father of Hitler's idol. It was the last of several books that Oma had given to me since childhood, each of which I had read eagerly in recent years, in the belief that what we read tells us something about who we are, and that these books might explain the mystery of my grandmother to me.

Frustrated with the density of *Der Vater*, I had turned to the author page at the back of the book and learned that while Klepper's tome had been ordered in bulk by the Wehrmacht during the war and been a favorite of the Nazis, he had himself become a victim of the regime. Klepper and his Jewish wife and her daughter had committed suicide in their Berlin apartment in 1942, having concluded that his considerable efforts to save his loved ones from deportation by making pleas in the halls of power where his story about the soldier king had been lapped up could not succeed. Oma had read Klepper's novel in exile in Brazil, and it had made its way back to Germany to become among the very last books on her shelf.

I imagined her in the Brazilian interior, sitting on a terrace, much like this one, though further back, careful to shield her delicate skin from the scorching sun, as she read Klepper's novel. By that time his fate was well known. His diary portrays a man whose faith in God had saved him from total despair and granted him joy and creativity, even as life closed in on his family. He kept his integrity, preferring death with his condemned wife and stepdaughter, rather than a pact with the devil. What must Oma, who had struggled between faith and the Führer, have thought as she read his work and why did she read it?

A black cat brushed up against my ankle as though to call me back from overthinking. I leaned down to stroke it, and it arched its back, purring with satisfaction. Footsteps approached, and the cat trotted away. "Ola, Julie!" exclaimed Mikael, as he and Lara continued to dote over one another.

During breakfast Lara asked what I had been reading and I told her the story of Oma devouring Klepper's book in the Brazilian interior. Her thick eyebrows rose, her intelligent mind immediately grasping the tragedy of it all.

Powered by his second plate of breakfast, Mikael took up the troubling conversation in the car from the day before about role models. Our trip to the falls had brought at least a temporary calm over his intensive search for a way to live; a way to be. "I believe in energies," he said. "Bad, good, you know. We need to find good energies; *be* in good energies."

It seemed simplistic at first, but the idea of energies and how they moved in us and through us had been a constant question for me. How often I had imagined myself to be a crucible into which the energies of the past poured like rain. It was frightening and alienating, because it meant that I was a receptacle for indignation, hatred, and violence too. How would I remix what gathered in me, and did I have the power to do that? I looked across the table at Mikael and realized that we were empowering one another: I with the details of history and he with his theory of energies. "Pappa changed when he knew you were coming to visit," he continued. "He became more relaxed, more open, happy. You have good energy."

Lara stroked the tortured muscles on Mikael's neck not far from the shortened collarbone, and the fallen bag of armor clanked as it washed away.

———

That evening, back in my apartment in Asunción, I emailed my sister the video clip that Lara had taken of the ritual stone-throwing. "It's done," I wrote. "Amen," she replied, with many emoticons.

There was another duty that lay ahead, one that I didn't look forward to. I had made a pact with myself that if Uncle Harty was who he said he was—and there could no longer be any doubt—I would inform other members of the extended family that he was alive and had his own family. Bibbi and Mikael were as eager for the list of uncles and cousins as their father was.

For myself, I longed to remain in the compassionate bubble in which we found ourselves. It felt like a small treasured space in time in which my Paraguayan family and I had known one another away from old family fears and resentments. I knew that there would be varying reactions, and that once the information had been sent there was nothing I could do to protect Bibbi and Mikael from some of the negative sentiment they would inevitably encounter from those who might feel threatened by the truth, which was that Uncle Harty was alive and that they existed. I hoped for the best, but now everyone had to decide for themselves. With a heavy heart I pressed Send.

CHAPTER 19

Asunción, March 2016

THE DAY OF DEPARTURE FOR BRAZIL HAD ARRIVED. AS I PACKED MY bags, news of the strangest presidential election race in American history blared from the flat screen on the wall in between CNN's exhausting canonization of its own reporters. The viciousness and cruelty playing themselves out on the political stage of the world's most powerful nation, one that had upheld the international order that had kept us from world war for so long, was frightening to watch. Where would it all lead?

An hour later Mikael loaded my luggage into the back of his pickup to take me to Uncle Harty's, where a farewell lunch was being prepared. "Pappa were awake in the night," he said in a deep, grainy voice after another late night's work. In Lara's absence, he spoke perfectly comprehensible English. "'Julie! Julie! Where is Julie?' he ask me." Mikael shrugged his shoulders.

"But he knew I was here in the apartment," I replied. "Was he sleep-walking?"

"Si, he sleep-walking in the house and this morning—early, early— he went to buy fish for you at the river."

"He went to buy fish for me?"

"Si, good Paraguayan fish. You eat bad fish in Iguazú."

On the evening after our trip to the falls we had visited a restaurant where I had ordered fish that was undeniably rotten. This travesty had been relayed to Uncle, and he wouldn't have me leave his home without tasting fresh Paraguayan fish.

As we pulled into the driveway, Uncle Harty closed his diary after making an entry. I wondered how he had written about these days, about our meeting and my questions, or whether he had written about them at all. Was he working through the memories, or did he continue to lament the floods that prevented him from renting out his farm machines? Secretly I hoped that something was happening inside of Uncle that would be reflected in the pages. In fact, I hoped that a shift was taking place for all of us.

As soon as he saw me he rose from his chair and gave me a long, warm embrace, as though I had gone missing overnight. It was different from his previous greetings—less theatrical, more sincere, relieved—and gave me reason to believe that something was under way, like the flowing river. Whatever this man had done in the past, his affection moved me, and whatever questions I posed, it seemed that I had grown on his heart. We had been essential to one another in more ways than one. His desperate search for me in the middle of the night seemed a sign of fear of being left alone to deal with the deluge of memories I had released. For whatever reason, he wasn't used to speaking about them with his family. He'd related so many boyhood accounts with a sense of humor and excitement that seemed a buffer before the abyss. In Uncle Harty's world the fall at Devil's Throat was always near. A part of me felt irresponsible about leaving and longed to stay to see him through the difficult thoughts I had provoked. Yet his family was unflinching in their love for him, and, no doubt, this was most important.

"Come and take some maté with me before lunch," he said. "Ola, Julie!" shouted Bibbi, Walter, and Luna in three distinct voices from the kitchen, where they were fully engaged in the preparation of an elaborate meal I hadn't expected.

I sat down with Uncle Harty in what by now had become my own familiar armchair. As usual, the mental list of questions I had prepared on the evening before ran out onto the sands of our conversation. This was right: these were my relatives who had treated me well, and my search for truth must never use them as pawns in a game of chess aimed at winning. Far from being a zero-sum game, truth was an elusive trophy that couldn't be won. It revealed itself to those who were open and vigilant, and whatever I had discovered, the nature of the information seldom felt like winning.

On the table was a plastic sleeve in which Uncle Harty had collected a number of papers. "I had these prepared for you," he said. He pulled the papers out of the sleeve and showed them to me: they were images of his farming machines, his *chaco*, and himself as a younger man standing before the various light aircraft in which he had traversed the untamed borderlands between Paraguay and Brazil. All of these were pasted onto large sheets of blank paper and told the story of how he would like to be remembered. The obsession with the land stared me in the face, as did my naïve hope that I had set about some sort of shift. Enthusiastically, he explained the photographs once again, and I thanked him, trying not to convey any disappointment.

Now Uncle became silent and stayed in that heavy-hearted pause for what seemed like a very long time. "Maybe I misled Mutti and Vati to come here. Maybe it was the wrong thing for them." There it was again. I'd seen it in Auntie Best's face and now I saw it in Uncle Harty's: the unconscious bearing by a child of a parent's unclaimed guilt. Written on the snapshot of this moment was the rejection of responsibility by parents unable to fathom the magnitude of their own crimes, and the self-imposed silence of an entire society that, in its exhaustion, had seen no other way than to trudge forward grudgingly under the yoke of collective guilt.

Despite his knowledge of his father's engagement in the SS, and the networks he guarded and drew upon after the war, Uncle appeared not to have understood that the principal motivation for his parents' departure from the Federal Republic had nothing to do with him. Perhaps Oma and Opa had made him the cover for that, preferring to sacrifice him, as they had their other children's well-being, in order to avoid confronting their own past. Or perhaps Uncle Harty had willingly sacrificed himself rather than call out a parent for abuse, turning the myth into his own reality along the way. The wild behavior that had followed had surely been pent-up rage. Gerhard Hoch's words rang like shrill church bells: "ungoverned guilt does its unholy mischief."

I imagined what that time must have been like: hurriedly applying for a tourist visa to Brazil in a climate of panic and unease among his father's former comrades who were afraid of being caught in the sticky web of Adolf Eichmann's confessions. The blond young boy with the skinny legs kept on running, now not away from his father but on his behalf.

"I don't think you were responsible for their decision to move to Brazil, Uncle Harty," I said.

"No?" he responded with a hopelessness that suggested the abyss—fear of the truth about what his father had done—was once again near.

"No," I said, shaking my head resolutely. "There were things that he did during the war, Uncle . . ."

"Ach!" Uncle shook his head. "Two years of denazification—he just wanted to get away from it all. The hotel business was going very well, mind you."

How I wanted to save Uncle Harty from this cesspool of nonsense; to take him in my own light aircraft of sorts to show him the landscape of that time, which must have been impossible to see living in it. Then he might conclude that he had been lied to, that he didn't have to protect his parent, and that it was all right to be the boy who had an "illegal" Polish friend and detested his father's violence. At the same time, I knew how hard it was to extract that parasite, shame, and Uncle had borne it for most of his life. It would take the salt of memories and more time, which I hoped his fragile aorta would grant him.

"Those Russians were animals anyway," he said. "Si, the Ukraine would have been better off farmed by us. And how I remember all of the great people that came through our hotel after the war. Vati knew them all." It was like an old reflex that kicked in whenever he came too close to the brink; a feigned racism which he conjured up to satisfy the ghost of his father.

As Uncle went down this beaten track once again, I recalled one of the important questions on my mental list. "What about Filinto Müller? Did Opa know him? Did you?" Brazilian researchers who had helped me to prepare for my trip had told me about the famous and infamous Müller, the governor of the state of Mato Grosso where Opa's *fazenda* was located in the sixties. Many towns in the state had streets named after this controversial figure, who had visited the Reich on the invitation of Heinrich Himmler in 1937. Müller had become mesmerized by what he saw as the effectiveness of the SS, which he thought provided a model for the reorganization of law and order in his native state. His part-enforcement of the idea as governor resulted in extensive human rights abuses.

"Si!" exclaimed Uncle Harty proudly. "He visited our *fazenda* with delegations and declared ours a model farm. He thought the Mato Grosso needed more men like Vati." My heart skipped a beat, and yet, it all made total sense. Uncle Harty had had little chance to form his own opinions. The boy who had feared and detested his father's brutality, yet, by no choice of his own, been immersed in the mentality of the SS, had become an adult in an oppressive environment where questions about the past were forbidden at the same time as it was given a silent nod. Before he knew it, the young man in his formative years found himself in an often-brutal wilderness where only strong men survived. It wasn't hard to understand how Uncle might have been susceptible to some of his father's thinking. Being tough, sometimes merciless, may have seemed justifiable in a setting where the rules of the game were determined by thuggish strength rather than by any considerations of morality or fairness. I felt sorrow for Uncle, a gentle soul sometimes invaded by brutish spirits. How difficult it was to say no to those whom we loved.

——◆——

Frustrated at our lack of time, I excused myself from the terrace. In the kitchen, Walter and Bibbi, both in aprons, joked with one another over the bubbling pots at the stove. According to Bibbi, her husband had saved her from the self-destructive behavior that was the result of an unstable childhood. He was a hard-working Paraguayan, who had broken out of poor conditions by his own wits and the love of a supportive mother. According to the others, he had an innate sense for what should go into the cooking pot. Bibbi and I had both been lucky to find partners who supported us in digging ourselves out of the rubble of the past.

Mikael had taken a glass of fresh fruit juice and milled about the kitchen. "You want?" he offered.

"No, it's yours," I replied.

"No!" He growled in his grainy voice. "For you. Take it." It was the same boundless generosity I had experienced from my cousins throughout my visit.

"How you make sourdough, Julie?" asked Mikael, who had become aware of my health and food projects of the past.

The thought of advising Mikael on making sourdough in a climate so different to the one in which I had composed my recipes worried me. I imagined a jar of it exploding within an hour of being made in this hot, humid kitchen. Lara held up the screen of her cell phone, which displayed a recipe I had published on the web. "Yes, follow that, but watch out," I warned. "It could explode on you!" This generated an infectious giggling from Luna who was clearly delighted by the presence of the whole family in the kitchen and our humorous, relaxed small talk, even if she didn't understand it all.

"You like your father, Julie. Pappa said he is a good man," said Bibbi, before tasting some sauce from a wooden spoon that Walter held up to her mouth. "And Mikael is like Opa. Good-looking!" Lara mused, and the others laughed. It was true that Mikael had inherited the good looks of Opa and Uncle Harty as young men, but, as always with such family comparisons, there was the lingering implication that the similarities went deeper.

"What you think, Julie?" Mikael asked, laying himself bare for judgment. I stared at the strained chest muscle under which there beat a very big heart. Everyone held their breaths.

"I think Mikael is like Mikael," I pronounced.

"I like," said Mikael, and a broad, gleaming smile came over his face as his brown eyes twinkled with a sense of freedom.

We were not simply our genes. That was an idea that the Nazis had pursued to the point of absurdity. Laughter broke out in the kitchen, and a spell was broken.

Bibbi took off her apron and returned after a few minutes with a solemn-looking elderly woman. It was Luna's mother, who had embroidered my name on all the fabrics I had received as gifts, and who had brought a pot of her best "Paraguayan soup," a dish that had been invented by a fluke of cooking. I thanked her for all the work she had done on my gifts, to which she nodded silently before sitting down next to Luna at the heavily laden table. She watched me throughout the meal, and I was certain that she wondered whether my entry into the family would be good for her daughter and grandchildren.

Uncle Harty and I sat at opposite ends of the long table. The Paraguayan fish took pride of place at the center. Uncle watched as I tasted a fork of the succulent white meat. "Bueno?" he asked.

"Si," I replied, and we both laughed, releasing a lively discussion around the table.

Once again as before, I was outside myself, watching a scene that I could barely believe to be true. I had a family in Paraguay, and all the truth that needed to be known right now was that we were alive, in good spirits, here together.

At the end of the meal, just before my departure for the airport, Luna asked all of us to rise and join hands in a prayer of thanks. In this circle each of us had done something to heal one another's wounds. Uncle Harty remained silent, but a few moments later at our parting his eyes teared over, and he clasped my arms as though it might be for the last time. "You've got guts," he said. "Thank you for coming."

Bibbi and Walter drove me to the airport, and at our parting, Bibbi expressed a wish to visit me in Sweden. "Just come any time," I said, wondering whether that air of the surreal would ever leave our friendship.

Shortly after landing in São Paulo, I learned that Uncle Harty had called Aunt Gise. He'd wondered why she had left home so abruptly at the age of seventeen. She was over the moon to hear from him. I hoped that they could heal one another's wounds.

CHAPTER 20

São Paulo, March 2016

MY RESEARCH IN BRAZIL BEGAN IN BETINA'S APARTMENT. IT WAS A modern place, sparsely furnished with wide open spaces and large, prominent works of art, reflecting the avant-garde character of its owner.

Betina poured two cafezinhos, small shots of strong coffee, and offered the sugar. Brazilians seemed to regard this as the only viable combination for making coffee worth drinking.

I recognized the feel and sound of this culture: in its penchant for sweet things; in the softness of its music; and in the language, my first, which I had learned as a toddler. An absence of forty-five years had left me a novice to the realities of its history, rampant crime, and poverty. I'd been warned against the cash machines that were rigged by gangs, and about wearing anything valuable that caught attention, including my wristwatch. I had left my handbag at home and instead wore a leather pouch attached to my belt. In it was my Brazilian passport that the embassy in Stockholm had issued to me before the trip. "Once a Brazilian, always a Brazilian," said the cheerful consular official. Without knowing it, I had remained a citizen by birth throughout life.

The connection to Betina was Paula the filmmaker's way of helping without being able to accompany me herself. It was no small gesture. Betina, a Brazilian artist, was conversant with my subject matter in a most personal way. Five years earlier she had been contacted by a group of elderly citizens in the community of Weisenau near Mainz to inform her that they had taken measures to preserve the Jewish history of that town, of which her family had been a part. Betina and her mother, who visited Weisenau soon thereafter, learned that the last Jewish child to be born there before all Jews were deported was a girl named Chana Khan, a close relative. Chana, her brother Gideon and their mother were murdered in Auschwitz and her father in Dachau. The daughter of the midwife, who was arrested by the SS for delivering the child, was a member of the group that had ensured a road was named after Chana, and a signpost was placed outside the house where she had lived. In addition to restoring the local synagogue, the group wrote a short book about her, and published several articles in local newspapers and magazines. Betina eventually returned home, committing herself to volunteer for academics who researched both Jewish and Nazi immigration to Brazil—thorny subjects in a country with a conflicted attitude toward the Third Reich.

We had gotten to know one another in cyberspace where she had first shared this story with me. Quickly I understood her deep commitment to facing history, but still felt compelled to offer her a tangle of reasons for venturing on what I assumed she too saw as an inadvisable journey. She'd listened calmly, but appeared never to doubt, and all my words became unnecessary. "Let's compile our joint list of contacts and I will begin to organize your meetings," she said. That was it. To her there was no question that our missions were inextricably intertwined and that everything was unfolding as it should.

Now as she sat before me, impeccably dressed in strong colors and angular designs, she handed me a plastic envelope containing a schedule of meetings and a detailed list of names, contact details, and descriptions. She had waded through the administrative jungle of various Brazilian archives to find individuals prepared to guide us. The fact that transparency was not the norm in public offices in this part of the world made this task especially difficult, frequently raising suspicions.

"Use my apartment as your office," she said, sipping her coffee through lips that reminded me of Rothko's "Red on Maroon."

Her phone rang. "Bom dia, Emerson," she said, listened attentively, and ended the conversation with "tudo bem," indicating her agreement. How strange it was to live in that twilight zone of knowing the feel of a language intuitively, but not being able to understand it all.

"He is coming up now. Delayed because of traffic. More coffee?" I wasn't yet certain of how many cafezinhos I could drink in one morning. Oma's voice piped up in my head. "Terrible coffee they have in Brazil," she complained, and insisted that the key to long life was not to have too much of anything. Cafezinhos were too much.

While Betina had played a critical role in organizing my visit, both of us knew that the fate of my trip rested in Emerson's hands. Dear friends of dear friends had put me in touch with this genealogist who had no connections to my subject matter except that he was used to pursuing the details of family history with very little prior information. At this point, Emerson's qualifications were no doubt secondary to the fact that he was the only professional conversant in both English and his native Portuguese prepared to make the journey with me into the interior.

Presently my traveling warrior stood before me: a timid, soft, balding man whose only weapons were the reading glasses strung around his neck and a folder with a pen attached to it. This was not the strong man with the rifle that Paula had recommended. Betina urged us to sit down and served another round of cafezinhos. I drank mine quickly, counting on the jolt of caffeine to power me through my worries. Emerson sat nervously on the edge of his seat, fiddling awkwardly with his folder. "I don't know anything about *Nazzies*," he said, uttering that word as though he'd never said it before. "But I will do what I can."

We'd all had previous contact with one another and now confirmed our plans. Yet the question mark of what could realistically be achieved, particularly without getting into trouble, hung over us, and the only measure of that just now was Emerson's character.

"I will meet you in Campo Grande," he said as we shook hands before parting. Emerson's handshake was loose and undecided, so that I wondered whether he might just slip out of our agreement, and what to him must seem a spurious project, at best.

According to Betina's plan, the next place I was scheduled to meet him was in this last modern city at the threshold of the vast interior where Oma and Opa had once buried themselves from the world like needles in a haystack. Emerson and I barely knew one another, and we'd have to hit the ground running. I'd hired him with my precious fellowship funds from Wellesley. Whatever the pay, Emerson had the upper hand. There was no one else who had stepped forward to do this unenviable job.

"What do you think?" I stared at Betina, the pendulum of my thoughts at a dead standstill.

"I think you will be fine with him," she said, unconvincingly. "Come—leave the coffee cups. We have a meeting to get to."

Within minutes we were in Betina's car headed toward a private address to meet a circle of academics she had been working with during the years since she had discovered her family's fate in Europe.

The late-morning sun baked the stone courtyard of an elegant mansion in an exclusive neighborhood of the sprawling city of São Paulo. The houses themselves could barely be seen behind the high security gates that fenced out the fear of crime. Only the bougainvillea that straddled some of the gates got a look-in. As Betina and I sat with her research colleagues in a small, comfortable alcove in a courtyard, we spoke in hushed tones in a meeting that felt clandestine, like a resistance movement. I couldn't help but wonder against what.

The researchers listened eagerly as I related my reasons for being here, although Betina had already made them aware. I assumed they had met many like me, the descendants of the fled perpetrators who sought explanations, many of them still living in Brazil.

"We must start by telling you how happy we are that you are here," said the lead researcher in Portuguese, which Betina translated. "It gives us encouragement in a situation where it is still difficult to carry out research on the Nazis who came to our country. We have never met anyone like you, only the people from Ludwigsburg who look for the last remaining war criminals, but most of those are dead now."

I recalled the white monastic building that I had visited in southern Germany. Those who had led that effort were, by necessity, focused on prosecuting war criminals, not on investigating the insidious after-effects of their legacy on families, communities, and whole societies. The rest of us were responsible for that, but so few were prepared to realize it, either out of fear or indifference. We needed another kind of

Ludwigsburg now: one that encouraged us to look and speak honestly about what had happened to us through the generations as a result of a monumental act of evil.

The researchers told me of the documents that suddenly disappeared when they visited archives, and of the threats they had received from proxies of the descendants in established families in Brazil. Another of their colleagues, not present, had experienced these effects intensively in her research on Filinto Müller, the governor of Mato Grosso who had revered men like Opa. According to the researchers, the state, in collusion with some of these families, had over decades built a cocoon around guilt and shame so that these would remain unstirred, and awkward questions would not have to be answered.

I began to wonder whether Emerson and I would be able to achieve anything, and whether the two of us were in fact headed for trouble. None of the researchers had volunteered to accompany us, despite the fact that they saw ours as a unique case and an opportunity to gain significant insights into a subject they hoped to give more attention to. So far, they had devoted their efforts mainly to historical anti-Semitism in Brazil, and the reluctance to accept Jewish refugees during and after the war. The next step was to immerse themselves in the Brazilian public sector's known historical partiality to admitting former SS because their specialist skills were needed in a rapidly growing economy and because their attitude of might-makes-right was familiar. Yet, as we continued to speak in hushed tones, I suspected that their reluctance to become more engaged at present was grounded in sensible reasoning.

"Don't say anything about the Nazis when you are doing your work here," one of them advised, confirming my suspicions. How fortunate it was that Emerson was a genealogist, not a historian steeped in Brazil's Nazi entanglements. We could simply argue that this was about family research.

"Did you know that Mengele once lived in a house in this neighborhood? His old housekeeper has given an interview," said one of the researchers. I remembered my friends at home, Hédi and Livia, sisters who had been separated from their parents at Auschwitz by this travesty of a doctor in the white coat who had decided over life and death and performed grotesque human experiments on the inmates, some of them children. After the war, he had traveled back and forth to the Federal Republic freely, often using his own name, and been afforded the chance not only to find shelter but to live comfortably in this affluent community. I liked to believe that in the end humanity could not tolerate such evil and that justice would eventually be done, but the knowledge that Mengele, who died of natural causes in Latin America, had lived just down the road in one of these spacious mansions was a reminder that justice only succeeded if we pursued it. How naïve I felt; how very naïve.

During the evening I visited the dear friends of dear friends, who had attempted to calm my nerves from afar.

"This is very interesting work that you are doing," declared Senhor Joaquim in his light voice from his wheelchair. "I have myself pursued the history of our family with Emerson's help. There are slaves, Portuguese, Indians, you name it," he said, before being interrupted by a storm of coughing.

His body was besieged by disease, but his family who surrounded us supported him in satisfying his insatiable curiosity as best they could. His cough began to subside and he took up a kerchief into which he muttered his annoyance at the physical deterioration of his body, which came at the expense of everything that was still to be known. Tucking the kerchief away, he insisted that we set the uninteresting matter of his terminal illness aside and continue with more important conversation.

"I would go with you if I could," he said. "But you have Emerson to help you and I hope my secretary has provided you with information about the town where you are going. Have you booked your *pousada?*"

"Thank you, yes," I confirmed, attempting to hide my unease about many things, including the safety of the inn we had booked to stay in.

"Now don't worry, and I look forward to a full report upon your return. Do you have repellent? Although, they've fumigated so thoroughly I suspect all the bugs have died." He broke into a chuckle that unsettled his fragile breath and left him coughing once again.

I would meet this dear friend of a dear friend once more before he succumbed to what he considered to be irritating mortality.

——◦——

The last stop before meeting Emerson in Campo Grande was Rio de Janeiro, where, under the pretense of visiting the National Archive, I had arranged to meet my longtime Brazilian contact, Fábio Koifman.

We met on a crowded street only a few blocks away from Copacabana. He was pale and sweaty from an illness that would soon lead to surgery, yet he greeted me with the warmth and sense of humor that I recognized from our communications over the Internet. With him was a younger colleague who worked on topics related to mine, with whom I had also started a conversation from afar about accompanying me into the interior. As with the other researchers, there was a generosity and willingness to help that stopped short of offering to make the actual journey. It was entirely understandable.

The waiters in white jackets sped around the tables in the cafe, occasionally barking questions at us that I could not comprehend. Fábio had not lost his appetite, an observation that cheered me. I had never forgotten the *abraço* or hug in his signoff that had been sent many times over the years in blind faith across an ocean.

The noise in the room demanded that we speak openly and loudly about our work, in contrast to the hushed tones of the meeting only a day before. Fábio questioned everything, including the potential danger in the research. It was his way, and without it I would by now have made a number of wrong turns in the work. He had encouraged me to go the extra mile, be skeptical of wild stories, and resist the urge to cast judgment upon people, including Opa. All this spoke volumes about Fábio's integrity, since he was himself a Jew, and the temptation must have been great to damn every former Nazi who had entered his country.

Yet when it came to the question of Baron von der Kleist, and the extra information about him that I could add from conversations with my uncle, Fábio's ears pricked up. This was a notable case, he thought, and one that warranted further investigation based on the potential new information it could yield about former-SS networks and so-called rat lines between Latin America and the Federal Republic.

The casual flow of pedestrians on the pavement was a relief from the aggressive lunch venue. As we sauntered past the many colorful vendors and street musicians, Fábio asked where I was born in Brazil. "Here," I said. "Right around here, although I don't know the address." "Ah! You are a *Carioca!*" The two laughed. I recognized the word. It meant someone who was born in the River of January, Rio de Janeiro. The connections between me and this place were growing. My birthday was in January.

~

After we parted, I walked along the waterfront along Copacabana Beach on that famous finely tiled pavement of swirling off-white and gray. My earliest childhood photo album attested to the fact that M and I had once walked here daily. Or she had walked and I had lain in a pram at first, and eventually tested my first shoes on this very surface.

I sat down in a café on the beach behind the pavement and ordered coconut water, a drink consisting of a green coconut, the top of which had been hacked off so that the milky liquid inside could be drunk through a straw. It was another of those flavors indigenous to my taste buds.

As it was a weekday, the tables were empty, with the exception of a few local surfers with salt-encrusted faces and wiry bleached hair that didn't tolerate combing. As they laughed and pointed toward colleagues riding the waves, I realized how comfortable I felt here, despite all the warnings of crime. I was once again the toddler with the sand-encrusted feet in the floppy pink sunhat mesmerized by the Rio seaside that was the only place I had ever known. Carioca indeed.

"It must have been nice for you to have been born in Brazil." It was a comment that had been tossed at me in defiance from behind a figurative wall that was quickly raised by a community leader in Schleswig-Holstein only a few months ago, as I had attempted to finalize my investigation of Baum, Opa's accuser.

I had stood in a small, local museum west of Hamburg before an anxious gathering of townspeople in their seventies with the same aversion to remembering as so many others of their generation in that region. They had been powerless children then, like M and her siblings. Why should they feel responsible for the legacy of events over which they'd had no say? Instead, they had put their energies to organizing a substantial collection of artifacts from the textile business Baum and a colleague—heroes to these people—had built up after the war. I hoped to be able to verify that this Baum was the same man as my grandfather's accuser. The business he and his colleague had steered with a steady hand offered them secure employment as young adults, and built up their communities so that the cruel ruins could be removed, and their children had playgrounds and parks.

"Look in here," said one of them, proudly opening up one of the many company pamphlets with tips for managing all aspects of life. The business had been more than a means of earning a paycheck. For many, it had been a lifeline out of chaos and darkness. How was one to live in a time when the previous generation could offer little credible guidance?

The many old brochures and photo albums of fine company events included pictures of an aging Baum through the decades. The earliest photographs, taken during the early fifties, confirmed to me that he was one and the same as the SS hero who had been personally decorated by Adolf Hitler and who, after the war, had denounced Opa. How could I raise all this amid these nervously smiling former employees and wards of the museum, eager to showcase their community at its best?

As I pointed at the photograph and disclosed to them that I knew Baum had known my grandfather, they quickly acknowledged that he had come to their community during the late 1940s. He wasn't a native of these parts, and yet he had become one of the patriarchs of their community. It seemed odd that for someone so important to them, no one seemed to want to mention where Baum had come from or how he had come to them. On the other hand, Opa, who had originally come from these parts, was regarded as a "refugee."

Briefly I mentioned the hunting hotel my grandfather had created in the nearby community. They seemed well aware of him and the place. The company had held some fine dinners through the years, they said, but the conversation soon came to an abrupt halt.

"You must bring your daughter next time." One of them laughed as he gave me a souvenir button from their collection for my daughter, who studied textile design. It was meant genuinely, but had the added benefit of being a friendly means of getting away from a difficult subject. Perhaps they didn't know who Baum had been, but in these parts not knowing spoke volumes. Everyone knew that this had been a melting pot for former SS and their postwar networks. Baum and Opa had moved into this area at approximately the same time in 1949. For Opa this was a return home, but for Baum it was a new place. Could it have been possible that it was Opa who had led Baum here, and that when Baum's star had risen sufficiently my ill-tempered grandfather, who had made a number of enemies, became dispensable? Former SS "comrades" were known for throwing their colleagues under the bus when they became a liability. In addition to the changing climate of public opinion, the reopening of war crimes trials and the ripples generated among former SS by the capture of Adolf Eichmann, this local spat may have been the last straw; and so Opa became someone who had always had an uncertain future in these parts and could be dispensed with: in other words, a "refugee."

Nele, who had accompanied me to this place, raised her eyebrows in frustration. To her it was all a familiar game of avoidance that she had experienced repeatedly throughout her many years of research into the mounted SS. I could see that she had given up on this crowd, but I wasn't ready yet. On the way out I asked the chairperson of the museum association whether he knew that Baum had been a decorated soldier in the Waffen-SS and had most likely been a significant catalyst in my grandparents' decision to leave for Latin America, where I was eventually born.

It was then that he had shot back with his comment about my being born in Brazil, seemingly unsurprised by the information about Baum. "It's warm and lovely there, isn't it?" he'd added, attempting to ensure that I was put in my place.

Nele bristled when I told her about the man's comments in the car, and I had felt snubbed at the time, but now all this faded into the question of why being born in Brazil had always evoked such mixed feelings in me. There was the sun-kissed child with the sand-encrusted feet longing for the magic of the waves, sweet fruit, and the swirling tiled pavement; and then there was the imposed nothingness of that entire experience. My child's Portuguese had never existed, according to M, as though it was something that had to be erased. As I sipped the last drops of precious coconut water, I was filled with renewed appreciation for this place of my birth, and a renewed right to feel it.

Almost a half century ago, Oma and I had sat on a mat under an umbrella on the trampled white sand below, her arm cupped around my chubby bare midriff, temporarily holding me in place for the photograph. Under my floppy sunhat I had no other thought than total fascination with the older children who splashed in the surf. But what thoughts did she and M have then? Both had left the interior where Opa had remained, and that Emerson and I would now venture into.

CHAPTER 21

Campo Grande, March 2016

A TEXT MESSAGE ARRIVED FROM EMERSON. "SORRY! BAD RAINS HERE. Stuck in São Paulo. Flight delayed." I had landed in Campo Grande from Rio, and began to suspect that my worst fears had been confirmed. Emerson must be jumping ship while he still could. There was nothing to do but hope and wait.

My taxi sped down the airport road that was wide and modern, like a triumphal Roman road, lined by well-irrigated carpets of green, palm trees, and intimidatingly colorful flowers. Man has won here, was its daring message in this wild interior, where nature had attempted to fight back in many ways. The smoothness of the road seemed to mask this brutal struggle.

As we entered the city, luxury hotels and shopping malls rose out of the wide empty streets like a Xanadu for ranchers, agribusiness, and less-honest sources of wealth. Dwarfed between these giants were small, air-conditioned legal and public offices such as the land registry or *Imoveis* that served the specialized needs of this region. Campo Grande, Opa's burial place, felt like a town that had skipped the usual stages of development in a hurry to serve the meteoric growth that the fruits of the land were expected to yield.

I checked in at the counter of a spacious, cool, marble-floored lobby that provided immediate relief from the baking sun outside. A fountain trickled against the carefree sound of a bossa nova that played from invisible speakers, and an overstaffed army of uniformed waiters served *cafezinhos* and cool drinks in the sparsely populated coffee lounge.

My large room with a view into the fishbowl of this strange quasi-city included every imaginable modern convenience. I changed into fresh clothes and collapsed onto the bed, imagining this to be my last taste of civilization for the coming week. My worries of whether Emerson would turn up were muted by exhaustion from the impressions of the last few days. I fell into a deep sleep, and when I awoke two hours later I found a text message from Emerson. "The plane is leaving now. I am boarding."

Upon arrival he vanished quickly into his room, saying that he needed some time to take care of business, which I assumed included other more straightforward archive jobs that he was running at the same time as making this somewhat unconventional and time-consuming journey with me. I imagined it might be like this all the way, but was beginning to dislike my skepticism, which was merely a reflection of how uncertain I felt about this entire undertaking.

We met in the lobby that evening before dinner. "I found these in the archives before leaving São Paulo," he said. "Very interesting. Look." He laid several photocopied pages on the lounge table that were a list of names and other accompanying identity details.

"What is this?" I asked, surprised that Emerson had already given some detailed attention to our project.

"Disembarkation list from the *Charles Tellier* in December 1960— the boat your grandparents came on."

I scanned the long list with several names that had been circled by past researchers. The French liner, which had left Hamburg in December 1960, had carried a mix of nationalities and faiths. Among them were Jews seeking a new life away from dark Europe where their kin had been murdered; and then there were my grandparents, former SS and once their oppressors. I wondered what the journey must have been like.

Under "Religion" Oma and Opa had declared themselves to be Catholic, most likely in order to facilitate their entry into a Catholic country. After the war, the Catholic Church saw benefits in welcoming back its former SS "black sheep" who had rejected their faiths in favor of the Führer, and in some instances had helped them to escape. I had no evidence that the Church had played any role in helping Oma and Opa to find refuge, but Oma's call for the pope to be shot began to take on different dimensions as I looked at this disembarkation list. She and Opa were now forced to use the same Catholic Church they had fought and persecuted in Poland as a cover for their own escape from what they may well have seen as their own persecution. Now I understood that the rage she had expressed in her peaceful apartment, and that I had found so unsettling, was in fact about humiliation.

"Look here," said Emerson, pointing to an address listed against their names. "That's where they went after the boat. Fazenda San Pedro, São Paulo, it read. "That's not around here. They stayed on a farm near São Paulo first. Maybe they knew someone there? Maybe von der Kleist?" Emerson knocked his forefinger against his temple, a habit that suggested he was mentally circling a problem that he would eventually find a way to solve.

My mind spun at every detail. Nothing was inconsequential and nothing could be dismissed as benign information. I longed to think like Fábio and to doubt my own suspicions, but found it difficult as I looked at this most revealing document. I needed many more days with Uncle Harty on his terrace, but I knew that wouldn't be possible. My family back home in Sweden and I had already been away from one another for too long. Uncle and I would have to settle for the telephone, which I knew would hamper communication with my tactile relative.

"Interesting, huh?" said Emerson, lifting his spectacles from his nose. "About land ownership—I have called the Imoveis. We will visit them." We had jointly determined that one of our strategies for mapping out my grandparents' life and networks in Latin America was to learn about what they had purchased, when, and from whom. Uncle Harty had told his broad-brush story of the land, but it had become such a contentious issue in our family that I wanted to see it on paper. From Uncle Harty's feelings of guilt about misleading his parents, it had also become clear to me that he did not know the whole story behind his father's Latin American contacts.

After this start, I knew I had been quite wrong to doubt Emerson's commitment. He had arrived anything but empty-handed.

On the following morning we pulled up into the small parking lot of the private graveyard on Avenida Senador Filinto Müller. To enter the graveyard one had to pass through an archway where there was a reception that recorded visitors. We suspected that this could also be a means of catching relatives who hadn't paid for grave maintenance. In a country where corruption was the norm, this could get very expensive. I decided to keep quiet, and Emerson proceeded, somewhat nervous about finding a way to ask for the grave number without explaining fully who we were.

A conversation ensued and eventually we were admitted without any request for payment. I didn't ask Emerson what he had told them. Now we entered a large, lush garden where there were no graves or the usual visible signs of Christianity. In the distance, two maintenance workers moved across the grass, dodging various parts of it. I looked down at my feet and noticed a metal plank pressed into the ground amid the thick grass. Emerson had gone ahead and cast his eye across the ground for the grave number. He couldn't find it, but it didn't matter because I couldn't hear him as I continued to wander through this pagan garden of the dead.

Only five months before, I had stood at Oma's grave in southern Germany. It too had been in a garden of sorts, devoid of visible religious symbolism, with the exception of a small chapel that looked like a hut on the hill below the graves. She too had settled for a plank in the ground, surrounded by the grass. She shared the space under a young tree with seven others. It had been in the autumn, and its leaves were turning to gold, like a maturing young god, so that the grave reflected perfectly her on-off desire to throw off the shackles of Christianity and to embrace Nature as her one true religion.

I remembered hearing her voice scolding the others for reaching what she regarded as pathetically low ages. None of them had made it past seventy-five. I imagined that she didn't like to share the same tree with many others, or with anyone, as this contradicted her tendency toward exclusivity. The dream of Lebensraum had come to a dismal end, or perhaps I was being unfair. Could it be her way of finally rejecting it, not only of saying that it had led nowhere, but also that it was wrong because it came at the expense of innocent lives? I realized I was making up stories in my head, and that until the end of my own life, I would look for signs of my grandparents' remorse, precisely as on this journey through Latin America I searched but found only evidence to the contrary.

At Oma's grave, I thought I would feel regret for my obsession with the truth, but no such emotions were forthcoming. Auntie Best, who always did things properly, had handed me three apricot-colored roses, which I placed next to the small plaque with the name of the deceased and dates of birth and death engraved onto it. Instead, I had felt an odd sense of neutrality about the way my relationship with Oma had ended. My husband had been right to advise me to face her with what I knew.

"Now Oma can rest in peace," said Auntie Best. At times I admired my aunt's determination to bring dignity to a family that had been grievously lacking in it; and at times I felt sorrow that she could not allow herself to scream. Not even once that I could remember.

Now I found myself next to a completely different type of tree, one that was being strangled by a vigorous climbing plant with large, draping, heart-shaped leaves and thick, woody tendrils. The gardeners had obviously decided to let the tree die in the luscious embrace of this plant. It was like the beautiful slow death one only saw in operas and ballets, but that in reality was plain murder.

I looked down at my feet and saw a name I thought I recognized, although it wasn't quite the same name. It had been so altered by the engraver, who most likely hadn't been able to read the handwriting or wasn't conversant with German names, that one could easily conclude that Opa had finally gotten his alias. But there was no hiding in death because there was an identification number. Grandfather, who had been complicit in reducing so many to a few digits, had become one himself. Unlike most of the other graves, this one was rusty and had a lock and chain on the tiny door to the underground compartment, where presumably the ashes were placed. A cross that could have been misconstrued as a downward-facing dagger had been engraved on the door. Had he been worried that someone might defile his grave? Was there something other than ashes in there?

I ran my fingers across the misspelled name that was mostly hidden under long strands of grass that grew over this untended plaque. There were two other blank metal strips on the plaque under Opa's, but who would join him there after all that had come to pass? I wanted to believe that there was some justice in a lonely end, under the murderous temptress with the heart-shaped leaves, but that was hard to conclude. He would remain in obscurity, under the protection offered by the street named after his friend, Senator Müller, and never have to explain himself to anyone.

Emerson snapped a photograph of me crouched behind the grave. How odd that I could smile, but then realized that it was my traveling partner who made me feel this way. I could summon neither pity nor rage. All I could think of was my longing to leave the stifling heat of this godless garden where time had stood still and secrets festered. Instead, I longed to stand at the great river and let its cleansing sound and the affection of my Paraguayan cousins wash over me.

Emerson asked one of the gardeners about the chain on Opa's grave, but the man just shrugged his shoulders. We returned to the car, successfully avoiding any questions from the receptionist, but, as he was about to turn the key in the ignition, Emerson looked at me and said: "Maybe his mistress visits him. Maybe they know where she is—whether she is still alive." He stared at the steering wheel, realizing that by going back to make such an inquiry he was risking stirring curiosity about who I was. He slapped the steering wheel, annoyed that he could not suppress his own curiosity. "Wait here," he said, and headed for the reception.

He returned empty-handed, but now I began to gain insights into the stuff that Emerson was made of. He turned over every stone and never gave up.

CHAPTER 22

Campo Grande, March 2016

"Eh! Which way to Maracaju?" Emerson shouted out the window of our SUV to a vendor selling bottled water at the entrance to one of Campo Grande's well-groomed roundabouts. The man shouted a friendly reply. "Not my beach, he says." Emerson sighed and then regained his composure. "Okay, we will find it. Don't worry."

We circled the roundabout twice and took a wrong turn before choosing another road that eventually offered a sign telling us that we were going in the right direction. The GPS didn't work in these parts. "Maracaju 158 km," read the sign. We were on our way.

"Do you mind some music?" Emerson asked, as soon as we had left the city and were on a wide open road with no other cars in sight.

"No, not at all," I replied. It was so easy to forget about beauty and pleasure inside the labyrinth of my family's tortuous history.

With one hand on the wheel, Emerson eagerly unzipped a folder of home-made CDs and inserted one of them into the player in the SUV. Soon the high-pitched swooning of the Bee Gees filled the car. "One of my favorites," he said enthusiastically. "Music from the seventies is great! I also like Brazilian lounge music from that time very much." He gripped the steering wheel hard with both hands and began to sing with a hurts-so-good expression on his face as Robin, Barry, and Maurice blended their inimitable voices.

"Mind if I roll down the window?" I asked.

"No!" he replied. "It's a great day and we're stayin' alive!" He chuckled, like Muttley, the snickering hound. He was right. It was a day made great by the azure sky and the tangerine sun that showed off the endless flat space at its mightiest. As I rolled down the window, the soft air hit my face and a feeling of freedom and peace came over me, despite the daunting task ahead.

Beyond the deep trenches on either side of the wide glistening highway, we saw only red stretching in every direction, as far as the eye could see. "It was everywhere; in our clothes and shoes and we couldn't get rid of it," Oma complained of the rich alluvial soil that had made this land such a bonanza for farmers. I licked lips that felt suddenly dry and grainy, and ran my fingers across my face to discover that the land had already claimed me.

Flightless brown-plumed birds on stilts, called rheas, picked at the remains of a harvested soy field; the same crop that, decades ago, Opa had hoped would make him a wealthy man. The clumps of trees—eucalyptus in these parts—and farmhouses that were sparsely scattered across wide open vistas, reminded me of the other landscapes I had been in as I had traced my grandfather's relentless quest for living space through Schleswig-Holstein, Wielkopolska, and Mato Grosso. It was the same but not the same, and each time the dream grew larger; so sprawling and uncontrollable that it overruled any other considerations, including family. There was no doubt that there had been a strong push for Opa to leave the Federal Republic, but now I saw before me the magnetism of this land for one who thirsted for more, which his friend von der Kleist would surely have portrayed during one of those Waffen SS weekends at the hunting lodge. That Uncle Harty felt responsible for all this was as grotesque as to claim that he was responsible for the crimes his father had committed.

"That's the old road," Emerson pointed out. "Much harder to get out here in your grandfather's time." Now I could see that the red path below the highway was a dirt road. What a difficult journey it must have been to get to Maracaju, and no wonder Uncle Harty had opted for light aircraft.

Occasionally, next to that road, there rose a few shacks made of wooden planks and old doors collected from derelict farmhouses. A small child in ragged clothes, with long black hair tinted by the red soil and feet caked in mud of the same color, gripped my gaze so that I turned my head to keep eye contact as our car passed his home without hope. The adults continued to move about, performing chores of survival, although there didn't seem to be anything to live on here; neither water nor food, only the remains of broken houses to cover their heads when the rains came, and the scraps of soy to share with the rheas in the harvested field.

Emerson looked unsympathetic. "The government pays them for votes. Just enough to keep them like that." Institutionalized helplessness and violence were the norms of this vast, rich land. We'd been forewarned that some of the landless poor had formed militias in order to try to retake land from the wealthy, which added to the danger of traveling in this country. The documents we had already seen, some originally provided by Igor, suggested that ownership of the land Opa had procured outside Maracaju was itself now disputed, and the possibility remained that Emerson and I might be walking into a conflict. Just as in the rural towns of Schleswig-Holstein and Wielkopolska, news that the relative of a previous owner had arrived traveled fast. People might wonder, as they had in the Polish countryside, whether I had come to reclaim property, but the difference was that here the guns might come out. Wherever the law was weak or uncertain, suspicion filled the vacuum.

Emerson had resumed his swaying to the sound of the Bee Gees. He had no rifle, only his curiosity and I wondered what else. "How did you become a genealogist?" I asked.

"I was an accountant—made me very tired and unhappy. Genealogy was a hobby. The story of our forefathers is fascinating! It's really about ourselves, you know. You cannot believe it, but sometimes people have hired me to trace their families far back into the past. They want to find some European nobility, but when I find slaves in their background, they ask me to stop the research. Many don't want to hear it! Senhor Joaquim was an exception."

Suddenly I realized just how qualified Emerson was for a job that was precisely about not closing our eyes to the past. What he had encountered was certainly racism, but there was more. It was our existential fear that in that web of tangled ugliness and beauty that we called history we might just discover something about ourselves. Pride and false facades might have to be relinquished. We may just have to renounce our imagined exceptionalism, and call ourselves regular members of the human race.

"Why do you carry on with this work?" I asked, wondering how he kept himself motivated in the face of such blatant racism.

"Not everyone is like that, and, besides, I believe in the spirits."

"Spirits?" I asked.

"Sure. You know, Allan Kardec and Spiritism," he said. "I mean, I go to church, sure, but that's social. The past, present, and future are all connected by spirits who wander through different lives, suffer, make good or bad choices, and experience the consequences in new lives. It's all connected by the law of karma."

Brazilians were famous for peppering their Catholicism with a heavy dose of indigenous supernatural belief. Yet Emerson, with his academic appearance and strong sense of practicality, didn't come across as one who hung talismans around his bed or participated in séances. It unnerved me that someone who had spent so much time examining ancestry had come to the conclusion that we were merely bodies that were the puppets of invisible ghosts.

Noticing my skepticism, Emerson burst enthusiastically into explanation. "What could a black child learn dying after one or two years of starving in Africa? Did he have a chance to make any choice at that age? What is the explanation about this suffering? Where is the goodness of God? Wouldn't he be paying for something wrong done in other lives?"

This reasoning bothered me, because it seemed to me that there could never be any justification for the suffering of a child. It also left me wondering what Emerson thought I might be paying for with this long, painful, midlife journey. Was I perhaps my own grandfather's spirit wandering in search of answers for what I had done? Noticing my silence, Emerson momentarily turned his sights from the road ahead, possibly aware of my dismay. "In only one life it is impossible to learn everything we have to. That's why we have other lives—to evolve spiritually and become beings of light."

An hour and a half later we crossed the old, disused narrow train tracks, entering the town of Maracaju, which was symbolized by a colorful parrot.

The center consisted of a few one-story government offices, among them the imoveis, a library, a museum, and a churrascaria or cafeteria serving grilled meats for hungry ranchers at lunchtime only. There were no other shops or restaurants.

It was the end of the day and these streets that I imagined were never really full were now empty. We drove into the residential area, which consisted of a few blocks of large, orderly bungalows that gave way to smaller, older row houses with rust that crept out from under the paint on the gates. According to Senhor Joaquim, the population of this place had swelled to 45,000 but it was still run by a handful of fearsome ranchers.

The pousada was a quiet, modest place with a spacious lounge where the staff sat on a battered leather couch watching with deadpan faces as the latest revelations about the corruption scandals—this time a staggering US$450,000,000 of kickbacks from the state-run oil company, Petrobras, and the Brazilian National Development Bank that had gone into the pockets of senior politicians—unfolded on the wide-screen television on the wall. So far, Maracaju was not the Wild West with drunken ranchers dueling outside the saloon that I had imagined.

Over a deep-fried dinner that could have served ten, I asked Emerson how we would proceed on the following morning. I knew that he was mulling it over, and perhaps it was strange that we hadn't discussed it before, but both of us knew that this trip had to be like riding the waves; we'd have to take each one as it came. Our problem was that we were strangers in a small town where everyone and everything got noticed, and where we didn't want to arouse suspicions. It seemed an impossible task. In the dining space next door to us, a large party had prebooked an event, and occasionally the guests craned their necks to see who the two strangers in the next room were.

"I think we'll go to the early morning church service," said Emerson, keeping his head low over his meal, either because he was hungry, or because he was trying not to be noticed.

"And what will we do there?" I asked, wondering whether he had decided to submit our problem to God or the spirits.

"We will find people with white hair," Emerson replied.

At first I thought it a strange idea, but soon understood his meaning. The Sunday morning service was as good a place as any to find locals who might have known where my grandparents had once lived. The cleverness of this move was that it could ingratiate us to the community; if we attended Church we must be all right.

"Any other plans?" I asked, eager to know what our fallback position was.

Emerson shook his head. "No, I think this is a good start."

We rose from our table, leaving most of the meal untouched. The crescent moon admired its own reflection in the small swimming pool on this mild evening in which the temperatures were neither too hot nor too cold. The allure of this land was becoming clearer to me by the minute.

"Wow!" gasped Emerson, and sat down in one of the chairs near the pool under the star-studded sky. "Come! Look! Incredible." Once again, Emerson lifted my attention out of the musty cellars of my family's history to the marvel of life and the universe.

"Do you believe in UFOs?" he asked excitedly, unable to take his eyes off the constellations in a sky so clear it seemed as though one could touch them. I didn't know what to say, and before I could respond he answered his own question: "I do."

In the past I would have reacted skeptically, but Emerson's sense of wonder and openness to mysteries we could not understand was irresistible and refreshing. People could be practical, even scientific, and they could believe in spirits and UFOs; they could be strangers and they could treat you like an old friend. Emerson touched something that was playful and serious, superfluous and essential all at the same time, and freed me from slavish linear explanations. I had struggled to understand how Robert, Nele, Betina, and all the others had appeared exactly when I needed them, and perhaps—just perhaps—there was no single rational explanation at all. In Emerson's world the evolution of my spirit had been passed on to another guardian, whose most potent weapon beyond curiosity was joy.

CHAPTER 23

Maracaju, March 2016

THE EARLY MORNING LIGHT STREAMED IN THROUGH THE LONG STAINED-glass windows, illuminating the spacious modern church with a rainbow of colors. The gray and white heads were already seated in the pews, and now the younger families arrived just before the start of the service. The church wasn't full on this Sunday morning, a reflection of the fact that the Catholic Church was slowly losing its iron grip on the souls of Brazil.

No sooner had we sat down in the second-to-last pew than Emerson began surveying the church for promising white heads. I felt ambivalent about imposing our agenda in this place of worship, but Emerson appeared not to be concerned about it. He tapped me on my knee and indicated that he wanted to approach the people standing in the back before the service started. The drum of embarrassment pounded in my heart as he squeezed his way past worshippers preparing themselves for the sacred hour. I turned to look behind me and saw that he had quickly struck up a conversation with a shrewd-looking man, who nodded in the affirmative.

A guitar struck up a tune, and a procession of choir boys and girls carrying the cross before them, followed by a priest in a white robe, began moving down the aisle toward the sanctuary at the front of the church that was a low stage, barely separated from the congregation. People sang the words that appeared on a large screen in the right-hand corner while a guitarist played. It was the gentle music of another religious tradition, not the sometimes-damning sound of Europe's organs.

As the priest began the service, I cast a glance at Emerson behind me. He had stopped speaking with the old man, and his head was bowed, hands clasped, as though already in prayer. He looked up briefly, his walnut-shaped brown eyes under the long eyelashes twinkling in the affirmative to indicate that his efforts had been fruitful.

I expected that we'd have to wait out the service in our separate places, but soon my impatience to know what Emerson had discovered was overtaken by the sound of the guitar in this temperate church of the gentle. Oma had spoken of an unbearable, scorching, primitive place, but I had difficulty matching the essence of this culture with her description. Certainly, many of the modern conveniences had been absent during her time, and I didn't doubt that the dangers my friends had referred to were real. Yet, as the young choir sang in this language without hard edges, I wondered whether her description was more a reflection of her inner state of being at the time. Forced into a lonely wilderness by fear of justice with a violent husband, she must have felt that God had sent her to hell.

Emerson slipped back into our pew during one of the pauses and went through all the motions, including taking communion toward the end of the service. As he kneeled I wondered whether he prayed to God or the spirits, or whether they coexisted and could both be entreated at the same time.

The service was over and without saying anything, Emerson urged me to exit the pew quickly. The old men were waiting. We greeted one another, one of them looking at me with particular intensity before speaking. Emerson paraphrased.

"He knew your grandfather—he had a reputation here."

"What kind of reputation?" I asked, aware that my facial expression, an attempt to smile kindly and keep calm, was out of sync with the storm inside.

"He says he remembers two beautiful girls who used to drive into town on tractors," said Emerson. Undoubtedly, he was referring to M and her younger sister, who had been brought to this place to work.

"But what kind of reputation?" I pressed on, trying to avoid distraction.

"He thinks it is better that we follow his grandson, who will go ahead of us on the motorbike. He will take us to someone who can tell you more. Dutch farmers, I think."

We thanked the old man and left through the side door of the church, where the grandson had started up his motorbike.

A few minutes later we halted in front of a bungalow that was different from the others. It was built like a chalet in dark wood, and in the front yard a miniature windmill turned obediently in the near-still air. A mountain of a man emerged from the front door and walked toward the gate on giant feet that were strapped into black gladiator sandals. The sun revealed a white head of hair, still tinged with its original strawberry blond, and fair skin that had taken a beating from the rays. I remained in the car as Emerson and the grandson explained why we were here. "Hollandaise," as I already thought of him since this was the nickname given by the locals to the descendants of Dutch settlers, kept one eye trained on me as he listened. From the stern look on his face, I wondered whether this was the farmer who would pull out his shotgun and tell us to back off.

Instead, we were welcomed into the house, where a pair of classic Dutch wooden clogs took pride of place on the largest wall. Everywhere there were symbols of the homeland, survival mechanisms of immigrants to avoid getting lost in the new land. Hollandaise offered me the seat next to his, while Emerson sat across from us. A young man with strawberry blond hair, likely in his early thirties, busied himself about repairing things in the backyard. I assumed it was Hollandaise's son and expected to soon see small strawberry blond children playing in clogs around another windmill.

Hollandaise began to speak to me in a language that sounded half familiar. Eventually, I worked out that it consisted of a blend of German, Dutch, and Portuguese. His father had immigrated to Brazil and had come to these parts to farm, so that the son, while clearly distinguishing himself as ethnically Dutch, was to all intents and purposes a Brazilian. I explained that we wanted to find the fazenda where my grandparents had once lived—maybe he knew where it was. "Naturalmente! We can go there," exclaimed Hollandaise, raising his large hand with the thick farming fingers that had gone arthritic. After this crescendo he went strangely silent. He seemed to know quite a bit, but remained guarded about his opinions.

As he spoke of peripheral things, I noticed his mastodon lower legs and feet that were clearly challenged by his body's great weight. How could he take us anywhere? Yet within minutes the Dutchman had heaved himself into the passenger seat of our SUV and guided Emerson out of his tree-bare neighborhood into the farmlands of corn and soy. There were no farmhouses in sight, or anything but crops and clumps of eucalyptus trees. Within a quarter of an hour Hollandaise indicated that we should turn off at a sign that read "Fazenda Meu Sonho 4 km." Opa's fazenda had been renamed "Farm of My Dreams."

The dirt road wound in ways that challenged determination, and eventually turned downward into a long road guarded by orderly rows of trees on either side. Another SUV passed in the opposite direction and Hollandaise waved.

Eventually, a bungalow that looked faintly familiar came into sight. The one existing black-and-white photograph of it in the albums was creased and ripped, and showed M as a young woman in work clothes petting a dog on the terrace. The doors and the windows had been modernized, and the paint was new, but there was no mistaking that we had found Opa's first chosen hideout in the interior of Brazil.

A horse grazed near a palm tree and two vulture-like birds followed our every move from an old telephone cable. I wandered across the red earth through an orchard of fruit trees, and encountered a long white stall that was empty with the exception of a single hen that clucked and flapped its wings in protest at the disturbance, then scuttled away. It was the pigsty that Uncle Harty had built for Opa's unwieldy genetic experiments.

It occurred to me that we were on potentially disputed land and that we had walked in without asking. Yet Hollandaise stomped across the property without hesitation.

"Where are the owners?" I asked in German, our common language.

"We drove past them—friends of mine—it's no problem," he reassured me. "We know one another well. Tudo bem."

There was no doubt that Hollandaise was a valuable passport in these parts. "We are lucky," whispered Emerson, in reference to the rapid course of events since the morning church service that had brought us to this place we thought would be so hard to find.

"Shall I take a picture?" he asked. Instinctively I didn't want it. Everything about this place seemed to me to be a source of suffering. A young M and her sibling had petted the dog in a rare moment of rest, forced to work in this place by their father's past. Oma had sat on the terrace reading Klepper's novel, her heart pounding with fear in anticipation of her husband's return home. There was no one to protect her, not even God, who she believed had shut her out. Uncle Harty worked the farm and tried to dream, but fought with himself and everyone else.

It was a place about which stories had been told that we children had been assailed with until we believed that it was our fault, even if we had never been here. The hard work that had taken place in the surrounding fields was admired and despised all at the same time, and cast upon us to suggest that we would never understand what real work was. In this way, it had become the source of our sense of worthlessness; but neither we nor the house or the crops in the field, nor the horse or the vulture-like birds, were responsible. The source, which I had attempted to unearth, lay decades back in history across an ocean, where millions of innocent people had been murdered in the name of a greedy, racist vision.

Once, during the travels of the previous autumn, half a world away from this place, I had experienced a similar gut-wrenching feeling of coming face to face with the source of pain and indignation that had been handed down to me, to my sister, and to our cousins. Now as I stood here in Oma and Opa's Brazilian hideout, my thoughts went to Verden on the Aller River, a small northern German town not far from Bremen that had been the first of their hideouts after the war. It was Oma's birthplace, and the haven to which the family had fled after its return from the East in the winter of 1945. I had driven around in search of the family farm, but found nothing, and eventually stopped for help at the only inn in a tiny community on the outskirts of town.

"Ah, *that* place," said the hotel owner, whose shortness of breath and plump fingers reminded me of the classic German sausage-eater of medieval European texts. "I tried to buy the place once but it was too expensive." He shook his head at life's lost opportunities, and then moved toward the doorway of this empty hotel that he suspected had become his fate.

"The farmhouse is hidden down there. Out of sight," he said, looking across the street down the side road that vanished as it curved downhill to the right behind the houses that lined the main road. "It's been modernized and divided into apartments, and the farmland has been sold off—not what it once was, but it is still quite a place," he conceded.

I drove down a few minutes later and discovered a formidable thatched mansion flanked by a redbrick coach house turned garage with newly painted green doors. Like the Fazenda of My Dreams, the property was nestled in a place that was difficult to find: in this case, far from the menacing gaze of Allied patrols and the prying eyes of strangers who had once driven past on the main road; and, on the other side, behind a dike built to protect the farmlands when the Aller and the Weser rivers, which met at this point, flooded. In the dangerous immediate postwar environment in which families and friends of victims were sometimes known to seek out their loved ones' torturers and murderers and take justice into their own hands, it must have seemed a gift to be able to nestle in this safe pocket off the risky thoroughfare.

I could only imagine what an eerie place it had been: full of Germans forced out of the East who were victims, bystanders, and perpetrators, all trying to survive. Amid the raped women and traumatized children, SS comrades on the run received a bowl of hot soup and shelter before fleeing to the next hideout. The challenge of the day for those who stayed was to buy and sell goods on the burgeoning black market without being caught. Oma and her children had returned home, but were refugees all the same.

Later on, I tracked down a man who had been a child refugee in that place. The bare outer order of his property seemed to me a reaction to the chaos and crowding of his early life experiences. Over his garden fence, the trim man in his midseventies with snow white hair squinted against the dim autumn sun. I explained who I was and that my family had once owned the place where he had worked. "What do you want to know?" he asked in a monotone voice. He wasn't pleased to see me and to be forced to revisit hard memories.

"Do you remember the family that lived there? The children? What was it like after the war?" I asked.

He continued to squint, unmoved. "Yes, I worked there. Don't much remember anyone from that time. There were so many of us squeezed into small spaces."

In this, as in other moments, I struggled with the feeling that in order to deal with my own pain I had become the selfish reminder of it for others, who preferred to try to forget. Yet as I looked around me and in my mind's eye the muddy autumn grass of Verden blended into the dry red dust of the fazenda, it struck me that past and present were like the cat's cradle, that child's game in which two polarities were inextricably linked by string.

"Shall we go?" Hollandaise asked, calling me out of memory.

Emerson snapped a photograph, but I didn't look into the lens. It was impossible.

———

Opa's farm had been split in two, the other part purchased by Dutch settlers, the Gijshofs, who were old friends of Hollandaise. Soon we were on the terrace of their home that in its Calvinist order was as much a statement of their ethnicity as Hollandaise's windmill and clogs. Willem and Veerle Gijshof, a couple in their sixties, could have been from any Dutch village, yet spoke the same blend of Portuguese, German, and Dutch as Hollandaise. Veerle spoke German without wandering as much as the men into the other languages. They were old friends, the children of Dutch immigrants from the same generation.

"Would you like coffee with milk?" she asked. How I welcomed a large mug of milky Dutch coffee with a butter biscuit, after all the cafezinhos with sugar.

The Gijshofs apparently hadn't known my grandparents, and spoke of their story of coming to own their farm, which they had purchased from an interim owner. As I was relating my reasons for being here, Hollandaise interrupted. "Do you know where your Uncle is? He was a troublemaker. I think he married Stroessner's daughter." His face flushed with anger that he could barely restrain.

I had stirred a swamp of old conflicts that I had little idea about. This feud was personal, and I wasn't here to settle Uncle Harty's unfinished business, which he had admitted to himself. The rumor that he had married the Paraguayan dictator's daughter was without substance, but said something about the shadiness in which Uncle Harty was perceived, not only as a result of his own misdeeds, but also because of his father's fascism. The latter seemed unfair to me, and all I wanted to do was get away from the subject.

"I'm not sure," I replied, at the same time as Emerson blurted out that, yes, he was in Paraguay. Both of us went quiet, silenced by the contradiction.

Hollandaise merely smiled at the conflicting information, tacitly acknowledging my desire not to get involved. "Never mind," he said, like an explosive disarmed at the last minute.

Veerle Guijshof was eager to leave the subject, about which she appeared to know nothing. "Would you like to see some of the land deeds and maps that can show you how all this land was divided?" Emerson was glad to escape the contentious subject of Uncle Harty and eagerly agreed. With all the land deeds and maps spread out on the table before us, Veerle took the opportunity to strike up a conversation with Emerson about genealogy, a subject of great interest to her, as she had been born in Brazil and longed for contact with her Dutch heritage.

"Still, I'm glad we don't live in Europe with all those immigrants—terrible," she said emphatically. Her husband nodded in agreement, but Hollandaise, who had a quick mind, remained silent.

The coffee at the bottom of my mug began to curdle in the heat. Who were these Dutch farmers if not the children of immigrants? Their spartan lifestyle and Dutch memorabilia began to feel like weapons in a tribal war; symbols in that museum of European white supremacy where the portrait of the heroic Aryans in the golden field that had once hung on Oma's wall also belonged. Tucked behind the vast rivers of the interior, away from the coasts and the constant ebb and flow of people, it was easier to avoid the reality, which was that all of us were the descendants of people who had wandered the world.

Emerson, who had begun to calibrate his behavior with mine after the embarrassing slipup concerning Uncle Harty's whereabouts, noticed that my expression had sunk. "Can we just photograph these before leaving?" he asked the couple hurriedly.

"Of course," said Veerle, without showing any signs of suspicion. With a few clicks of his cell phone, Emerson photographed the deeds and maps.

After the meeting, we drove Hollandaise home. As we said our farewells outside the gate to his Dutch microcosm, I felt a tinge of guilt for my dishonesty about Uncle Harty. Hollandaise seemed a decent man and had been generous with his time. "I am sorry . . ." I said, but didn't get to finish my sentence before the giant passed his huge hand across my cheek and clasped both of my hands in his.

"Good luck and enjoy your life," he said, as though imploring me not to live in the shadows and accepting my apology because family is no easy thing.

—◆—

"Hungry?" asked Emerson, and as usual during these journeys I couldn't answer. The past fed me with its stories, and I had lost touch with my appetite. Emerson decided for both of us, and parked our SUV alongside the many pickup trucks lined up outside the churrascaria.

Inside, the waiters and waitresses, dressed like butchers in stained white aprons, moved from table to table carving roasted meat of different sorts from long skewers. We made our way to one of the few remaining free tables, amid the ranchers feasting on the meat with their families. I felt tense. If there was any moment in which these fearsome ranchers could question or intimidate us, this was it. I sensed the many eyes watching us over the lunchtime banter, but Emerson wasn't bothered. At present, his only mission was to satisfy his hunger.

I loaded my plate with vegetables from the buffet, but declined the lashings of meat that were offered as soon as we sat down at our table again. It was a preference that I was certain made me even more suspect.

Within a few minutes the elderly man we had met in the church who had known my grandfather came to greet us at our table. Emerson spoke to him in Portuguese, I guessed confirming a successful morning. "Obrigado!" said Emerson, thanking the old man.

"Yes, thank you," I added.

The old man's attention turned to me, and he began to speak solemnly. Despite the fact that I barely understood anything he said, save the word "Hitler," I nodded in the affirmative, assuming that he rejected anything to do with the Third Reich. Emerson kicked me lightly in the lower leg and kept his attention focused on our visitor as though nothing had happened. Confused, I stopped nodding. The old man finished and patted me on the shoulder, suggesting that he thought we understood one another, and left to pay for his lunch at the cash register.

Emerson leaned over the table, looked around cautiously, and under his breath said, "He knew your grandfather was SS—everyone here knew at that time. But he agrees with him! He said it was a pity Hitler didn't win the war—things would have been much better."

I wasn't sure whether I felt embarrassed or annoyed. Shared blood didn't mean shared ideology. Once I had got over the initial shock of having foolishly agreed with everything the elderly man had said to me, it struck me that there were insights to be gained. Hundreds of thousands had taken to the streets in the cities of Brazil to protest corruption in government. It was a seemingly intractable disease that drove people to the extremes. Lack of trust bred desperation that, in turn, bred nihilism disguised as the desire for greater order than messy democracy could deliver. Anger was an unreliable partner that could lure us to overturn what was most sacred to us, namely our freedom.

Disheartened by the misplaced perception that I might be here to pay homage to my grandfather and his ideology, and feeling guilty for having stirred up Uncle Harty's unfinished business, I suggested to Emerson that we retire to our pousada. It seemed that an eternity had passed on this day of rest.

I attempted to read, respond to emails, plan, but to no avail. The events of the day kept rerunning in my head in slow motion. It was like being in the eye of a storm. Once again, I had no idea what would come of all this. Had someone stopped me in that moment and asked me why I was here, the only answer I could provide was that it was because of the unbearableness of not knowing.

As time for dinner neared, I wandered down to the pool and sat down to watch the deepening night sky. It was clear and crisp as the night before. Emerson soon joined me. In just a few short days he had become a brother.

"I have to show you something," he said, placing his spectacles on his nose and unfolding the heavily creased disembarkation list from December 1960. He pointed his finger at a name that I recognized. Willem Guijshof had emigrated to Brazil with his parents on the same ship as my grandparents. Seventy-eight souls had spent three weeks onboard the *Charles Tellier* together. Perhaps he had known, perhaps he hadn't. He was only a young boy then. Yet if he had, why hadn't he said anything about it: this defining trip of his family's life? It could mean something and it could mean nothing; so many coincidences that could too easily be dismissed.

CHAPTER 24

Maracaju, March 2016

It was Monday at 8 am and the floors of the Maracaju town library were still wet from the early morning mopping. I looked down a swept street that was a far cry from the disease-ridden town of my imagination. I hadn't noticed a single mosquito since we'd arrived and was certain that Senhor Joaquim had been right: the fumigators had wiped out every last proboscis.

We waited outside the open double doors until a heavyset woman, who shifted with difficulty from one leg to another, heaved past the entrance, stopped briefly without looking at us, then flicked her hand to signal that we could come in. We followed and watched as she dropped into one of the chairs at a round table where two other women had draped themselves listlessly. They were silent when we entered, staring blankly at the floor or the ceiling, or through the tiny windows of this crowded space with a few rows of half-filled book shelves.

"Bom dia," said Emerson, breaking the malaise.

"Bom dia," mumbled the sprightliest of them, with the anger of injustice lurking below the surface that neither of us could miss.

Emerson explained that we were here to learn about my family. Without looking at us, the same woman rose, walked behind the librarian's counter, then slapped a book on the surface. We moved closer as she opened it and leafed through the pages, which featured black-and-white images of a bygone world: the fierce ranchers of the early twentieth century in gauchos and overbearing mustaches next to their equally fiercely clad women in tight corsets with strict middle-parted updos and baggy

trousers. Emerson and I observed with polite interest, but quickly concluded that there was nothing to be found here.

Noticing our lukewarm response, the librarian closed the book and
asked Emerson a pointed question, her eyes investigating the relationship between him and me. He replied and there was a silence until she
shouted out to her colleagues. "Si, tudo bem," they replied absently, one
of them wiping the sweat of boredom off her forehead.

The librarian tucked the book back under the counter and replaced
it with a local phone book. She dialed her cell phone and exchanged a
few quick words, which resulted in a fourth woman, someone from the
local administration who could approach the town's citizens in an official
capacity, soon pulling up outside the library in a hatchback.

Words were exchanged with Emerson, and soon the entire library
crew became animated with conversation, until silence descended as a call
was made to another Dutch farmer who had apparently known my family.

Our convoy traveled through town, back to the residential area,
where we were soon welcomed onto another shaded veranda of one of
the orderly bungalows. A man in his eighties with a rancher's swag-
ger walked out of the house and sat down across from us, placing his
Stetson on the table next to him. His wife, a native woman decades his
junior with thick round glasses, served us hot tea and then vanished
inside the house again, her face appearing occasionally like a gray
shadow behind the netted veranda door. The skin on the Dutchman's
exposed lower arms was so dry that it had developed scales and looked
reptilian, and the large black cankers on his lips were an unavoidable
distraction. It made me wonder whether we Caucasians were meant to
live in this land at all.

He spoke Portuguese with a Dutch accent and the occasional
flat-voweled word tossed in as a reminder of his original nationality. All
of us fell between different worlds in one way or another, but in the case
of the Dutch in the Brazilian heartland it couldn't be more apparent.

"He says your uncle was a Nazi," said Emerson. It was an abrupt way
to start a conversation. Unless the term "Nazi" simply meant troublemaker to this man, the burden of the past had once again unjustly been
placed on the wrong shoulders.

"Please tell him that it was my grandfather, my uncle's father, who was a Nazi," I replied. Emerson translated and the rancher looked at me puzzled, as though to ask: what mission, exactly, did you come here to accomplish? How could I explain the legacy of unclaimed guilt for war crimes in the jungle of Dutch and Portuguese we'd have to hack through? Sometimes I hoped for understanding without speaking between the eyes of fellow humans, windows to the soul where the intolerable awaited relief.

"There is an old Nazi living in this town," Emerson translated. "Ninety-seven years old. No one wants to speak with her anymore. He knows her and will take us to her." Was it merely another aged local troublemaker we would meet or had the term been used with any substance attached to it?

We followed the rancher in his giant pickup to a poorer residential neighborhood marked by row houses with crumbling turquoise paint discolored by the red dust. The rusty gate creaked as we opened and closed it, and a local woman who appeared to be the housekeeper ushered us into a cramped living room dominated by the smell of worn upholstery and things no one wanted.

"Bom dia, Alice!" said the Dutch farmer, lifting his Stetson. Emerson merely nodded a greeting, wary of what a real Nazi might say.

"Guten tag," said the old woman, as she balanced shakily on a cane and what was left of her pride. The blond dye had washed out of the gray roots of her thin hair, and her dress hung from the shoulder pads over a caved chest and a body bent by time. She beamed at me through blurred glasses that needed cleaning and, eagerly taking my hand into hers, led me to sit next to her on the couch with springs that screeched.

Alice's blue eyes devoured me hungrily as I explained why I had come to Maracaju. She ignored everyone else as though at last she had found that being upon whom she could offload her stories and her loneliness; because I was the descendant of "her kind," I must be someone who understood. Emerson and the aged rancher sat on the couch across from us chatting superficially, witnessing this hoarding with grim fascination.

Sometimes as Alice spoke, she became Oma, and I was transported back to that apartment with the noise-absorbing green wall-to-wall carpet. She clasped my hand and stroked it as Oma often had, and once again I could not scream or shout or object—"I am not like you!"—because there before me was a tired, deserted old woman moldering into the ground behind the crumbling turquoise paint. The red dust would be cast upon her as it would upon everyone else who lived and died in these parts. It was the great denier of all exceptionalism.

"We were anti-communists," Alice said of her husband and herself. "We joined the Belgian Blackshirts during the war because we didn't want the Bolsheviks to take over. Peter, my husband, played various roles and eventually in 1944 we fled to Germany where he joined the secret service because he was good at languages." She smiled coyly at a passing memory of her husband, whom she regarded as a hero.

I was as hungry to listen as she was to tell, gathering everything she said so I could rummage through it later and perhaps find the answer to that question that had hung over me since I had first held those hundred pages from the German Federal Archives in my hands: "Why?" Emerson and the Dutch farmer seemed ever farther away from us as I followed her slavishly into her catharsis.

"After the war he and I were both imprisoned, and all we could think of was getting out of Europe to Latin America. I was released and followed Peter back to Belgium where he received a sentence of eighteen years. It was shortened to five and a half, and when he was released we left immediately on tourist visas. We weren't allowed permanent visas." She stopped and waited for a sympathetic reaction, and I felt my face warming with embarrassment as I rummaged around inside trying to find something that approximated it.

"Rosa!" she called with a sense of urgency, issuing a directive in Portuguese. Soon the housekeeper returned with an envelope that she handed to her mistress. A broad smile came over Alice's face as she removed a greeting card with a curious hand-drawn picture on the cover. "His SS comrades made it for him in 1946 as a birthday present while they were in prison together. It's very fine. Don't you think?" She handed it to me, as though the sharing of this secret treasure would seal our affinity.

I looked at it, my heart seized by the fear of seeing those withered souls, the creators of the card, who had surrendered themselves to become part of a merciless killing machine, and by the fear that I might see into Opa and feel the forbidden twinge of sympathy.

The cover of the card portrayed a man with an orderly haircut and spectacles wearing no more than a loincloth, sitting on the back of a turtle playing the trumpet for a fascinated monkey that dragged a map of faraway islands carelessly along the ground. Two other monkeys sat on a rope a short distance away, their tails affectionately intertwined, one with a half-eaten banana in its hand, enjoying the entertainment. In the distance two palm trees rose from the ground next to an adobe hut. There were no other people and no other signs of civilization.

The privilege of expressing oneself openly and loudly, away from the prying eyes of human judgment and fickle morality, was their gift. Now that they were imprisoned and faced an uncertain future—possibly the hangman's noose—the hunters had themselves become the hunted and thus discovered the value of freedom. These young men, who had been told that they were the masters of civilization, could now only dream of living out their days with the apes.

"Look inside—they wrote a very fine poem," Alice urged with the excitement of a child. I read the three stanzas in elegant red and black script that rhymed perfectly in German:

For Pitt's 28th Birthday—6.3.18

Our dear, good Peter
Earlier was an A-trumpeteer:
Where the negroes smoke,
He lives peacefully under the palms.

He allowed himself to be driven by instinct
To embrace Europe:
As an interpreter he spoke not only languages,
He represented the foulest things!

Full of thanks—all joking aside—
We wish from the bottom of our hearts:
Keep us from punishment!
But if you eventually become free,

Be filled with that lusty cry:
Onward into the paradise of the Apes!
6.III.46—Your comrades in the camp

The poem blew a final, irreparable hole through all the lies I had been told and had willingly lived by for so many years. The Paradise of the Apes was exactly what Oma and Opa had sought. My anger raged like a storm inside, but that was where it would stay until it subsided. For now, I forced myself to listen, to keep a balanced façade, and to remain focused on the goal, which was to obtain as much insight as possible.

"We went to Paraguay first," Alice continued. "He worked for a time—quiet job, low visibility so that we could live peacefully—but he quickly succumbed to heart disease. We really didn't want to see anyone and kept to ourselves. After he died I moved here across the border. The city seemed too dangerous—too exposed—and no one would bother me here."

The air had become like soup, and I felt a monstrous headache coming on. "Do you have any children?" I asked, sucking in whatever oxygen I could find.

Her face hardened and her voice cooled. "Our son moved to France, became a Communist, and learned Russian. He doesn't want to know about us. But my adopted son—a Brazilian—is a good boy. He comes to visit sometimes." Her voice softened as she spoke of her second son, but overall she was uncomfortable with the subject of her children and quickly shifted to another subject.

"Do you believe in God?" she asked, and without waiting launched an attack on the Catholic Church. Like Opa, she had been a Catholic, but didn't attend church, which she said had polluted religion. While the Catholic Church hardly had an innocent history, I couldn't help thinking that hers was a desperate effort to justify the Reich's systematic murder of priests, and, not least, the fear of being deserted by God at life's end, which must come soon. I had the feeling that she too had consented to the inner desertion required to pursue the outer trappings of the Reich, and now felt lost in a no-man's-land. I'd heard it all before in my grandmother's apartment.

Toward the end of our conversation, Alice looked lighter. She had unburdened herself, at least temporarily, without the need to show a moment's remorse. Had I done for Alice what I hadn't done for my own grandmother, which was to help an old Nazi die with less doubt and to rest in some modicum of peace?

Yet I couldn't miss this chance to be sure that there was no light in the abyss—no remorse for wrongs done. "But Alice, what about the Jews and the Holocaust?" I asked.

"Oh that," she said without the slightest trace of unease. "Well, they were a part of it, of course, and some sacrifices had to be made for our cause. Germany deserved to be made great again and we wanted Belgium to be a part of that."

My search for the Holy Grail of remorse seemed over.

———

The old Dutch farmer waved his hand out the window of his pickup truck to signal that he was turning off to head back home and that Emerson and I should continue straight ahead to get back into town.

My head hung low. I had been digging for so long, doggedly committed to finding that sense of wrongdoing in my grandparents that would provide evidence that they had somehow freed themselves from bitter selfishness. Yet all I found as I kept going was a deeper, darker hole that it was increasingly difficult to climb out of. Alice had never really escaped prison, just as Oma and Opa had never really evaded it. Their unwillingness to say they were wrong kept them breathing thin air, cut off from the oxygen of compassion.

"Do you still want to go to that museum?" asked Emerson, sounding doubtful. "You look tired. What did you talk about with that old Nazi?"

"All the same things I once discussed with my grandmother," I replied. "Like my Oma, she couldn't get any further."

"*Tsssss!*" Emerson hissed at the tragedy of it.

I couldn't make any decisions, and soon we were outside the modest white building that housed Maracaju's history museum. Inside, an enthusiastic young man greeted us and asked how he could help. Emerson responded, and presently the museum curator showed us to the collections of local newspaper clippings that had been gathered together in large, musty-smelling, leather-covered albums. After he'd dropped one of the collections, retrieved it from the floor, and then shuffled it around with his own bare hands, the young man equipped us with two sets of gloves. Emerson's big eyes grew even larger, as they always did when confronted by the self-contradiction of bureaucracy in his country. I thanked the young man and left my gloves on the table to wander through the various rooms of the museum. The visit with Alice had drained me.

Two of the rooms were filled with gun belts, rifles, saddles and saddle bags, leather cowboy hats, and armor. Bull horns filled the empty spaces on the wall. A third room exhibited a series of black-and-white photographs of the strongmen who had governed these parts. Beards gave way to thinly twirled mustaches and eventually clean-shaven faces with thick glasses—a gallery of small dictators in different fashions. The military uniforms and gleaming medals reflected a society that had long known no other way to be governed than by might. They gave the outer impression of order, while letting the privileged—which included people of European origin—get away with their own exploitative chaos. Small wonder that this place had remained a strange time capsule in which Oma, Opa, and Alice could exist without being judged, and, on the contrary, even admired for adhering to their ideas about the natural right of the strong over the weak.

I returned to the reading room, where Emerson flicked through the last pages of a folder with interest but not the excitement of a find. "In Guarani Maracaju means green parrot with yellow head." He grinned, pointing at a sketch of the bird in the collection. Emerson never tired of nature and color.

The curator reentered and asked whether we had found what we needed, eager to gather evidence that the museum was of use to someone. "Si, tudo bem. Muito obrigado!" Emerson reassured him.

On the following day we returned to Campo Grande before catching our flight to Brasilia, the capital, where we would visit the National Archives before returning to São Paulo. Emerson revisited the *imoveis* to see whether any further land registration documents had been found, and exchanged a number of frustrating phone calls with Martha, a bureaucrat at the *imoveis* in Maracaju, whose intransigence had temporarily become the bane of his life. Despite this, a clear picture was taking shape concerning just how much space for living Opa had amassed during his years in Brazil. The nearly two thousand hectares he had purchased in Mara-caju had been only the beginning. Emerson laid out all the land deeds on a table before me and shook his head.

"We won't make it to Bara do Garças, but, oh my God, look at his holdings there," he said, glasses poised on the tip of his nose as he leaned over the documents. Collectively, the urban, cultivated, and grazing land presided over by Opa came to more than 15,000 hectares, larger than 15,000 football fields. It wasn't Baden-Württemberg, as Oma had once suggested, but nevertheless. According to the documents, he'd also owned a "beautiful house" overlooking the river in that town. How had it all been afforded? Through various loans and guarantees—we were still not certain of the source—that eventually could not be repaid because of Opa's resistance to learning the language and because the dream of Lebensraum had quite simply been self-defeating.

Why did it matter to me? All this had begun and ended in the first years of my life, but it had cast a very long shadow of bitterness and betrayal over the world in which I had lived. We had lost something so valuable that it had left a gigantic wound. It wasn't the land. It was our capacity to speak with one another about events tinged red by the blood of unclaimed genocide.

"Look, this guy purchased all of your grandfather's urban holdings in Bara do Garças more than a year before his death." Emerson pursed his lips and inhaled deeply, always the sign that he knew he was going to have to do something he didn't really want to. Dr. Nando de Souza was an attorney in Campo Grande. Oma had mentioned the name in a forlorn tone, as though it somehow held the answer to the question of what had happened to the land. De Souza—here it was on paper. It was too late for us to visit him now, so Emerson calling him once we got back to São Paulo. We wouldn't make it to Bara do Garças. The land had overcome our means with its size.

"Oh. Here, bought you this," said Emerson as an afterthought. It was a book filled with photographs that attested to the meteoric growth of Campo Grande from the 1960s on. Brazil had been hungry for land managers then, and it was prepared to turn a blind eye to the past mis-deeds of some of the newcomers as long as they were capable. Some of its leaders went a step further: they welcomed the SS, with whom they were ideologically aligned.

We dined at a McDonald's before the flight, throwing my thoughts back to southwestern Poland where I had bought Robert a couple of burgers after a day of scouring the countryside looking for eyewitnesses. I often wished that someday Emerson might meet Robert and Nele and all the others who were a daily reminder of the integrity and generosity that humans were capable of. At times I imagined that when I was all done with this work I would bring them together in the same big room so that they could laugh and converse in the company of kindred spirits. What would they say to one another—these people of great hearts who would never want to be known as extraordinary?

While sipping our soft drinks, Emerson and I became so absorbed in our reflections and plans that we nearly missed the flight. As the aircraft lifted off the ground I watched the neon-green grass that grew out of the red soil. In time it would grow over the plaque full of misspellings in the private graveyard off Avenida Filinto Müller. No one would remember it, or maybe it would be removed if no one paid for its upkeep; the lock unopened, the secret of the grave gone forever.

My life's work had been a dead man's trial. Now as the aircraft rose over the huge tracts of soy and corn, I asked myself whether there was any justice in it. What could be worse than being tracked down by your own flesh and blood without the possibility of defending yourself? Yet there remained a lump in my throat as suddenly I was next to him again, a toddler unawares next to her grandfather, who held the newspaper with his one good arm.

CHAPTER 25

Brasilia, March 2016

OUR TAXI HONKED ITS WAY THROUGH THE ANGRY PROTESTERS BEING held back by riot police outside the presidential palace. The car braked sharply as a fight broke out when one of the protesters hurled himself past the police at an angry counterprotester among the throngs that continued to support the embattled Rousseff government. Uncle Harty had said that lying, stealing, and cheating were the ways of this land, and that there was nothing to do about it. One had to adapt to survive, so who was to blame? It was easy to surrender to this barren argument, which could also be an excuse for one's own bad behavior. Yet three and a half million people from all walks of life had taken to the streets nationwide during the previous weekend to protest the endemic disease of corruption that had plagued this country for so long. Quietly I wished the protesters well, and hoped that they would stay with messy democracy in order to solve their problems.

In the shouting there were sometimes echoes of a conflict that was rising all around the world, even battering democracies that once seemed secure. It was between those who thought like the old man in the churrascaria and advocated drastic solutions that, without exception, would lead to suffering; and those who advocated incremental change and the evolution of systems that might eventually arrive at something we called humane. This very same fight had been inherent in the seed of my grandparents' extremism.

Our taxi crawled through the shouting crowds, but we made it in time for our appointment at the national archives. A friendly official greeted us in a dimly lit room where men in black trousers and dark ties worked on antiquated computers with the sleeves of their starched white shirts rolled up to provide respite from the stuffiness. On the way to the reading room, he conducted polite conversation that tested the boundaries of what he could find out about our motives for reserving a mountain of files containing immigration and naturalization applications from Germans during the 1950s, '60s, and '70s. The reality was that we were interested in piecing together as many of the detailed links that had secured my grandparents' temporary visas, permanent residence, and eventually Opa's naturalization. I said that I was born in Brazil and interested in tracing my family's history, but left out the rest. The double standard inherent in truth-seeking crawled on my skin like an insect I couldn't catch.

"These may not be complete," warned the official as he left us with the files in the room, as though he knew for a fact that documents were missing. Maybe all of us were toning down the truth in order to seek or avoid it. What a strange game.

Emerson and I leafed through the files of letters to immigration authorities. Behind the restrained words was the desperate cry for a different life, away from the memory of killing and destruction, away from blame for the war. They attested to the perversions that Germans in the postwar world lived with, in which anyone could be accused of being a former Nazi, in particular by those who had been ardent supporters of the Party and now wished either to wreak revenge or deflect attention. Some applicants shared instances of working or dining with Jews as proof of their innocence. Guilt was like a hot potato seeking an owner; small wonder that so often it had been tossed down through the generations.

We left the archives without any of the documents we had sought, but I couldn't say that I had left empty-handed. Emerson hailed a taxi by waving his folder with the pen clipped over the top that seemed a permanent attachment at the end of his left arm. "Don't worry," he said. "I have made inquiries with other archives in São Paulo. We will find the information."

Soon we were in the heart of this capital city that looked like a government campus with some convention-defying structures, and streets that prioritized grandeur rather than pedestrians. It was eerily empty for a weekday, the people either in government offices or concentrated at the protests that continued in smaller numbers in different parts of the city.

As we walked into the Cathedral of Brasilia, Oma's voice followed me despite myself. It was never far away when I walked into any place of worship, like an obstinate child who wanted to tag along but refused to show it.

There was a magic in this place that gave the impression of a mind that had seen other worlds. The skies and the deep seas were reflected in the patterns of the blue-green stained glass of the dome, which was held together by a white star or a starfish, depending on where one preferred to be. Angels hung from the ceiling over the pews, among us rather than over a distant altar reserved for God's earthly messengers. The largest of them held out his palms in a sign of surrender.

Emerson, who sat in one of the pews, had returned to his natural state of wonderment. Oma's voice became a distant whisper, and the quiet that she had so coveted but never attained triumphed over history's shouting to bear witness to grace.

⸺

Betina sat across from me at our lunch table in a fashionable São Paulo café, her elaborate makeup reminding me of a performer's in kabuki theater. We had just visited the academics who had prepared me for the journey to the interior and debriefed them on my findings.

"What you've done is important to us," she said, her red lips leaving their imprint on the rim of the espresso cup. It was a sentiment that echoed our earlier meeting. Apparently, the heavy door to researching former Nazis and SS in Brazil had been pushed further ajar. Research work that had been set aside due to its difficulty would be taken up among them once again. One of the researchers would soon visit Poland with her husband to learn of the fate of his Jewish family. A man in his sixties, he longed finally to know more about the source of his mother's agony, far away in Europe where her family had perished in the gas chambers. He'd looked at me with tears of gratitude that I could never really understand. I'd spent the past six years bullheadedly conducting work that I suspected was selfish, and at times thought that those who had refrained from opening the Pandora's boxes of their family's pasts were wise. It hadn't been my way, but I certainly didn't expect anyone to thank me for it. Seeing my doubt, Betina intervened. "What you have done is beautiful," she said.

There were colors and forms that were beautiful. A person or their spirit could be beautiful; but what in this troublesome project matched the quality that this word implied? Perhaps it was like the weeds that grew through the cracks in the pavement, that sought out the light, whatever the obstacles. Betina had urged me to see it in the most unlikely things: in the clear plastic sleeve that held my schedule and list of contacts; in the tears I had wept at her kitchen table when the pressure and the fear had become unbearable.

"What are your plans?" I asked, curious as to what such a resourceful and aesthetically conscious person would do after her own harrowing journey into the past.

"Work with art and children," she said. "I have an idea that I have been thinking about for a long time and now I will pursue it." It was no coincidence that those of us who had stared into the dank caves of the past sensed the urgency of devoting our energies to the young.

"Look—I want to show you something," she said as she played a video on her phone. A Portuguese voice narrated an image of black polka dots in varying densities against a white background. As the camera zoomed out, the dots formed an image of the face of Adolf Hitler. "It's like you said: If you look up close, evil becomes diffuse, something else." What was it then? Maybe the children could tell us.

꧂

Emerson waved from the street corner, keeping his distance from a crowd of angry protesters and counterprotesters who flung their arguments at one another without listening. It was my last day in Brazil.

"Bom dia!" he said enthusiastically. "I have more informations about the permanent residence, but we can look at it later or I can send it to you."

"What is it?" I asked, curious what new documents Emerson had managed to unearth.

"Don't worry," he said. "Let's get away from these crazy people. Today we enjoy São Paulo. It's a great place!"

I felt impatient but went along with Emerson's plan. We left the safe street where my hotel was and wandered through the city, in and out of the subway system that surprised me with its modernity. Brazil, with its shantytowns en route to polished airports, remained a mystery to me.

As we walked, Emerson told the stories of the streets and the buildings, until eventually we reached the Museu de Arte de São Paulo. His ebullience about his hometown made me forget about whatever new information he had found.

"This was my hometown as it was over a century ago. Amazing paintings!" Emerson exclaimed. Most people bragged about faraway places they'd traveled to or expressed their longing for them. To Emerson, the most spectacular finds were at one's feet, in the sky overhead, and in one's hometown. Opa had become addicted to the horizon. It was all that we had lost but could never have owned.

We came to a painting of Portuguese conquistadores landing at a beach where Indians, some of them hidden behind bushes, waited apprehensively to learn what sort of people the newcomers were. "I have both of their bloods in me," said Emerson. "I did a test. If most people would be ready to realize these things there would be peace. Genealogy is peace, you know."

"Yes, but my grandparents believed in the power of genealogy too," I countered, remembering the exhaustive family trees they had submitted to demonstrate their so-called racial qualifications to join the SS.

"Sure, sure! But that's the fake genealogy," replied Emerson. "Catholic priests had to do the same into the nineteenth century to prove they didn't have Moorish blood. Not possible!"

I looked at the painting again. The futile struggle of all racial ideology was in attempting to suspend the moment in time captured by this painting: them and us; suspicion the only substance of our connection.

We stopped at an elegant café where Emerson insisted that I taste one of his favorite Brazilian desserts, quindim, a creamy sugar bomb with intimations of coconut. "Now I can tell you what I found out in documents from the São Paulo archive—I also made a call to the fazenda in San Pedro," said Emerson, passing his fork through his dessert with pleasure. He took a first bite and let the sugar and cream dissolve before continuing. "Try it," he said. "Good!" I tasted some, but my digestive juices dried up at the threshold of every new discovery.

"Von der Kleist was the fazenda manager in San Pedro where your grandparents first stayed when they came here. Your uncle was his apprentice until all moved to Maracaju eight months after your grandparents arrived." The pieces fit together perfectly. I had learned from the academics that the town of San Pedro was one of the places that offered a sort of welfare network to fleeing Nazis, not uncommon in German communities in Latin America. Oma and Opa had taken advantage of this until they parted paths with von der Kleist in the autumn of 1960 and left for Maracaju. It was easy to blend in on streets where German was commonly spoken. I knew all this, but now I also knew exactly how and why von der Kleist had been such a valuable link.

"Another bit of information: your grandfather applied for permanent residence four months after he arrived—I found the papers." With all the other evidence, it confirmed that he had never had any intention of returning to Europe.

We wandered back in the direction of my hotel, the newly found pieces of the puzzle still settling into place, transforming the picture. We stopped on a bridge that ran over a busy street lined with tall, modern buildings. "That's where I met my wife—right over there." He pointed toward the bus stop, below. The most mundane of places could become a paradise in Emerson's eyes. "And that is where your grandfather once stayed." He pointed at the tallest of buildings nearby. "It was a modern, luxurious apartment building then—expensive to stay in." It was a testament to the game played by the old man who had given off the impression of wealth but seemed to have left nothing behind for his family, except the barbed wire of guilt and shame.

"Von der Kleist lived in a nice place too after San Pedro. Moved to the same neighborhood that you visited, where Mengele also lived." Maybe my search had been the trial of more than just one dead man.

Emerson and I parted before the turnstiles in one of the subway stations. His home was in a different direction from my hotel. I realized that this was the first day that I had seen him without his folder and pen, though his spectacles still hung faithfully from the string around his neck.

"Thank you for making this difficult work such a joy," I said to him, my heart filled with the sadness of parting.

"It is a pleasure, my friend, always," he replied.

Once I had walked through the turnstile I looked back one last time. The protesters had begun to stream in and fill the underground with their chants. Yet Emerson stood completely still, watching me through the angry bodies until I couldn't see him anymore. I thought I saw his spirit wave. "Don't forget the stars, the universe, the wonder," it said.

—◆—

On the following morning Shalom Taxi Service delivered me to the airport. Lilien, who had flown from Asunçion to São Paulo for the transatlantic flight, was there to meet me, carrying as many overflowing bags as she had departed with.

"How was it, Lilien?" I asked, happy to see a face that would ease me back into my old life back home.

"Totally wonderful—couldn't resist buying lots of presents!" she exclaimed. My bags contained a few slim offerings for my husband and children that I had bought at the last minute. She made me feel stingy.

At security, Lilien unpacked and repacked her many carry-ons full of maté and other things that could only be found in Paraguay, reluctantly forced to relinquish some to the trash can. Now we were back in that eerie space between countries where all eyes awaited the first signs that boarding would soon start. Many were Europeans, including Germans with bronzed skin from days in the sun. Lilien too radiated the glow of a warm holiday, but I was the same shade as when I had set foot in Latin America three weeks ago. There had been no time for sunbathing, only for history and searching.

We had settled into our seats. Lilien couldn't fit all her bags into the overhead compartment and had packed them all around her like insulation. "So tell me. How was it? Did you enjoy yourself?" she asked.

I never expected to feel that way because the trip had been nerve-racking and at times stretched belief to its limits, but I said yes. "I met a loving family, and someone who wanted me to see the beauty in the country of my birth," I said.

"See! I told you it would all work out," said Lilien, turning to look out the window as the maintenance trucks backed away from the aircraft so that the engines could start.

The aircraft lifted off with barely a sound; not the dramatic heave from the ground I remembered as a child. I fell asleep quickly, exhausted by the many impressions, awaking only sporadically until the reflection of the bright sun on the snow-covered Swiss Alps brought me back to full consciousness. The cabin had chilled to match that familiar feeling of displacement, prompting me to pull the thin blanket provided by the airline up to my chin.

I fished for memories of the past weeks: Mikael with the flowers at the airport; Bibbi's tears behind her shaded glasses in the Asunçion traffic; Uncle Harty and the green book; Luna's forgiveness; Betina's dramatic red lips; Emerson at the wheel of our SUV as it made its way through the red landscape with the ostrich-like birds pecking at a harvested crop. Yet it was the rusting turquoise of Alice's house gate that colored everything. To me it had become the bright future that we hoped for when we were young, eroded by the weather of time and our own mistakes. It was Oma as I had known her, but had not wanted to see; and it was in beholding this imperfection that I truly learned about myself.

CHAPTER 26

Stockholm, May 2017

"SORRY I HAVE BEEN OUT OF TOUCH—BUSY WITH MY GRANDSON'S CHRIStening," Emerson wrote in one of the many communications that ensued between us during the months after my return from Brazil.

We had blasted a mine of information together, and the pieces were still being gathered and organized. In the email Emerson revealed that he had been out blasting on his own and had placed a call to my grandfather's old lawyer.

"I spoke with Dr. Nando. Long talk. He says your grandfather was a serious person and punctual. Angry—liked to scream and had a short fuse." The descriptions of Opa by people in Schleswig-Holstein, Wielkopolska, and Mato Grosso were all strikingly similar.

"He drove well without use of his left hand, which he lost fighting when he was in the army in Africa." Memory often inadvertently bent history, but it didn't sound like Dr. Nando de Souza had forgotten much about my grandfather. In the case of that arm, I had come to the conclusion that all the stories Opa and others had told about it were just made up. Serving in the Army in Africa sounded better than serving in the SS in Poland or having hunting weekends with former SS colleagues in Schleswig-Holstein.

"He used to say that he would like to visit Germany, but only if Dr. Nando accompanied him, and Dr. Nando didn't want to, so he never visited." De Souza had been a young and inexperienced Brazilian lawyer when my grandfather had known him, and even if he had accompanied Opa back to Germany, it was unlikely, if ever called upon to do so, he could have protected him under the law of the Federal Republic. In reality, this was an admission by the wily Dr. de Souza that he was well aware of his unruly client's dark past.

"He kept his bank account in Dr. Nando's name and a house he owned in Campo Grande in the name of his 'second' woman. He said he doesn't know where she is, but I don't believe him." The money trail had been covered, as had several property transactions, which had taken place in de Souza's name. A family connection that preferred for the die-hard Nazi and SS man not to resurface had arranged bank guarantees for the largest property purchases. It was a pattern consistent with other cases I had heard of.

Overall, academic research of the last few years showed that most former SS in Latin America were unlikely ever to face trial or even be hunted, protected by a coalition of powers uninterested in pursuing them. The remnants of the Third Reich in the Federal Republic and the Vichy regime in France littered public offices, including the diplomatic services and police forces. While the Adenauer government felt pressured into a new phase of war crimes trials by a confluence of international forces in the late 1950s, there was no widespread support for coming to grips with the past until the eighties; despite the youth who protested in the streets in 1968, incensed by the many former Nazis who continued to hold influential positions; and despite Chancellor Willy Brandt's spontaneous kneeling at Warsaw's monument to the ghetto heroes during his visit to Poland in 1970. Latin American regimes that bore the blood of their own people on their hands were not only uninterested in turning the spotlight on their own human rights violations by extraditing former Nazis—putting up legal smokescreens in cases where inquiries were made—but were ideologically aligned with fascism and didn't look favorably upon the forward march of liberal democracy in Europe. In the case of Brazil's military regime, the United States, which had mostly been a source of pressure for pursuing former Nazis, looked the other way as it saw a stalwart partner in the fight against communism.

Of the thousands who escaped to Latin America, six were successfully brought to trial and sentenced, not least through the tireless efforts of Holocaust survivor and Nazi hunter Simon Wiesenthal. In each of these cases, public pressure had been built up over a long period of time, and a rare, sometimes bizarre, confluence of events resulted in capture and extradition. In 1964, Franz Stangl, former commandant of the Sobibór and Treblinka extermination camps, was arrested at the Volkswagen factory in São Paulo. Not long after, Herbert Cukurs, "The Butcher of Riga," who ran his own flight tourism business out of São Paulo, was lured to Uruguay and assassinated by Mossad agents. Neither of them had felt the need to conceal their identities. A photograph of Oma at one of her daughters' weddings in São Paulo during that year came to my mind. There was a glimmer of fear in her eyes, and Opa was conspicuous by his absence. Perhaps it was these captures that had motivated him to venture across the Rio dos Mortes, and to tuck himself farther away in the interior in Bara do Garça with the help of his young Brazilian attorney. Despite the coalition of governments unwilling to pursue former Nazis, his situation became ever less comfortable as the cause of human rights advanced globally. Ultimately, as inadequate as it was, his punishment was that there could never have been a moment after the war when he wasn't looking over his shoulder.

"And before I forget it," Emerson continued, "de Souza said something that caught my attention: he bought your grandfather's grave. God forgive me for thinking like this, but the way he said it and everything else I heard from him makes me think he was saying: 'I stole a lot of things from him, but at least I bought his grave.'"

Deep inside I felt sorry that Emerson's sunny personality had been invaded by the cynicism inherent in my grandparents' story, but it also took a Brazilian to understand the powerful role that superstition played in the decision to confess. When I was a young child the Brazilian nursemaids who had rocked me in their arms were all members of the Catholic Church at the same time as they maintained a fervent parallel belief in the power of Macumba, the threat of black magic. In life they saw a need to take active measures to avoid the evil eye and to ward off evil spirits, and allegedly they had hung talismans around my crib in order to protect me. De Souza's confession could easily be explained in the light of this widespread belief.

The lawyer's story was supported by our findings concerning the purchase and sale of Opa's properties. It strengthened my theory that Uncle

Harty had been a pawn, not only in Opa's game but also in de Souza's. One had used the other, and the losers were the children.

Subsequently, I wrote an innocuous letter to de Souza but never received a reply. "Se correr o bicho pega, se ficar o bicho come"—"If you run the bug will get you, if you stay the bug will eat you"—Emerson wrote, reflecting his opinion that there was no preferable avenue for pursuing de Souza any further.

Overall, when I reflected on these past six years, it struck me that I had stayed with the bug rather than run from it. Sometimes I thought I could feel not one but a thousand bugs eating me, like the termites that had infiltrated Oma's belongings in Maracaju. In my dreams they stung me when I cranked open those crates.

"A big hug, my friend," Emerson signed off. I knew instinctively that he felt the sorrow of my family story, a puzzle that would always be incomplete, but that nevertheless had become a more comprehensible picture as a result of our efforts.

Was this closure? I understood why many had wished it for me, but still wondered what it was. Maybe a sort of emotional landing in which I could get on with the everyday and return to "normality?" Yet I was still floating without gravity in a universe of question marks, with a heart pounding with both the agony of knowledge and the love of those I had met along the way.

Over the years I was often in the classroom with a group of youngsters who, one way or another, faced me with the question of what I would do about the long shadow cast by my family's legacy. Whether it was through my nonprofit that engaged youth in storytelling about the enigma of human behavior, or the research itself, working with students forced me to consider what we could do to change the patterns of history. The warning signs that the world was unraveling in ways similar to Oma and Opa's past intensified with each year.

On one occasion in 2014, a group of third-graders had drawn a swastika, among many other images of birds, trees, and human stick figures, on the long sheet of paper that we had placed on the floor. The teacher and I stared at it with dismay as the nine-year-olds who had drawn their story kneeled or sat in lotus positions in a semicircle around the offending image. A chain reaction of mischievous looks ensued. Who had drawn that symbol and how should we handle this moment?

During the previous night, a swastika had been spray-painted repeatedly on the exterior walls of this small school on the rural outskirts of Stockholm. The principal and staff reeled from shock as they considered why this had happened and how best to respond to it. The same had been experienced by other schools around the country since the election into the Swedish Parliament of an anti-immigrant party with a neo-Nazi past.

The story we had set out to explore together on the large sheet of paper was about the fate of a Muslim girl, a newcomer to our country, and how we would interact with her. The swastika temporarily halted all creativity and conversation, like a wall behind which those who didn't want to know retreated. Yet the children on the floor around us were too young to understand the history of the symbol, or to comprehend the significance of the shift that had taken place in national politics and beyond. They were like tender sponges that absorbed everything their elders said and did.

My colleague, who had been running a similar exercise in the room next door, rushed in, flustered. A child in her nine-year-old group had blurted out that "Hitler was a great, strong leader." To me this was the underbelly of a new time in which thoughtlessness abounded under the guise of freedom of expression.

We could have discarded the paper and the comments and scolded the children, but this would only increase the desirability of forbidden things and sow resentment. On the following day, I unrolled the long sheet of paper. "What do you think this means?" I asked, pointing at the swastika, struggling to hide my sadness. The children were silent, because none of them knew. I cannot remember how I explained Hitler, his ideas and symbols, without exposing such young hearts to horrors that no heart should ever have to bear, but in the weeks that ensued, the children changed the story. They removed the symbol of their own volition and focused instead on how to enjoy life with the Muslim girl, who eventually became just a girl to them.

Since that time, the overall climate in which the young ones who sat before me were growing up had worsened. Jews and other minorities once again feared for their safety, synagogues were attacked, and young men bearing the symbolism of white supremacy marched in the streets under police protection. The far right attempted to legitimize themselves, exhibiting their publications in the same forums as other parties as though they offered a serious alternative, yet they had little idea about the future of anything except their anger. Mass migration from war-torn countries had become an excuse for bad behavior—a sort of nihilism that I recognized—at the same time as the intolerance and mistrust imported from those wars fueled a vicious cycle.

Each occasion that I stepped into the classroom felt new, equally harrowing, and all the more necessary. "Was he a bad man?" I asked a group of seventh-graders, including my son, who looked at me eager-eyed. After an hour's discussion, we had arrived back at the photograph of Opa as a young man in his oversized merchant's suit hugging the foal. I'd started our session with that photograph to give the youngsters, who lived in an area where horse paddocks abounded, an accessible way into the complexity of the personal history I had uncovered.

My son remained silent, and I worried about how he and his sister, who went to another school, felt about my work. An eager student waved his hand in the air. "It's hard to say. So many things happened along the way." And with that the youngsters had grasped the duality that all of us live with, between being caught up in the relentless onward current of history and the choices that we make.

"So what happened?" I asked, and a discussion ensued that transformed all the years of fumbling in the dark into the light of learning. I imagined Betina in her own classroom, half a world away, showing the sum of the polka dots and challenging her students to question each dot. Maybe closure was turning our stories into questions for the young.

At home a few hours later I asked my son how he felt about the class. "It was really good, Mamma. A lot more interesting than some of the other stuff we have to learn. Good you showed your grandfather with the picture of the horse. Made him more real." With those words, he wandered to the kitchen to satisfy the ravenous hunger that follows a day at school.

I didn't know whether my children would walk the earth more lightly than I did because of what I had done. It could, after all, have the reverse effect or no effect at all. In a world that spewed old-new problems at an accelerating pace, what could one reasonably hope for? The news that Bibbi and Mikael were both expecting children with their partners, and the images my sister shared with them of her toddler, brought both joy and apprehension. It all seemed so right that we should know one another's families—triumphal in moments—but what could we tell our children based on the past we had come from? Even more difficult to contemplate was how we, their past, would affect their lives and the lives of their children.

The spring rain had begun to fall outside the window to my study, where the shelves were laden with binders stuffed with documents from the many archives I had visited. I found solace in observing the antique wooden statue of an angel that presided over the small pond next to the plum tree in the back yard of our townhouse. I had salvaged her from a scrap heap, and placed her on a pedestal there after my last trip to Poland, where I had learned of the Madonna in the field that Opa had struck down.

As the water gathered in her cupped hands, it seemed to me like the formation of a life out of the droplets of the past. Still, I imagined that she had the choice of how to hold it: with awareness and reverence, or with fear and indignation. The former was much more difficult, because it demanded the self-respect to acknowledge kindnesses and admit one's own injustices; and the inclusion, not merely of one's own life or the life of one's "tribe," but of all life. The rain intensified, insisting that we must never stop trying, for this was the way out of the wasteland and into hope.

Acknowledgments

This book is dedicated to the angels of hope, not merely with an abstract idea in mind, but with reference to real people who lit my path and who, to me, represent sides of humanity that make speculation about the future more bearable. Some of them are characters in my journey, others remain in the background. They are my mentors, my co-researchers, my critics, my readers and early editors, my little mothers, and, not least, my friends. In the dark valley where I feared I might walk alone, I rarely experienced loneliness, and eventually found that I had entered a new world of listeners and conversation partners who understood instinctively how essential it is that we attend to the past, helping one another to dig deep and find courage. Whenever I prepared to explain myself—the tension evident in my furrowed brows—they smiled with clear eyes that said: we're already behind you.

To be a nomad in research and writing, without attachment to any institution that endows one's work with credibility and structure, is difficult at best. As my work progressed, I was fortunate to gain the support of some highly respected organizations that put a roof over my head when I most needed it. In 1984 I arrived at Wellesley College a fresh-faced eighteen-year-old with a heavy inner burden. Little did I know that just over thirty years later, Wellesley, with its unstinting belief in the power of women to make a difference, would become one of my most ardent supporters on a dark journey. The Swedish Author's Fund generously looked beyond the confines of language and sponsored the completion of a book in English, thus adding to Sweden's increasingly culturally diverse literary repository. University College London kindly bestowed the title of honorary research associate, opening doors that might otherwise have remained closed.

One of my mentors, an experienced historian, asked the legitimate question of what such tortured stories about the past written by descendants can contribute to the study of history. As family members, it is impossible for us to leave behind emotions that might cloud our perceptions of truth. Equally, it is precisely those emotions that can be the driving force of learning, and, as I quickly found during my journey, many historians of the Third Reich and its aftermath have deeply personal motivations for pursuing their academic interests. I have had the great fortune of coming into contact with some of the best, personally and through their books, who have informed my search. Some of the many archives, libraries, and other repositories of primary documents I consulted in Brazil, Germany, and Poland are named in this work and their staffs are to be commended not only for tolerating but also for being helpful and understanding toward a descendant in desperation.

More than twenty years ago, I had the good fortune to meet a person who understood aspects of me better than I understood them myself and allowed them to take their course. It requires more than patience to watch your nearest fall apart and painstakingly put themselves not just back together again but together in a different composition. My husband, Claes Lindahl, has the fierce, wise heart of a lion. Together with our children, he put me first.

Suggested Reading

In seven years of intensive research, I have had the benefit of learning from many primary and secondary sources that supported me in untangling the threads of my own story. Below is a selection of sources I found most valuable.

Alberti, Michael. *Die Verfolgung und Vernichtung der Juden im Reichsgau Wartheland, 1939–45.* Wiesbaden: Harrassowitz Verlag, 2006.

Arendt, Hannah. *Eichmann in Jerusalem: A Report on the Banality of Evil.* New York: Penguin, 1964.

Baldow, Beate. *Episode oder Gefahr? Die Naumann-Affäre* (Dissertation zur Erlangung des Doktorgrades). Berlin: Fachbereich Geschichts- und Kulturwissenschaften der Freien Universität Berlin, 2012.

Bode, Sabine. *Kriegsenkel: Die Erben der vergessenen Generation.* Stuttgart: Klett-Cotta, 2009.

Böhler, Jochen. *Der Überfall: Deutschlands Krieg gegen Polen.* Frankfurt: Eichborn, 2009.

Böhler, Jochen, and Stephan Lehnstaedt, eds. *Gewalt und Alltag im besetzten Polen 1939–1945.* Osnabrück: German Historical Institute, Warsaw, 2012.

Browning, Christopher R. *Ordinary Men: Reserve Police Battalion 101 and the Final Solution in Poland.* New York: Penguin, 1992.

Eichmüller, Andreas. *Keine Generalamnestie: Die Strafverfolgung von NS-Verbrechen in der frühen Bundesrepublik.* München: Oldenbourg Verlag, 2012.

Epstein, Catherine. *Model Nazi: Arthur Greiser and the Occupation of Western Poland.* Oxford: Oxford University Press, 2010.

Evans, Richard J. *The Third Reich in History and Memory.* London: Little, Brown, 2015.

Fahnenbruck, Nele Maya. *". . . reitet für Deutschland": Pferdesport und Politik im Nationalsozialismus.* Hamburg: Verlag Die Werkstatt, 2013.

Haffner, Sebastian. *Germany: Jekyll & Hyde.* Translation by Wilfrid David. London: Secker and Warburg, 1940.

Harvey, Elizabeth. *Women and the Nazi East.* New Haven: Yale University Press, 2003.

Heinemann, Isabel. *Rasse, Siedlung, Deutsches Blut, Das Rasse und Siedlungshauptamt der SS und die Rassenpolitische Neuordnung Europas.* Göttingen: Wallstein Verlag, 2003.

Igra, Ludvig. *Den tunna hinnan mellan omsorg och grymhet.* Stockholm: Natur och Kultur, 2001.

Klemperer, Viktor. *LTI*. Stuttgart: Philipp Reclam, 1975.

Klepper, Jochen. *Unter dem Schatten deiner Flügel: Aus den Tagebüchern, 1932–42*. Stuttgart: Deutsche Verlags-Anstalt, 1956.

Levi, Primo. *If This Is a Man—The Truce*. London: Penguin, 1979.

Łuczak, Czesław. *Documenta Occupationis XIII*. Poznan: Instytut Zachodni, 1990.

Mai, Uwe. *Rasse und Raum, Agrarpolitik, Sozial- und Raumplanung im NS-Staat*. Paderborn: Ferdinand Schöningh, 2002.

Mallmann, Klaus-Michael, and Bogdan Musial, eds. *Genesis des Genozids—Polen 1939–41*. Published by Wissenschaftliche Buchgesellschaft on behalf of the German Historical Institute, Warsaw, and Forschungsstelle Ludwigsburg der Universität Stuttgart, 2004.

Mueller, Andreas. *Tatort Warthegau: Leben und Sterben im "Pflanzgarten" der SS*. Gelnhausen: Wagner Verlag, 2007.

Nyiszli, Miklós. *I Was Doctor Mengele's Assistant*. Kraków: Frap-Books, 2010.

Pollack, Martin. *Der Tote im Bunker: Bericht über meinen Vater*. Wien: Paul Zsolnay Verlag, 2004.

Roth, Markus. *Herrenmenschen: Die deutschen Kreishauptleute im besetzten Polen— Karrierewege, Herrschaftspraxis und Nachgeschichte*. Göttingen: Wallstein Verlag, 2009.

Rosenthal, Gabriele, ed. *The Holocaust in Three Generations: Families of Victims and Perpetrators of the Nazi Regime*. Leverkusen Opladen: Barbara Budrich Publishers, 2010.

Sands, Philippe. *East West Street: On the Origins of "Genocide" and "Crimes Against Humanity."* London: Weidenfeld & Nicolson, 2016.

Sebald, W. G. *On the Natural History of Destruction*. London: Hamish Hamilton, 1999.

Stahl, Daniel. *Nazi-Jagd: Südamerikas Diktaturen und die Ahndung von NS-Verbrechen*. Göttingen: Wallstein Verlag, 2013.

Stangneth, Bettina. *Eichmann before Jerusalem: The Unexpected Life of a Mass Murderer*. Translation by Ruth Martin. New York: Vintage Books, 2014.

Steinacher, Gerald. *Nazis on the Run: How Hitler's Henchmen Fled Justice*. Oxford: Oxford University Press, 2011.

Tucci Carneiro, Maria Luiza. *Weltbürger: Brasilien und die jüdischen Flüchtlinge (1933–48)*. Zürich: LIT Verlag, 2014.

Ventzki, Jens-Jürgen. *Seine Schatten, meine Bilder: Eine Spurensuche*. Innsbruck: Studien-verlag, 2011.

Welzer, Harald. *Täter: Wie aus ganz normalen Menschen Massenmörder werden*. Frankfurt: S. Fischer Verlag, 2005.

Wiesel, Elie. *Night*. Translated by Marion Wiesel. New York: Hill and Wang, 2006.

About the Author

Julie Lindahl is an author and educator living in Sweden. During her six-year journey in which she visited archives and interviewed eyewitnesses in Germany, Poland, and Latin America, she was named Stevens Traveling Fellow by Wellesley College in 2015–16 and Honorary Research Associate, University College London 2013–15 in connection with their work concerning reverberations of war and genocide in later generations.

Julie writes and speaks widely about her experiences at schools and other learning institutions and is a contributor to WBUR Cognoscenti (National Public Radio Boston). The writing of this memoir was supported by the Swedish Author's Fund.

Julie holds a bachelor of arts in English literature from Wellesley College and an MPhil in international relations from Oxford University. She was a Fulbright Scholar in Frankfurt, Germany. She was raised in ten countries on three continents and has worked in many countries as a consultant in the developing world. She is the founder of Stories for Society, a nonprofit organization for renewing the art of story-making among youth for social transformation. For further information, see www.julielindahl.com.